DUE DATE	RETURN DATE	DUE DATE	

HISTORICAL RECORDS AND STUDIES

THE MONOGRAPH SERIES

UNITED STATES CATHOLIC HISTORICAL SOCIETY
MONOGRAPH SERIES XIV

———

GONZALO DE TAPIA

(1561-1594)

FOUNDER OF

THE

FIRST PERMANENT JESUIT MISSION
IN NORTH AMERICA

W. EUGENE SHIELS, S.J., Ph.D.

———

GREENWOOD PRESS, PUBLISHERS
WESTPORT, CONNECTICUT

Library of Congress Cataloging in Publication Data

Shiels, William Eugene, 1897–
    Gonzalo de Tapia (1561-1594).

    Reprint of the 1934 ed. published by the United
States Catholic Historical Society, New York, which
was issued as 14 of the Society's Monograph series.
    Bibliography: p.
    Includes index.
    1. Tapia, Gonzalo de, 1561?-1594. 2. Indians of
Mexico—Missions. 3. Jesuits—Mexico—Biography.
4. Jesuits—Missions. I. Title. II. Series: United
States Catholic Historical Society. Monograph series ;
14.
F1219.3.M59T367 1978   266'.272'1 [B] 74-12835
ISBN 0-8371-7758-8

IMPRIMI POTEST
        C. H. CLOUD, S.J.,
            Praep. Prov. Chicagiensis

NIHIL OBSTAT
            ARTHUR J. SCANLAN, S.T.D.,
            Censor Librorum

IMPRIMATUR
            PATRICK CARDINAL HAYES,
            Archbishop of New York

Reprinted in 1978 by Greenwood Press, Inc.
51 Riverside Avenue, Westport, CT 06880

Printed in the United States of America

UNITED STATES CATHOLIC HISTORICAL SOCIETY
MONOGRAPH SERIES XIV

———

GONZALO DE TAPIA

(1561-1594)

FOUNDER OF

THE

FIRST PERMANENT JESUIT MISSION
IN NORTH AMERICA

W. EUGENE SHIELS, S.J., Ph.D.

———

NEW YORK
THE UNITED STATES CATHOLIC
HISTORICAL SOCIETY
1934

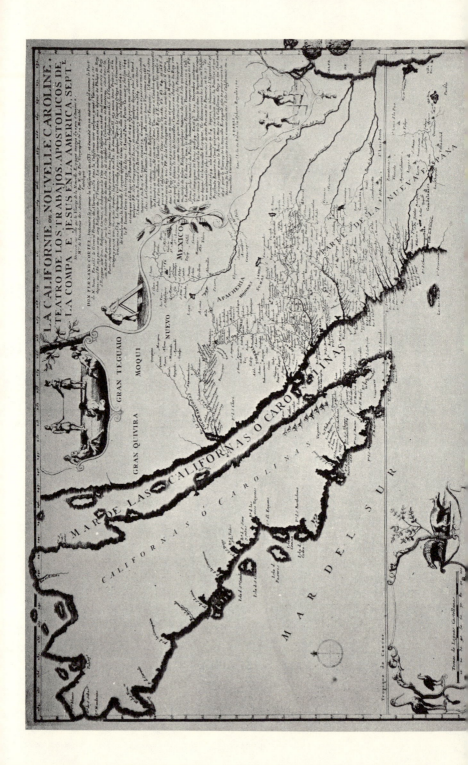

LA CALIFORNIE ou NOUVELLE CAROLINE.
TEATRO DE LOS TRABAJOS APOSTOLICOS DE
LA COMPA. E JESUS EN LA AMERICA SEPT.E

GRAN TEGUAIO

MOQUI

NUEVO

GRAN QUIVIRA

MEXICO

APACHERIA

PARTE DE LA N. NUEVA ESPAÑA

MAR DE LAS CALIFORNAS O CAROLINAS

CALIFORNAS Ó CAROLINAS

MAR DEL SUR

Tropico de Cancer

CONTENTS

[vii]

LIST OF MAPS

PREFACE

The story told herein is that of the founding of the first permanent Jesuit mission in North America. The narrative revolves round the founder of that mission. Both the man and his work are unknown to American readers. Both were equally unknown to the writer, until an amount of searching and sifting revealed the main lines of their history.

The sketchiness of the account will be clear at first sight. That is a blessing, for it may lead others to improve and expand. The work is meant as a beginning.

If the operation has proved in any way worth the effort, the writer again calls on his loyal colleagues and helpers, to thank them for their guidance and long hours of patient assistance. Before all he wishes to extend this meed of gratitude to one whom he is proud to call his friend, the scholar by whom he was so highly favored in counsel and encouragement, Dr. Herbert Eugene Bolton.

San Francisco, March 31, 1933.

GONZALO DE TAPIA

CHAPTER I

THE JESUITS OF NORTH AMERICA

I

Some sixty years ago Francis Parkman wrote a remarkable book[1] on the Jesuits of North America. The story was new to men of his day, for it took courage to surpass the narrow limits of the contemporary New England thought.[2] Yet vision and genius were his, and his narrative marked a definite advance in American literature.

Parkman was an artist, and he sought a subject that would thrill his audience. He had pored over the pocket volumes of the Cramoisy series,[3] and he was acquainted with the records of the fur traders and the early Indian wars. In these studies he came upon that band of heroes whose careers had run like wildfire through the imagination of Europe in the two centuries before his time. With his fine feeling for words, and his power of pic-

---

1. *The Jesuits in North America in the Seventeenth Century,* 1867. Parkman is surpassing "in mastery of style, and in fusion of the writer's vigorous character" with attractive materials. Guilday *Shea,* 53. Cf. note 3.

2. The New England School of Historians (cf. Bassett, *Middle Group of American Historians;* Jameson, *History of Historical Writing in America;* also Bolton, *Anza Expeditions,* I, ch. 1) wrote in the settled tradition that New England is the cradle of America. The notion has not yet died, in spite of the very un-New Englander character of our population in race and national affiliations, in spite, too, of the varied origins of our social and economic institutions.

3. Cramoisy in Paris published forty volumes of "Jesuit Relations," 1632-1673. (Cf. introduction to Thwaites, *Jesuit Relations and Allied Documents;* also Guilday, op. cit., 55.) The "Relations" were formed in this manner: every year the French Jesuit missionaries in North America sent to their superior at Montreal a written account of their labors. As the year drew to a close, this superior made a redaction of the several accounts and forwarded this compilation, called the annual letter, ("lettres annales," "litterae annales," "anua" in Spanish), to the Provincial in Paris, who had them printed by Cramoisy. The series was suspended in 1673 because of royal hostility and was never afterward resumed. The Spanish missionaries followed the same practice, but aside from stray accounts as in Purchas or the *Lettres Edificantes* these annual letters never came to light. The pioneer in directing American historians to the riches of these "Relations" for colonial history was John Gilmary Shea. Guilday says Shea knew the missionary history of the priests of New France better than any historian of his time, not excepting Parkman. Shea himself added twenty-five volumes to the forty original Cramoisy's. He and O'Callaghan, in the 'fifties and 'sixties, did much to bring these treasures to the notice of historians. Parkman was indebted to them for his inspiration.

ture and telling effect, he produced a work that stormed the mind of his generation. Followers in many camps[4] took up his theme. The story crept into lecture halls and the public press, and in a short time a new orientation had been given to the beginnings of Colonial history. Missionaries became characters of importance.

With the march of time the writing of American history was bound to broaden the concepts of the pioneers. Adventurers, cattle men, and dealers in land pushed over the thirteen original borders.[5] Round the lower Appalachians, down the Cumberland and the Ohio, and beyond the headwaters of the lakes, swarms of restless men found new homes and new opportunities. The Mississippi was crossed from source to mouth. Over the great plains they went, and through the high passes of the Rockies, until the immense stretch from Atlantic to Pacific became the country of the white man. Wealth came, and leisure and education. Horizons broadened. Contact opened minds, and a new history found its springtime.

As late as forty years ago the study of the origins stopped with the travails and successes of Massachusetts and Virginia, and rising students were asked to believe that the full harvest of our life was reaped from that old and heavy soil. Then a rebellion took place in the seminar of which Frederick Turner was a member.[6] A fresh idea was given to a startled public. "The Sig-

---

4. Cf. introductory note to Hughes, *History of the Society of Jesus in North America, Colonial and Federal*, I.

5. See Roosevelt, *Winning of the West;* Riegel, *America Moves West;* Branch, *Westward;* Adams, *Epic of America.*

6. The story is this: Turner, a graduate student at Johns Hopkins under Herbert Adams, was beginning the third year of his history seminar. Adams thus addressed his students: "Boys, we must look to other fields this year. We have finished the study of American history. Last year we studied Virginia and the evolution of the parish into the county; the year before we covered New England and the influence of the towns. That is all there is to American history." After class Turner joined with his fellows, Haskins, Ely, Scott, etc., in an indignation meeting. He said: "That view of American history is too narrow. (He was from Wisconsin). The story must be a larger one." The revolt began. From that day Turner worked on his thesis, that most of American history deals with frontier expansion, the factor that has made the character of our people.

Even Turner was circumscribed in outlook. He treated the expanding Anglo-Saxon frontier, but there were two other great frontiers. For example, when the Treaty of 1783 ended the Revolution, the Spanish line in North America extended roughly from Vancouver down through St. Louis

nificance of the American Frontier" bade the old school of doctors and publicists listen to a newer voice, sounding a call to more generous interpretations and larger points of view. And the promise was fulfilled. The men of Harvard and Pennsylvania and Johns Hopkins drifted west with the course of Empire. Far away, as often happens, they got their finest view and appreciation of home. These were scholars who turned their eyes on the primitive foundations from a distant vantage point. Not that they felt less fondly for the fine old things, but they saw all round the tiny stream of Jamestown and Plymouth, rivulets of other water courses. They understood, too, that the northwest and southwest frontiers were set down upon other and older frontiers. And a third and wider interpretation[7] of our national beginnings found place beside the former two. It might be stated in these words.

Three large forces went to found the people and the parts of North America. Taking their start in diverse sectors, they made their separate ways through primeval conditions, until at last they converged. That was the first point of the new teaching. It was followed by its necessary counterpart, the European viewpoint. A new and complete meaning of the term "America" emerged, none other than the original meaning given by the sixteenth century. The present study of America begins where that history actually began, in Europe. It sees our hemisphere as a whole. It follows the different European experiments and adventures in this western world. It traces the institutions set up by the several colonizing nations, seeking in this light to paint a full and balanced picture. The three main lines are clearly marked in their distinct sites and operations, their cultures and ideals.

---

and across the Mississippi southeast to the Floridas. *The Significance of the American Frontier* was published in 1893. The viewpoint of Turner has been merged into the broader continental idea. See note 7.

7. This idea is well developed in Bolton's presidential address to the American Historical Convention of 1932 in Toronto. Cf. *A. H. R., April 1933.* He takes a wide perspective, that of the Western Hemisphere.

II

In keeping with this new historiography, an entirely fresh treatment[8] must be given to the history of the Jesuits in North America. Parkman set his gaze on a purely local phenomenon, the Great Lakes missionary sphere. He was truly inspiring in the magnificent characters that stand out in his glowing pages, yet he scarcely revealed the Jesuits in their full meaning. With all his brilliance he failed to find the larger aspects of the situation, and indeed a great part of the situation he did not see at all. In common with a later writer who did very much to enhance the historic position of the Jesuits, Reuben Gold Thwaites,[9] he thought the St. Lawrence and Mississippi Valleys formed the theatre of Jesuit action in colonial days. These men saw with the eyes of their day, a day that conceived the North and East as the whole of America. It was left to their successors to find in other sources the well-rounded account of the Jesuits of North America.

Today the historian of colonial days first looks across the Atlantic from east to west. Thus he sees that the Society of Jesus in Europe sent out three successive waves in the advance on North America. With varying fortunes, under stress of every conceivable handicap, their labor carried on. They knew the sunshine and the storm, and the black night of a suppression that they little understood. And when the cloud of obloquy was lifted they returned to a new existence in far happier times.

The story as Parkman tells it lacks another essential quality.

---

8. To date the attempt has not been made. Hughes, though most scholarly of all, has designedly limited his scope to the Atlantic Coast. Garraghan, his continuator, will undoubtedly remedy this oversight. Thebaud, whose autobiography, *Three Quarters of a Century,* is the best running account of the middle nineteenth century and connects the recent Jesuit movements, has no mention of the early beginnings. Campbell (*The Jesuits, 1534-1921*), who writes the best compendium of Jesuit history in the English language, has no special point of view in dealing with American colonial times. He gives the foreground to Kino and the martyred saints. His series, *Pioneer Priests of North America,* covers the St. Lawrence sector rather thoroughly, but the large field of New Spain remains practically untouched in his writings. The entire story is a unity to one who will take the pains to see it. John Gilmary Shea has achieved this idea to some extent, in his *History of the Catholic Church in the United States,* though obviously he was not dealing with the Jesuits as his chief subject.

9. Cf. note 3 above; also his *History of Wisconsin.*

His heroes are personalities of unique fiber and excellence. Yet a Jesuit must know that this is not half the story. He understands quite well a fact that passes the notice of most observers, that the chief part of his effectiveness is due not so much to his individual power of heart and mind as to the Society of which he is a member.

It is difficult for men who live no corporate life to comprehend this fact, a matter that is patent to him who is bound in the much larger organism that is a Religious Order. Men of the world are accustomed to make their single ways, up from the raw strife of youth through trial and failure to final achievement, so that they can often say of themselves that they are self-made men. They carry their thoughts and ambitions in their separate souls. Help comes to them from isolated friends or enterprising builders of projects, but in the final analysis they are alone in the quest that forms the ideal of their lives.

With a Religious such as a Jesuit, things are otherwise. Here, too, is a man, for all that, but he is something more. He is part of an organization with an ideal larger than his single self, with means that surpass his solitary powers, and with a bond of union that puts in close conjunction the abilities of many men. His outlook overreaches his own limitations. For him the first consideration is always the Society, that moral being that holds him and his brothers as one. He has an esprit de corps, as a private in a company that is linked in its component parts by a surpassing charity, by prayer, and by a unique obedience. This vital force of obedience runs up and down the whole gamut of the structure in that special authority which is held in the hands of the General and his subordinates.

Jesuits are in a sense an army. They have their brilliant men, their heroes, intellectuals, and martyrs, in every rank and grade. Yet none of them would be known as he is were it not for the Institution and the obedience to a common leader. One who reads of such feats of civilization as the Reductions of Paraguay,[10] will

10. See Charlevoix, *Histoire du Paraguay;* Pastells, *Historia de la Compania de Jesus en la Provincia del Paraguay;* Cunningham-Graham, *Vanished Arcadia;* Huonder, "Reductions of Paraguay," in *Catholic Encyclopedia.*

look beyond the talents and virtues of the individuals, to the cohesive and directive force implicit in the activity of the Jesuit. Each single person must reach his own best development; but the planning, the initial movements, the regime, the constant assistance, the encouragement in success and the care in distress, all devolve from what he calls with sincere affection the Society. And the true history of these men must stress that capital point.[11]

III

The Jesuit Order dates its origin from the vows of Montmartre on August 15, 1534.[12] For six years the small band carried on a quiet labor in the functions that are proper to priests.[13] During this time the scheme of organization was maturing. Frequent counsel was taken as occasion allowed. The mind of the master spirit mulled over the various forms of government. At last, on September 27, 1540, the Pope, in the Bull "Regimini Militantis Ecclesiae," approved the "Institute of the Society of Jesus," and on the following Easter Sunday, April 17, 1541, Ignatius Loyola was chosen as General. The papal approbation gave the formal character and right to exist as a legitimate body of Religious; the election of the General constituted the living authority; the renewed vows of Ignatius Loyola, Laýnez, Salmerón, Le Jay, Broet and Codure furnished the body of subjects. The constitution, written by the founder, sealed the permanent character of the organization.

One important member, Francis Xavier, was not present for these ceremonies. He had been sent by Ignatius in 1540 on the momentous journey to India.

The departure of Xavier for the East Indies opened a new chapter in Jesuit history. He and Simón Rodríguez were given to the King of Portugal for the mission of the Indies. He left Lisbon April 7, 1541, and on May 6, 1542, he disembarked at Goa. With a company of but ten men the Society could ill afford

---

11. This point is neglected in biographical studies of such men, thus making of them rather preternatural automatons than living human beings.
12. This date is traditional in the Order, rather than the date of papal confirmation.
13. See the excellent brief study by Goodier, *The Jesuits.*

to lose one from its European contingent, and him the best of all. Yet the parting words of Ignatius to Francis, "go, set the world on fire,"[14] indicate the high resolve and the confidence in victory that are typical of Loyola. This is the central idea of his celebrated Spiritual Exercises. The Society of Jesus was the Company, the advance guard, the light cavalry that would go out to the farthest regions to set up the standard of the King. Enough for them to be told that He wanted such action. He would guarantee the victory.

With the inspiration of Xavier and his example of intimate fellowship with his brothers back in Europe, the Jesuits began to extend their lines along the newly discovered routes of travel. Within forty years, from 1541 to 1581, they had circled the globe in both directions. Xavier blazed a way eastward as far as Japan before he died on Sancian Island. Alonso Sánchez in 1581[15] went from Mexico to the Philippines, and the following year he continued on to China and Macao. And with typical thoroughness of organization, connected centers were set up all along the way. Worldwide vision fitted in with unified control.

IV

The sixteenth century presented a marvelous opportunity for this new Order, though it revealed much that is paradoxical to the modern reader. Northern Europe seemed ripe for religious revolution, while the southern countries went to the diametrical opposite and produced a missionary development that is unparalleled in history. Spain led the way in the enterprise, but it is a mistake to find the solitary impulse in the Iberian peninsula. The seed of religious expansion lay broadcast over the continent, and the different turns in affairs are due rather to diverse leadership than to a plethora of evils in the old Church or to a much exaggerated Teutonic pragmatism. Why the Lutheran movement arose in Germany contemporaneously with Loyola in Paris and

14. See Schurhammer, *St. Francis Xavier,* and other works reviewed in *A. H. S. I.,* 1932, pp. 158, 159, 160, 161, 162, 171, 172, 174.
15. Sanchez is well described in Cuevas, *Historia de la Iglesia en Mexico,* II, 326.

Rome is more than mere mortals can tell. History but records the fact ·and its resultant.[16]

The Spaniards were indeed prepared by centuries of struggle, for the epic effort that began with the Columbian expeditions. Roused to supreme achievement after eight hundred years of conflict for national and religious freedom, they had just lately reached the coveted liberation in the fall of Granada.[17] Such forces were marshalled, such enthusiasm kindled in that traditional attitude of battle and daring, that an excess remained to overflow into the newly found countries of the Indies. Who does not thrill at the conquests of Cortés, or the gigantic expansion that within a hundred years gave the Catholic king a realm wider than ever was ruled by a Roman Emperor!

The religious heart of such a race demanded equal opportunities, and found them. To America they came, first of all from Europe, with portions to choose from as wide as a hemisphere. Franciscan and Dominican, Augustinian and Hieronymite, and representatives of many another Order, aflame with the vision of so brilliant a field for labor, rode the caravels beside the bold *conquistadores,* intent on the quest as *conquistadores de Diós.* They[18] and their queen,[19] the rare Isabella, cherished one ideal, to protect, to civilize, to Christianize the natives of this virgin land. To keep what was good, to add what was better, to stamp out what was base: the nation with a destiny!

From the ramparts of the city to which all roads lead, the General of the Society of Jesus saw this ardent emulation. And he had other Xaviers pleading to be sent into this wide realm. Later than their religious fellows, as their Institution was subsequent; the least, too, of all, according to their profession;[20] they were happy to have the rougher parts for their allotment, if there was anything left over. The turn in events gave them the opening they desired.

The Kings of Portugal and Spain were engaged in a royal race

---

16. An enlightened survey is Belloc, *How the Reformation Happened.*
17. Chapman, *History of Spain,* 1, c.
18. Fiske, *Discovery of America,* II, 272 sq., on beginnings of repartimiento and encomienda in Espanola.
19. Walsh, *Isabella of Spain.*
20. Proemium to S. J. Constitutions, n. 1.

for control of South America. Admirals and fleets, captains and cavalry began the conquest. But they could not finish it. The land was too vast, the peoples and tribes too many and often recalcitrant. Here was a problem that would have stopped the Roman legions, but later times had given a new agent to civilization, the monastic Orders.[21] The wise rulers now turned to these gentle folk,[22] and entrusted the task of taming the barbarians to the soldiers of the Cross.

North America saw a similar change in colonial policy, as the first experience of the Spaniards taught them a salutary lesson. Military power could not force the bronzed races; and, what was more, it failed altogether to respect the rights of the weaker aborigines. Charles V, as early as 1524,[23] in a *cédula real* (royal message), gave orders that more peaceful weapons be used to subdue the natives. For fifty years the crown held the leash over distant subordinates, and by 1573[24] there was a fixed system of using missionaries as the royal tool to pacify and civilize the Indians. France borrowed the idea when her first doughty warriors encountered fierce opposition among the savages of New France. England was unable to profit by the wisdom of her fellow imperialists, though she copied them in many another matter. She had no missionaries of her Established Church, and she persecuted those of any other Church. It was left to those Englishmen who had not found freedom at home to set out on their own account and do a work that officialdom could not countenance.

The coming of the Jesuits to North America formed part of this general operation. In the established centers of population, the older Orders labored at the task of amalgamating the various elements that gathered there for a livelihood. Sporadic efforts had been made to send Religious out beyond the frontiers, but their numbers could not sustain the demands that were made of them. To fill this need, to find a body of men who would set

---

21. Montalembert, *Monks of the West*, preface.
22. Williams, *People and Politics of Latin America*, is a good survey. Better arranged is the incisive work of Bertrand, *Histoire de l'Amerique Espagnole*.
23. Cuevas, op. cit.
24. Bolton, *Spanish Borderlands*, 166. Streit cites a pertinent cedula in his *Bibliotheca Missionum*, II (Amerika, 1493-1600), 210.

their whole endeavor on converting the tribes in the wilderness, was the motive that prompted the king to ask the General of the Jesuits for assistance.[25] This is clear in the letter of Philip II to St. Francis Borgia, May 3, 1566. The General assented, and in the same year the first band sailed away to Havana.

Then followed that continuous flow of Jesuit priests and lay Brothers to the northern new world, until the stream was cut in the suppression of 1767. To Mexico they came,[26] and built a line of missions that reached from Guatemala to California, the most notable missionary work of all the Jesuits on the continent. In 1611[27] the brave group of Frenchmen began the second wave in the advance. Up the St. Lawrence to Quebec and Montreal, and on into the wide lake country and the territory of the Illinois; down the Mississippi where they met their fellows marching upwards from New Orleans; thrusting aside meantime into New York and northward to the vast Canadian stretches; these chevaliers of the spirit left enduring marks of all those qualities that captivate the imagination.

Not long after the opening of that French mission, the third contingent disembarked[28] from the Ark and the Dove, on the morning of the Annunciation in 1634. They came in the Baltimore party, and they landed on a spot in the Chesapeake which they called St. Marys, not far from the Bay of St. Marys[29] where their forefathers had met death in 1571. Their ways were harder

---

25. See Chapter II, especially p. 17.

26. See Astrain, *Historia de la Compania de Jesus en la Asistencia de Espana*, II. For the foundations see Florencia, *Historia de la Provincia de la Compania de Jesus en Nueva Espana*. On the missions see Decorme, *La Obra de los Jesuitas en Mexico durante la Epoca Colonial*, the best summary of the individual mission works. Bancroft, *History of Mexico*, II, and *History of the North Mexican States and Texas*, I, are invaluable guides to materials, not superseded by any later work. Cuevas, op. cit., II, gives a skeleton treatment. The master book on the Sinaloa missions is Perez de Ribas, *Historia de los Triunfos de Nuestra Santa Fe*. Venegas, *Noticias de California*, is the source of histories of the California (baja) missions.

27. Thwaites, and the epitome of his work by Edna Kenton; also Parkman, op. cit., and the scholarly Fouqueray, *Histoire de la Compagnie de Jesus en France des origines a la suppression, 1528-1762*, I, sq., for good background. Campbell has a useful series, *Pioneer Priests of North America*.

28. The authoritative treatment is Hughes, cited above.

29. Cf. p. 21, infra.

than those of their French and Spanish fellows. Devoted to religious liberty,—it was their Provincial who had urged this grant on the Proprietor—,[30] their hands were chained by tyranny, and many of them went off in irons to inhospitable England. Still they managed somehow to stay on, until the day of freedom broke over the land whose savages they had come to teach in freedom's name.

Thus the ranks of these missionaries moved into North America in three separate divisions. Spaced by years according to the circumstances of time and men, the apparently segregated operations actually followed a quite definite arrangement. First in order was the decision to enter the open field. A pioneer group went out, carefully instructed, to locate in the uncharted country, to investigate the ground, set up a permanent establishment, and report back to headquarters. Pursuing their advantage, they won success in the campaign; and the example of their deeds together with the knowledge thus gained urged on and guided the next expedition. A third came on, from a different port, but just as in the first and second attacks, it took its motive force, its authority and direction from the center at Rome. The same system was set up, the same methods were used, as far as the terrain permitted. The same reports were returned to the General, who in this way led the battle over a wide and diversified front.

The vanguard of this enterprise, the Spanish Fathers, set foot on Florida soil in 1566. They reached Mexico, their first important conquest, in September of 1572.[31] These were the trail breakers. They first faced the wild savages. They mapped the field and found the best methods of attack. Back in Europe their fellows caught the enthusiasm of their victories, and begged to be sent to open new countries and give their lives in the same glorious combat.

The following pages are meant as an introduction to the story

---

30. Hughes, I, 249 sq.
31. Florencia, cited above, is a well-documented account of the founding of the Province of New Spain. He liksewise recounts most fully the previous efforts in Florida (his native province), Virginia, and Havana. He should be read in conjunction with the later Alegre. Nieremberg, *Varones Ilustres,* has several excellent biographies of the men engaged in these operations.

of these *conquistadores* in Mexico. The central figure in the story is a young man who came out of old León, and led the opening charge in the active campaign. He founded the first permanent Jesuit mission in North America, from which all the others in some way developed. He sealed his work with his blood. Such a man made history, and tardy memory at last arises to portray his life.

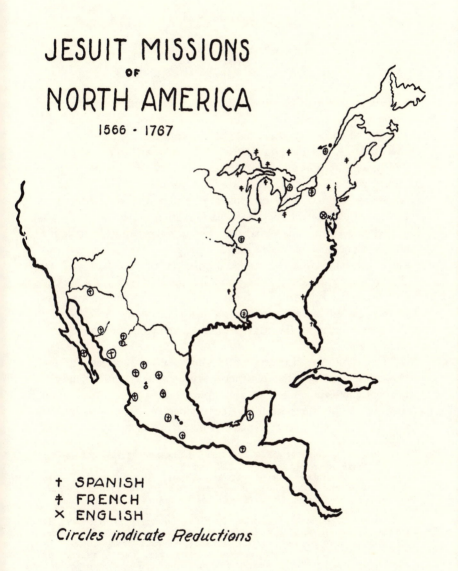

JESUIT MISSIONS
OF
NORTH AMERICA
1566 - 1767

† SPANISH
‡ FRENCH
✕ ENGLISH
Circles indicate Reductions

CHAPTER II

THE COMING TO NEW SPAIN

I

The continent of North America first admitted the white man through its southern gates. The chart of the voyages of discovery shows that the sailors followed the currents that sweep down past the Canaries, and then on the North Equatorial Stream they bore gently west and up into the Antilles. The tropical wealth of these Indies was a rich reward,[1] and the sovereigns of the old world never lost sight of Havana and its environs, the key to the first three centuries of international relations in America.

Stepping over from Cuba, the *conquistadores* quickly took the strategic positions of Panamá and Vera Cruz. While the isthmus always remained the highroad of transport, the province of New Spain became the finest colony in all America.[2] By 1521 Mexico City recognized the rule of Hernando Cortés. Twenty more years were occupied in reducing the Nahuac confederacy, in exploring the nearer parts of the Mar del Sur, and in building over all a solid regime.

Then came the discovery of the mines near Zacatecas, at the very moment when the Northern Mystery[3] was enthralling the intrepid pioneers. Onward and upward they went, this nation that was duplicating itself in the occident. The planter, the rancher, the urban entrepreneur—who were the really rich men,

---

1. Priestly, *Coming of the White Man;* Bolton and Marshall, *Colonization of North America;* Andrews, *Colonial Background of the American Revolution.* All three volumes stress the critical position of the Indies in American colonial history. See also Moses, *Establishment of Spanish Rule in America;* Maynard, *De Soto and the Conquistadores;* and Bourne, *Spain in America.*

2. Bancroft, *History of Mexico,* I; Fiske, *Discovery of America,* II; Prescott, *Conquest of Mexico;* Ixtlilxochitl, *History of the Aztecs;* Bernal Diaz, *Historia de Verdadia de Conquista de Nueva Espana;* Cortes, *Letters to Charles V;* Sedgwick, *Cortes the Conqueror;* Lew Wallace, *The Fair God;* Wissler, *The American Indian;* Brinton, *The American Race.*

3. Bolton, *Spanish Explorations in the Southwest;* Obregon, *Sixteenth Century Explorations;* Bancroft, *History of Mexico,* II; Sauer, *Road to Cibola.*

and not the miners, as many believe—laid the firm basis of enduring economic life atop the rather well-developed Aztec system. Political organization followed, as the *cabildos* arose, and the viceroyalty with its *audiencia*. Marriage of Indian and white brought a mixture of races and a sharing of what was best in either culture, sure proof of the breadth of mind and heart in the makers of America Hispana.

One further social factor must be provided. The elements of this new amalgam might be locally self-attractive, but taken in the mass they were centrifugal.[4] All these diverse forces must be fused into a unity.

The Spaniards realized, as has every nation in history, that "of all the dispositions and habits which lead to political prosperity, religion and morality are indispensable supports." Royalty desired in the subjects a conscientious respect for law. The rights of mutual happiness and possession urged the recognition of duty. Diversity of blood and priority of occupation made imperative a code of morals whose ultimate sanction lay beyond brute force. And a decent care for the inferior classes could be guaranteed solely by an all-embracing religious fealty. Moreover, the conquering people understood the meaning of Christianity, both as a law and as a power for progress. They had a living sense of their relation to the God of all, and they looked back on their national tradition with a lively gratitude. For they were the Crusading Christian Nation.

The religious history of Hispanic America is thus inseparably a part of the full picture. The Cross and the regal standard rose together. Royalty and people were frankly Catholic.

Philip II met the problem before him, as did his predecessor Charles V, in his supreme capacity under the *Patronato Real*,[5] and a large part of the *Codigo de Indias* reflects their serious attention to this function of government. Bishops, too, and statesmen, and other men of consequence, raised their voices often in petition or approbation of the work. And this zeal and interest

---

4. Note Zumárraga's expression "la babylonia de esta tierra." See Cuevas, I, cc. iii, x; II, c. 1.

5. See Note on the *Patronato Real*, p. 172 sq., infra.

resulted in the conversion of immense numbers of the natives and in a vigorous religious life among the immigrants.

Three ancient Orders,[6] the Franciscans, Dominicans, and Augustinians, entered on the colonial scene within twelve years after the initial settlement. Theirs was a vast work, and they did it well. And yet there was always room for more of these men. In fact, those on the ground were so busy in the cities and pueblos that the tribes beyond the reach of corporations were rarely touched. The report then came that a new Order of men had been formed in Europe and had received Papal authorization. These were the Jesuits, and they were rumored to be having high success in their endeavors.

At once a flood of letters[7] begged these new Religious to come to New Spain. Father Antonio de Araoz wrote to St. Ignatius from Madrid in 1547: "in Mexico, which is the principal city of the Indies of the Emperor, there is a gentleman,—I believe his name is Negrete—, who is an old and devoted friend of Your Reverence. And he writes to a man here that if he know anyone of the Company, he will have him write to Your Reverence that you send some (Fathers) there, for he has an excellent endowment for a house. Now if we were to be in all the places that ask for us, it seems to me that we should have, even in Spain alone, more houses than men."[8]

Polanco, in his life of St. Ignatius, develops the same point. "There are many who ask for the members of the Company, or even for whole Communities, and to obtain what they ask they urge their readiness to furnish habitations and all else that is necessary. Such a one is a certain bishop of the diocese of Michoacán in New Spain. Whenever he meets any of us he at once asks that some of the Company be given to him. He speaks of a bounteous harvest, in greatest distress for lack of husbandmen,

---

6. Bancroft, *History of Mexico,* II; Cuevas, I, passim; Alegre, *Historia de la Compania de Jesus en Nueva Espana,* I, 55. The years were respectively 1524, 1526, 1533.

7. See letters from Mexico reproduced in Florencia, Cuevas, Alegre, Astrain, l.c.

8. *Monumenta Historica Societatis Jesu,* Ep. Mixt., I, 360. See also Astrain, II, 299.

and he offers to provide all the needed funds. But that mission has not yet materialized."[9] This was written in 1551.

Nor would it materialize for many years. The background of the late arrival of the Jesuits in Mexico is involved in many difficulties that are not yet settled to the taste of historians.[10] The plain fact is that only in 1571 did the king permit their entrance, decades after their brother Religious took up their labors there. In 1566 Philip II sent a most friendly letter[11] to the General, Francis Borgia, asking for Florida missionaries. He wrote:

> Because of the good relations that we have with those of the Company, and the great fruit that they have borne and now bring forth in our domain, I have come to wish that some of the Order go to our Indies in the Ocean Sea. There is a daily increasing necessity for such persons. And Our Lord will be much served if the said Fathers go to those parts. For they are known for their Christianity and their virtue. They are, too, the *"gente de proposito"* (chosen group) for the conversion of those natives. And now for the devotion which I hold toward the said Company, I desire that some of them go to those lands. To this end I beg and urge you to name and order twenty-four of the Company to go to the said our Indies. Let them be approved by the members of our Council. They should be men of learning, of integrity and good example, such as you judge fit for such an enterprise. Finally, for the service which you give Our Lord I shall receive great pleasure and shall give orders that all necessary things be provided. And in their coming, that land will receive great contentment and benefit.
>
> I, THE KING.

Still, the main point is not settled by this letter. On the one hand, the king had early forbidden any but the three older Orders to cross over to New Spain.[12] Again, there was the matter of the tremendous drain[13] put on the scanty membership of the new Order, by the many other establishments so recently set up. A

---

9. Polanco, *Vita Ignatii Loyolae et Rerum Societatis Jesu Historia*, II, 321.
10. E. g., see Cuevas, II, c. iii.
11. Reproduced in Nieremberg, III, 321, and Alegre, I, 4. Cf. Florencia, l.c.; Astrain, II, 286 sq.
12. Cuevas, II, 322, 326.
13. See e. g., Astrain, II, cc. v, ix.

third cause of the delay has been uncovered by the late researches of Father Leturia;[14] it was a diplomatic problem.

For some years the General, Francis Borgia, had been striving to found a Congregation of Propaganda[15] in Rome. This congregation was to have complete control of mission work, under direct papal supervision, and one of its first aims would have been to install in the field the newer Orders, especially the Discalced Carmelites and the Capuchins. The Spanish crown found trouble in meeting this situation, and the movement was dropped.

Appeased by this turn of affairs, and urged by the many voices in New Spain, Philip II convoked the Junta of 1568. The upshot was that instructions were given the new viceroy, Francisco de Toledo, which would open little by little the territory of New Spain to the Jesuits. The road was now clear, and the Order responded quickly.

Francis Borgia wished the invitation to come from the king, as became the position of that monarch in the ecclesiastical field.[16] Their mutual friendship[17] made the matter easy, once the propaganda project was out of the way; and on March 26, 1571, Philip II directed a *cédula real* to the Provincial of the Toledo Province, Father López, asking for twelve Religious for the city of Mexico. On May 4, six weeks later, he sent another letter directly to Francis Borgia, and the General decided not only to send one contingent but to found a province which would be independent of Spain and would be called the Province of Mexico.[18]

---

14. See notes to Note on the Patronato Real infra, and bibliography in *A. H. S. I., 1932.*
15. Ibid. Cf. Corrigan, *Die Kongregation de Propaganda Fide und ihre Taetigkeit in Nord-Amerika;* Pastor, op. cit., XIII, 100-117; Rousseau, *L'Idee Missionnaire aux XVI et XVII siecles,* 74, 77, 85; Fish, *Guide to Materials for American History in Roman and Other Italian Archives.*
16. One should overlook the slant of Miss Hosea on this matter. See her *The Jesuits in New Spain in the Sixteenth Century,* University of California Master's Thesis, 1930. See also on Philip II in this connection Alegre, I, 4, 45; Astrain, II, 299 sq.; Cretineau-Joly, *Histoire de la Compagnie de Jesus,* II, passim.
17. Borgia had been Duke of Gandia. Cf. his biography by Bartoli, and see Sommervogel sub "Borja."
18. Philip II to Lopez, reproduced in Florencia, 72, and in Alegre, 1. c.; see also Astrain, II, 298, and Cuevas, II, 326.

II

The letter of 1566, quoted above, found its response in the prologue to the history of the Jesuits in North America, the temporary and dismaying attempt on the Atlantic coast.[19] Philip was inspired to write that letter through the insistence of Pedro Menéndez de Avilés, the *Adelantado* charged with the reconquest of Florida, from which he had expelled the French in so vigorous a fashion. Menéndez negotiated with the king for a complement of Jesuits to assist in this royal undertaking. Happy at this opportunity of entering a new missionary land, Francis Borgia replied to the sovereign by assigning several select men to begin the work. They were Fathers Pedro Martínez, Juan Rogel, and Brother Francisco de Villareal, the founders of the brief but significant operation in Florida, Georgia, and Virginia.

The missionaries left Cádiz on July 28, 1566. Together with the fleet that was bringing supplies to Florida, they sailed as far as the entrance to the Gulf of Mexico, where the Leeward and Windward Islands divide near Martinique. After following along the upper coast of Santo Domingo, the ship of the Fathers, a Flemish storeship,[20] left the fleet and made for Havana. Here they stopped for some days. Many soldiers and other laymen offered their services in the peaceful crusade, not for profit, but for the devout motives that are so often seen in the better class of Spanish colonists.[21] The mind of the Fathers opposed this assistance, and they set off in a small ship with only a crew to guide them.

By some mischance, the charts of the Florida Sea misled them, and for a month they cruised back and forth in search of the port of San Augustín. One day Father Martínez with a few sailors put off in a dory to call on some shore Indians. A storm blew

---

19. Shea, *History of the Catholic Missions in the United States*, l.c., and Astrain, II, 284-298, are the best short accounts. Much data will be found in Florencia, l. c., Alegre, I, 4-35, Hughes, I, 317 sq., Perez de Ribas, c. xiv, Nieremberg, III (on Segura), Ribadeneyra, *Vida del P. Francisco Borgia,* c. vi., The *Historical Magazine* throughout the 1860's, and the studies of Miss Mary Ross.

20. See documents in Astrain, II, 287.

21. See Astrain, II, IV, and Cuevas, II, passim, for documents and letters on the point. Passing proof of the same lies in this present writing.

up, and the main vessel was quickly carried out of sight in the tempest. Lost, the missionary and his companions begged for food in the name of the Cross. But the savages, the Tacatucuranos, who were then at war with the Spaniards, set on Martínez and the Flemish sailors, and the missionary and two of his guides were killed.

Father Rogel and Brother Villareal returned in distress to Havana without having found their fellows. The survivors of the massacre reached the same port by good fortune, and it was one of them who later gave to Father López the facts that are contained in his *relacion*[22] of the episode.

Two years afterward a larger contingent was sent out to aid the pioneers in the Florida enterprise. Father Juan Bautista de Segura was appointed their superior and Vice-Provincial of Florida, as they intended to set up the administrative unit that is called a province. Once in Florida, Segura recognized the fact that such a large number of missionaries could not remain there without burdening the few Spaniards and friendly Indians. He decided accordingly to return to Havana and begin a college, the first Jesuit college there, to be a center of operations in Florida and the islands of the ocean, and on the upper mainland. Menéndez gave his consent, and the foundation began its humble life.

From Havana several groups were commissioned to work in the vicinity of Santa Elena, our modern Port Royal in South Carolina, and in the territory of Guale or Georgia. They got along quite well for several months. But when the military commander put to death some mischievous natives, the opportunity to proceed in peace was ended and they came back to Havana.

Segura then planned a bold undertaking. It was to go to a land in which there would be no soldiers or merchants to enslave the converted Indians, and there to open an untouched field. Menéndez gave his word that all opposition would be removed. Segura was moved to this venture by a dusky convert named Don Luis, who hailed from a district called Ajacán.[23] He had

---

22. See Astrain, II, 288.
23. Ajacan is the land fronting on the Bay of St. Mary's (old Spanish name, but in Alegre's time called Bay of St. George: cf. I, 26), at the mouth of the Rappahannock. See Shea, *Spanish Mission Colony on the Rappahannock,* in Beach, *Indian Miscellany,* 333-344.

been picked up by Menéndez on a voyage of exploration, brought to Mexico and baptized and educated there, and then taken over to Spain to be shown at the court of the king. Don Luis made the return trip with the group of Jesuits. He now begged the Fathers to go to his tribe, assuring them that he was a potentate among them, and that he would act as interpreter and do everything to make their labor a succes. His secret motive seems likely to have been a wish to return to his people.

A small fleet was put in readiness, and the superior, with Father Quiros and six Brothers, said goodbye to Havana and civilization. At Santa Elena they took on board a young Spaniard named Alonso, in a capacity similar to that of the later French *donné*. The ships left Santa Elena, and continued to a point a hundred and seventy leagues beyond, in the bay called Santa María on the northern shore of the estuary of the Rappahannock. They disembarked on September 11, 1570. The fleet was sent back to Santa Elena, with orders to return in four months with provisions.

The Brothers built an excellent house, and set aside the best room for the chapel. In the fields nearby the soil was broken and seeds planted, in an effort to begin a self-sustaining life. The Indians in the neighborhood were quickly brought into contact with the mission. Don Luis was making good.

Then the catastrophe broke. Don Luis ran off to his family. Won by the allurements of savage freedom, he renounced his recent conversion to Christianity and refused further converse with the Fathers. They were dismayed at losing their one strong hope in the whole enterprise. They tried to win back Don Luis, and made several visits to the home of the fugitive. On their last call—they were begging for food, as the four months were up and the ships had not returned—Don Luis gave a word of command and the massacre began. It ended with the death of all the eight missionaries. The memorable day was February 4, 1571.[24]

The news of this debacle reached the General through the *relacion* of Father Rogel.[25] The fleet had come back too late to

---

24. Astrain, II, 299.
25. Cf. Carta del P. Rogel, in Astrain, II, 648.

save the Religious, and all they found were some Indians wearing the clerical garb, whereon they concluded that there had been an uprising. The Spanish layman of the expedition escaped the slaughter. After hiding some time, he at last made his way down the coast and over to Havana. And he told the story.

From Havana Fathers Rogel and Sedeno wrote to Borgia to tell of the death of the missioners. They had gone with Menéndez on the punitive expedition. They told the General that the Indians on the east coast were intractable and barbarous, and asked that no more men be sent to Florida, but that a visitor be appointed to come and close the mission. They could do more good in New Spain, in Sinaloa and New Mexico, for example, where they heard a vast open field was ready for the Order.[26]

Francis Borgia lost all heart on hearing of his fine men so fruitlessly losing their lives, and he begged Philip II not to ask him for further help in Florida.[27] With all the courage that he saw in his subjects, who were daring death in many parts of the world, he had no wish to make a useless sacrifice and expose his brethren in a land that plainly held no promise of success.

III

A change came over the General when his advisers brought word of a new request for the Fathers. With a natural eagerness they had longed to enter the province of New Spain. This district, in the fifty years now gone since the overthrow of Moctezuma and Cuachtemoc, was become the richest and most populous of all the western lands of His Majesty, King of Spain and Emperor of the Indies.

Growing with astounding rapidity,[28] Mexico already had its university and its cathedral. Trade flourished. Fine residences lined the palm-rimmed avenues. Caballeros curvetted in the plaza, and little folk dressed in old world costume sang the new world folksong. At evening the Angelus reminded all of the Christianity

---

26. Florencia, 41-66; Alegre, I, 48 sq.
27. Florencia, ibid.; Bancroft, *History of Mexico*, II, 700.
28. See Alegre, I, 38-43; Priestley, *Mexican Nation;* Bancroft, *History of Mexico*, especially II, cc. i, xviii, xix, xxv, xxvi.

that had come to stay, most Spanish of all the institutions of this wealthy, strange new Spain.

To the oncoming Jesuits this was a different sort of enterprise from the attempt on the Atlantic coast. Here was civilization. It is true that the Order was commissioned by Philip II primarily for work among the natives.[29] Creole education was a secondary objective. Yet all along the highways and on the border lines where barbarians roamed and fished and hunted, Spaniards had built their haciendas, and the mines and cattle runs were intermingled with the village of many a native tribe. This situation ensured a certain sense of order and peace, and a beginning of contact between the races, quite a fair prospect in comparison with the wilderness of the Rappahannock where Segura had attempted the impossible. There were, of course, nations beyond the frontier who were far from tamed; and these were the ultimate aim of the Fathers, as they were the hope of a government that looked for missionaries to hold an otherwise untenable territory.[30]

This new expedition was under the direction of the man who was named Provincial, Father Pedro Sánchez.[31] He was a doctor of the University of Alcalá, had been rector of that institution, and had twice held the office of rector in the Order. He was in charge of the college at Alcalá when he received the appointment from Francis Borgia in these terms: "go, my Father, with the blessing of Our Lord; and if we do not see each other again on earth, I hope in the Divine Majesty that we shall meet in heaven. And now, take the group of men from your province and assemble in Seville with all speed. I name you Superior and Provincial of New Spain. . . . At Seville you will receive your formal letters patent, and your royal license will, I think,

---

29. See cedula in Alegre, I, 56.

30. Bancroft thinks that even as the Jesuits left the port of Seville on June 13, 1572, the spot for the first mission had been chosen in the wilderness of Sinaloa. Still, nineteen years must elapse before that work was undertaken, and in the meantime a thorough-going province would sink its roots deep into the life of New Spain. See *History of Mexico,* II, 703, and Florencia, 65.

31. Appointed on July 15, 1571. Alegre, I, 46-47, quotes the letter to Sanchez and to the head of the Toledo Province. The men were chosen from the three Provinces of Castile, Aragon, and Toledo. See also Florencia, 73, and Cuevas, II, 326.

be given you in Madrid. I shall take care of that. It will be good to arrange at once in Seville for your traveling money, freight carriage, and equipment for the voyage."

The king at the same time addressed a *cédula real* to the Board of Trade in Seville.

The King. To our officials who reside in the city of Seville, in the Casa de la contratación de las Indias. Having seen the great benefit which the Religious of the Company of Jesus, who have gone to some parts of our Indies, have produced and still do produce, in the instruction and conversion of the natives there, We have ordered that Doctor Pedro Sánchez and twelve other Religious of the same Company should go to New Spain and reside there. The said Doctor Pedro Sánchez is going as their Provincial. And as it is my wish that you give them all that is needed for the expedition, I order our treasurer to provide as many maravedis as are required for the journey, to the same Provincial and the other twelve and the servants that they must bring for their help. Store their ship with enough provisions to last until they reach New Spain, conformable to the nature of the season at which they embark and the measure which you have set for other members of the said Company who have passed over to the said our Indies.

And to the Provincial and each of the other said twelve Religious you will give one vesture of black cloth, according to their normal custom, and to each a mattress and a blanket and a pillow for their ocean trip; allow to each, one real and a half a day for their entertainment and support during the time that they are in your city, or in Jérez or Cádiz or the villa of Sanlucar de Barrameda awaiting their departure. See to it too that when they leave the city, they are enabled to bring from their houses the books and clothing which the said Religious may have gathered together to take with them.

And with this *cédula* or its copy, signed by a public notary, and the bill of credit of the said Religious or whatever they have as a surety for the muleteers and their other expenses, I order that there be accepted and taken as remuneration whatever they shall show. Do you adjust the cost of the passage of the said Provincial and the Religious and servants and books and clothing, with the master or masters of the ship or ships in which they shall ride as far as the port of San Juan de Uloa. Arrange a cabin for each six of the said Religious and provide the like for their attendants according to my *cédula* or its copy, signed by the public notary.

In virtue of the same, I command our officials of the said New Spain or their substitutes, to pay for the said Religious on arrival, to the master or masters of the ships which bring them, whatever their cost has been. Let these officers provide animals to carry their books and clothing from the city of Verapaz to Mexico. And I order that this *cédula* or its copy, signed by the public notary, and the bills of the said masters and testimonies of the other expenses, be received and passed in account of the costs of the same Religious. In their Masses and sacrifices let them beg Our Lord to enlighten Us that We may govern well in the affairs of those parts. Do you procure their happy and rapid departure and a safe journey with all good will. Done in San Lorenzo del Escorial, August 6, 1571.

I, THE KING.

ANTONIO DE ERASO, SECRETARY.[32]

This document is interesting in its many revelations. There is the king who is so powerful as to control both sides of an ocean, and who can still care for the minutest details with precision and considerateness. There is the *Patronato Real,* seen in actual operation. There is the very simple arrangements made for the Religious, who are thus placed in a clear light as men surely not content to serve an earthly lord who would give them such paltry treatment, but who must have some great motive for this enterprise:—learned men, physically strong men, of good family, embarking for a strange land and cutting the ropes behind them. The lack of ostentation should not cloud the majesty of their ideal.

A rather long and rough journey, with stops at the Canaries and Hispanola, brought them to San Juan de Uloa on September 9, 1572.[33] Within twenty days they were all in Mexico. The viceroy sent word that he wished to give them a public reception. But the Provincial declined and they entered at an evening hour when few were about. They were a new Order, coming to begin a new work, and they preferred to go about it quietly. During the courtesy visit to the viceroy, Don Martín Henríquez, the

---

32. Given in Astrain, II, 301. Running comment on the Jesuits awaiting the fleet is found in Alegre, I, 46-47.

33. Florencia makes Sanchez stop at Havana to execute his duty of Visitor. Alegre straightens out the story.

Provincial handed him a *cédula*[34] of the king commending "the Fathers and Brothers who are sent to Mexico to sanctify both Spaniards and Indians."

This important *cédula* of Philip II to Henríquez reads as follows:

> You know, my viceroy, governor, and captain-general of New Spain, what great affection I have for the Company of Jesus. Their exemplary lives and works have made me decide to send some of their best men to our Indies in the Occident. I have high hopes that their teaching and conduct will product great fruit among my subjects and vassals, and that they will be an important force for the instruction and conversion of the Indians. Hence, by these presents, I send to you Father Pedro Sánchez and his twelve companions of the Company, who are coming to lay the first foundations of their Order in the province of New Spain. Therefore, as it is our intention to give them every assistance, and their work will do much for the service of God and the exaltation of the holy Catholic Faith, I order that when these said Religious come to your country you receive them with love and good will. Give them all the favor and help that you see needed for the establishment of their Order, so that they can reap the benefits that I expect from their work. Advise them, as one who understands the ground on which they will carry out their operations. Assign them land and materials so that they can build their house and church as I direct.
>
> I, THE KING.

The beginnings of the Jesuits in Mexico were extremely humble and straitened. They spent their first night in a poor hospital, their home for the next three months. Viceregal interpretations of royal generosity, contrary to all hopes and promises, found them no source of support. The voyage, too, had gone hard on them, and they were stricken with severe stomach disorders from which one of the Fathers, Francisco Bazán, died within a month.[35] After long privation, they finally began to see the future in a brighter color. The viceroy wrote the king on December 6, 1572: "Alonzo de Villaseca gave them a plot of ground and an unfin-

---

34. The cedula is in Alegre, I, 56. It is the charter of Jesuit work in America.

35. P. Francisco Bazan. Cf. Cuevas, II, 329; Alegre, I, 59.

ished little house. They are gathering material to enlarge it. So far they have nothing more than this. Your Majesty may be thanked that He is so well served. Here they have been well received. They have begun their work and the results are apparent."[36]

On December 11, 1572, they moved into their new dwelling, which became the central house of the entire province. This was the Colegio de San Pedro y San Pablo, the one true college which the Company had in New Spain in the sixteenth century.[37]

The idea of establishing a college came from the Provincial. Recognizing his prime purpose in coming to America as missionary, he deemed it best to set up a permanent base of operations before beginning the campaign. Here at the Colegio Máximo he would have a house of studies for members of the Order, embracing every step from the novitiate to the tertianship. Here, too, he would have a school of Indian languages and a complete secular curriculum. Here in the center of colonial life his men would come to understand the ways of the people, the climate, the economic system, the place of the natives in the scheme of things. It was a master stroke of organization, and for two hundred years this institution continued to be the hub of Jesuit activity in the viceroyalty.

To complete the equipment of the new province, it was necessary to inaugurate what is called the "Casa Profesa."[38] This professed house means a place wherein at least some Jesuits who

---

36. Henriquez to Philip II, quoted in Cuevas, II, 329. On their early work in Mexico see letter of P. Plaza to Aquaviva, Oct. 20, 1583, in Cuevas, II, 346 sq. Astrain, IV, 424, gives their numbers, as found in the catalogues and letters: in 1580 there were 107; in 1590, 200; in 1599, 314; in 1603, 345. The increase was rapid. Creoles were received, and former immigrants, as well as many volunteers coming from Spain for mission work, and after 1590 from other nations. Of course some of these were on their way to the Philippines and the Far East, but the large remainder is a sign of enthusiasm and zeal. Cf. Alegre, I, 72-73.

37. All the historians describe the Colegio Maximo. The best summary is found in Decorme, I, 15-17. See infra pp. 51-52. This present is a very sketchy account of the founding of this great college. Florencia adds much to the story. Note that Alegre, I, 75, says that Borgia forbade a college for externs until the Order was soundly established and well received.

38. See *Epitome Instituti Societatis Jesu*, passim, especially nn. 29, 2⁰; 493; 504. Cf. Alegre, I, 248-250.

are engaged in strictly spiritual ministries may live according to the highest ideal of their Constitution. The residents must be Professed Fathers, the first grade in the personnel of the Order, with a complement of Formed Coadjutor Brothers. This professed house may have no endowment whatever. If any property be given it, beyond the house, gardens, and a villa, it must be sold at once. For "in the professed houses that manner of life must be followed which is most remote from any contagion of avarice."

Such a house the *ayuntamiento* of Mexico offered to the Fathers in the first years. Again in 1584 Don Hernando Núñez de Obregón left them $4000 to build a Casa Profesa. The matter was deliberated in the 1587 Provincial Congregation, but on applying to the General the petition was refused. The reasons given were that the Jesuits had come principally to labor among the Indians, not the Spaniards, and that as the colleges were not well supported these latter could not support a Casa Profesa. A contrary decision was given in 1591, when $50,000 were given by Don Juan de Rivera, and in 1592 the Casa Profesa became a reality.

The Fathers who lived there spent their days working in the hospitals, prisons, teaching the little children the *doctrina* in the plazas, and assisting in other charitable works. These functions of the Casa Profesa continued for the full span of a hundred and seventy-five years, and at the suppression many people lamented the ending of this center of charity.[39]

In due time smaller institutions were begun in Pátzcuaro, Oaxaca, Puebla, Vera Cruz, and Guadalajara.[40] The Order was spreading its lines before opening a thorough-going advance in the missions. Meanwhile ambitious young creoles asked to be admitted, and the numbers increased rapidly. Generous and philanthropic men offered financial assistance. The authorities wrote to the court in praise of the Institute. The permanence of the province was assured.

---

39. E. g., Edmund Burke, *European Settlements in America,* I, 240; Decorme, I, 40.

40. Bancroft, *History of Mexico,* II, 703, gives the reason why the Jesuits first began schools rather than missions. They worked into the missions gradually. See Alegre, I, 65, 152; infra, p. 58.

As the terms of office expired and new superiors were appointed, a change of viewpoint characterized the regime. Were they attacking the main problem for whose solution they had come, the Indian missions? Was the momentum of the province slowing up after the first twenty vigorous years? Much work was being done, and on an increasingly wide scale. But letters of suggestion and criticism began to come to the General, the great Aquaviva, and he determined to send a Visitor to inspect the situation. The coming of this Visitor, Father Avellaneda, marked a profound change among the Jesuits of New Spain. With him the story enters a new phase, and the chief character is introduced.

CHAPTER III

THE BOY OF LEÓN

The Spanish peninsula is crossed from east to west by four great rivers, the Duero, Tagus, Guadiana and Guadalquivir. Each of these marks a chapter in the story of the Reconquest, as the warriors maintained their steady pressure southward, from the remote regions of Asturias to the splendid ramparts of Seville and Granada. In the watershed of the most northerly of these streams, the Duero, the gigantic struggle had its beginning. Santiago and Don Pelayo inspired the persistent fighters in the Cantabrian Mountains to drive out their Moorish rulers, and as the battle surged toward the Tagus a great State arose in the Christian territory. The tenth century found the Kingdom of León occupying all the land between the Duero, Navarre, and the Great Ocean. With the change of years and masters this ancient monarchy merged into the wider domain of León and Castile, until at last under Ferdinand and Isabella it was incorporated into the glorious unity of all Spain.[1]

This highland corner of a rugged country had and still has a population whose character fits the natural features of their land. Over the massive blue-gray hills is scattered a race noted for loyalty and dogged perseverance. In some parts the ground yields such sparse results that husband and wife must part to gain a livelihood, the man to find work in town industries while the mother guards the poor home and wretched farm. Other sections, though exposed to a biting climate and rare atmosphere, produce abundant harvests and pasture large flocks of sheep and herds of cattle. Roaring torrents cut wild ravines down the mountain slopes. Roads are few and communication is difficult. But with all the barriers that nature has put in the way, the people retain the spirit that brought their homeland liberty and renown.

The capital of the venerable province is León. This city of some 15,000 inhabitants has a strategic setting at the confluence of the Torio and the Bernesga. The name derives from the Latin

---

1. Cf. Phillips "Spain" in *Ency. Brit.*

legio, and mute evidence of its antiquity appears on the red
bricks of the old city walls. Each brick has stamped on the con-
cave upper surface "Leg. VII." This is the mark of the Roman
contingent that marched under the patronage of Gemina Pia Felix,
and in the early third century garrisoned this outpost of Pliny's
"urbs magnifica," Asturica Augusta.[2] Visitors who wander through
the city find in the cathedral, in the remains of the royal tombs
in San Isidro, and in the old fortified walls, the only reminders
that León was once the proud seat of a rule that stretched from
Oporto to the Pyrenees. The cathedral is considered one of the
finest examples of Spanish Gothic, smaller indeed than those of
Burgos or Toledo, but exquisite in design and execution. On its
walls is engraved the date of consecration, performed by eleven
bishops on March 6, 1149. And antedating that day by many
generations was a race of men, stout in freedom and in faith.
These sturdy mountaineers bent back the lines of the invader
and led their compatriots in reconquering their country. In time
their southern neighbors came to outstrip them in wealth and
population. Yet these hardy folk always remained the backbone
of the national cause.

One of the most illustrious families of the city of León in the
middle sixteenth century was the house of Tapia.[3] Rich and
landed with extensive holdings, they likewise made themselves
conspicuous in the annals of culture and of arms.[4] Chroniclers
name at least five men of the name who won signal renown in
letters and art. But lance and sword seemed to be their special
field of distinction. Andrés de Tapia figures in the story of Cortés.
His kinsman Cristóbal carried the first government message to
the conqueror of Mexico, and after the famous trial became among

---

2. Pliny, *Naturalis Historia,* III, c. iii.
3. Thus in all the biographical notices mentioned below in note 23, and
in the bibliographical chapter. Accounts of Father Tapia occur widely in
the seventeenth century.
4. See Espasa, *Enciclopedia;* Salvat, *Diccionario;* Bancroft, *History of
Mexico,* I, II, passim; *Memoirs of General Miller;* Bolton, *Anza Expeditions,* I, 243. Three other men of the same name were notable Jesuits:
Jose Tapia (1645-1698) was Superior of the Sinaloa mission, begun by
Gonzalo; Luis de Tapia (1613-1684) was Rector of Tarragona; Matthias
de Tapia (1651-1717) was Rector of New Granada. P. Juan de Tapia,
O. F. M., was killed by natives in the Zacatecas Mountains about 1556.
See Bancroft, *History of North Mexican States and Texas,* I, 117.

other things alcalde mayor of San Miguel de Culiacán in 1535.
Three centuries later General Miller encountered a Major Tapia
leading a Spanish attack in the South American wars of independence. Another Tapia was in a troop of Anza that founded
San Francisco in 1776. The title Vizconde de Tapia was created
in 1873, and today is held by the Marquis of Casariego.

In 1571 Gonzalo de Tapia was the fifth lord[5] of Quintana de
Raneros. Raneros stands some thirty miles to the west of León,
high on a tableland that is favored with a rich soil and a salubrious
climate. It is the center of an *ayuntamiento* of the same name.
Its thirty families are grouped round the parish church of San
Nicolás, whose spire dominates the neighborhood. Fourteen pueblos lie within its jurisdiction. Nearby is a hamlet called Tapia de
la Ribera, on the banks of the Rio Seco de Tapia. Time has
altered the ownership of the land—Tapia de Casariego near Oviedo
is now the domain of the Vizconde—but the name is carved deep
on the honor roll of León.

Senor Don Gonzalo was a lawyer of note.[6] As a youth he
had shown a marked leaning toward the ecclesiastical state and
manifested great interest in the problems of canon law. For this
reason his parents had given him a university education and got
him appointed judge and canon of the cathedral church of León.
In those days it was not unusual to find a layman in such positions. The chanting of the office does not appear to have been
a burden to a devout Catholic of Spain, and the holding of a
canonical judgeship was quite common for men in the world.
Even today a doctorate *"utriusque juris"* is an ordinary thing in
Europe, and the Spanish law student must study the text of canon
law as well as that of the civil code.

Medieval life developed a large number of non-clerical ecclesiastical lawyers. The profession was in honor, and it was lucra-
tive. Church law became rationalized much earlier than the civil
statutes of the new nations, and the latter codes owe much to

---

5. Alegambe, *Mortes Illustres*, c. i. p. 172 sq.; Tanner, *Societas Jesu
Militans*, 451; Albizuri, *Historia de las Misiones*, B, 3. On Albizuri see
Uriarte y Lecina, I, 81. "B" signifies the copy loaned by Carlos R. Linga of
Mexico City.
6. Albizuri, A, 208 sq. "A" signifies the Bancroft Library copy.

the rise of the canonical digest. Professor Maitland[7] has shown this in reference to the English law. His writings, too, make it clear that the prospect of practicing in the continental code of Christian Europe offered more concrete rewards of prestige and wealth than was the case in the courts temporal.

The don was thus preparing for a career of dignity suited to his standing, when an event occurred which changed the course of his life. The Council of Trent was convoked in 1546. Full thirty years passed, after the Wittenburg opening of the Lutheran revolt, before the reformation within the Catholic Church got into full swing. Of the necessity for reform this is not the place to write. The point here is that this Council set as its prime purpose to restate in clear terms the doctrines of the Church, and to make some needed changes in the material aspects of ecclesiastical life. The abuses in the administration of Church benefices called for special consideration. It was a very thorny and intricate question, and its solution forms an important event in history. The sum of the decision was that only clerics—and those in actual residence—might be admitted to prebends, and lay canons were ordered either to receive Sacred Orders within a year or else to give up their canonries.[8]

The exact date at which the Bishop of León promulgated this ruling is not evident from the accounts at hand, but it must have been in the early days of the Council, somewhat before the year 1562 in which the general regulations for benefices were sanctioned. Tapia, informed of the episcopal edict,[9] accepted the alternative proposal and resigned his canonical office to his younger brother. He gave up the judicial post at the same time and for the same reason. For it was declared that, according to the age-old practice of the Church, the clergy should be judged by their peers in causes that came under the cognizance of the courts spiritual. He then took a wife, and retiring to the management of his estate devoted himself to the rearing of his family.

7. Maitland, *Roman Canon Law in the Church of England.* See also Pollock and Maitland, *History of English Law,* and Stubbs, *Constitutional History of England,* passim.

8. Denziger, *Enchiridion Symbolorum,* l.c.

9. Albizuri A, 210-211. On the law see *Codex Juris Canonici,* l. c., and "Magna Charta," nn. 20-22.

He married the daughter of a royal councillor, a lady noble in blood and heroic in character.[10] She mothered a family that was known for its generous support of every worthy cause. She must have had something of the martyr in her, for she lived to see her first two sons give up their lives as officers in the wars of Philip II; and had she remained long enough on earth she would have witnessed her favorite child, the Jesuit priest, meeting death in another kind of warfare.

This boy, who bore his father's name, Gonzalo, was born in 1561.[11] His christian name implies that he was the beloved son from the beginning. His family had departed from that fixed formality that appointed the first male child to the future lordship, the second to the army and the third to the Church. They were of the new stock that the victory of Granada brought forth, the vigorous people in whom the full life of their country emerged. The older sons all took to arms[12] from youth. This one, too, would get a virile training. But he showed such marked traits of character that his parents watched his progress with close attention. Fortune, too, marked him for her child. At ten the untimely deaths of his soldier brothers left him the sole prospective heir to the ancestral title and the patrimony. More than that, he came into a world that opened the highest opportunities to genius and devotion.

His sovereign was the grandest monarch in all the world, with possessions from Cape Horn to Antwerp. The wealth of Zacatecas and Potosí, of the Netherlands and the rich peninsula, poured into his treasury. Yearly, almost monthly, news arrived of fresh victories and discoveries in the Indies of the Occident. In the Mediterranean his ships of war dominated the northern shores,

---

10. Ibid., A, 213.
11. Albizuri gives 1562 as the date, alone of ten who mention the fact. He copied Ramirez' lost biography. He sometimes misreads dates, as in his confused version of the canonry of Gonzalo Sr., and later on in the story of the governorship of Rio y Loza. He wrote at St. Ignatius Mission, Vampoa, in upper Sinoloa, in 1633, a situation scarcely permitting flawless scholarship. His censors corrected his manuscript and added enough data to clarify his statements. For example, on the date of the birth Father Varela notes: "mas parece esta errado. Vease al P. Puente en la vida del P. Balthasar Alvarez, c. 27, f. 113," in B, 3.
12. Albizuri, A. 213; Perez de Ribas, 131.

and from the South and East they warded off the incessant attacks of Islam. Elizabeth of England thought it well to win his favor, with her persistent game of coy coquetry and evasive promises. The Low Countries might be prosperous and aggressive and ready to break from their guardian—and here lay the trap that would soon precipitate his failure.[13] Yet everywhere the Spanish arms and ambition and intelligence carried the day. The whole world was in an uproar of achievement for this king and his vassals. And it counted little for his followers that they died on the battle field, if only they could die in the service of so great a king.

Nor only in things military was the nation alive. A recent novel, *By the King's Command*,[14] portrays the intellectual refinement of that century. Dona Isabella de Bobadilla moved in a world fit for Dantean Beatrice. The music and poetry, the drama and painting, are classic. That age of St. Teresa, of Lope de Vega and Vittoria, of silver and velvet, dreams and adventure and conquest, scarcely finds its equal in the ages of men. Wealth, magnificent castles, university life abound. Learning is in flower, and new groups of educators arise. Among these are the Jesuits, and the year 1571 finds them in their new college in León.[15]

To the door of that college in the very same year, Senor Don Gonzalo brought his son and heir. He was a boy of ten, of average build and dark complexion. His trim clothes and trappings fitted the poise and affability of his manner. He had been trained according to his birth in the best traditions of the land. The untimely death of his brothers made his future important, and his parents gave him all the care that love and family pride could suggest. The recent coming of the celebrated educators offered the instruction that a young noble demanded. His father felt happy in this further aid to ground him in "chivalry of character and a sufficient knowledge of the sciences to enable him to take his place in the world of men."[16]

---

13. See splendid analysis in Belloc, op. cit.
14. By Mary Brabson Littleton.
15. Cf. Astrain, II, 241, 598. The deed was signed on Nov. 22, 1571.
16. Albizuri, A, 215, quoting announcement of the college.

The college was popular and immediately successful.[17] In its eighth year it had six hundred students. Chroniclers call the course *"latinidad,"* a regime based on the classics of the ancient world with a final two years devoted to systematic philosophy. The first years were given to mental discipline and the rudiments of language structure and use. After that came a broad reading of the best authors, always accompanied by productive literary work. Verse and prose were written and declaimed; plays were composed and acted. During the classes in language, history and geography were introduced, not as separate subjects but as illuminating the chief subject, the everlasting man. The biennium of philosophy included a definite acquaintance with physics and mathematics, which were supposed to accompany and form an integral part of the scholastic investigations. The system aimed to turn out a well-balanced man, one who could think, speak, and act as a cultured gentleman.

These schools were called *"escuelas publicas"* or public schools. They were open to all who applied with good character and ability sufficient to warrant trust in their grasping the studies. And they were free,[18] though men of that day had no illusions of universal education, the so-called democratic doctrine that every child is capable of higher training. The funds for the support of the schools came from the donations of well-to-do citizens. People considered it a Christian duty to endow the education of youth, as clearly as they felt the obligation to establish and support hospitals, lazar-houses, almonries, magdalenas, and the many other social works that are the admiration of scholars. The Bishop of León[19] had founded this college, and it was called after him the College of Don Juan de Sanmillán. In the spirit of the time, that of the Council of Trent and of sixteenth century Spain, he was

---

17. See Schmitt, *Synopsis Historiae Societatis Jesu,* l. c., a very accurate and useful work to one studying Jesuit history. See also Albizuri, Ribas, Duhr, *Studienordnung,* Schwickerath, *Jesuit Education,* Herman, *La Pedagogie des Jesuites au XVIe siecle.*

18. Cf. Albizuri, A, 215-216. Almost every Jesuit school, college, and university (of which there were several—see Sommervogel) was endowed and furnished tuition and often board freely.

19. Cf. Astrain, II, 241, 598-599, in which latter pages the letters of the bishop are printed.

an enthusiast for schools; and he kept a close eye on his institution to see that it produced the results that he expected. His letters to the local Provincial and to the General of the Jesuits reveal his watchful solicitude for its success.

Gonzalo spent five years in this course of *latinidad*. The records of that time, as told by his early companions[20] who later sailed away with him on his great adventure, portray him as ranking high among his fellows. He is praised for his general talent. His memory was as imprinted wax that hardens. His mind was curious, eager, steady, sure. His later linguistic achievements in Mexico will bear out the truth of what here seems the vague glorification of eulogy. In his manner of life and dealing with his associates there was equal matter of approval. The constancy of life-long friends, who are in themselves estimable men, always connotes genuine worthiness, and the manifestations of sorrow on the death of Tapia force the conviction that he meant a great deal to those who knew him constantly from boyhood. One of them wrote in 1595: "I never knew anything base or mean in him. The brilliance of his heart shone in his face and every bodily movement." He was a leader of his set, and he led several of them to share in the glory of his later life.

An incident of those school days[21] shows what kind of boy he was. The quotation is taken directly from one of his contemporaries:

In the winter 1572-1573 three Jesuit fathers were traveling through France on their way to Rome to the General Congregation, to elect a successor to the deceased General, Francis Borgia. They were Aegidius González de Ávila, Provincial of Castile, Juan Suárez, Rector of the Professed House in Burgos, and Martín Gutiérrez, Rector of Valladolid. Other members of the Company were making the same journey. Some Calvinists of Cardelat, blood enemies of Catholics,

20. E. g., Ramirez, Santiago, Villafane, etc., who will be quoted later on. Ribas, 131, urges this point, and he was a most reliable historian.

21. This story seems to be correct in essentials, though doubtful in some details. It is quoted from Albizuri, A, 221 sq., more to give a sidelight on contemporary life—the times of St. Bartholomew's Eve—than for its intrinsic value. The data may be checked by comparison with the letters of Juan Suarez and Gil Gonzalez, in De Ponte, *Life of Balthasar Alvarez* (Trans. anon), II, 18-22. See also Chandlery, *Menology*, on Gutierrez.

brutal fellows clothed in sheep's soft garments, recognized them as priests and Religious. With eyes sparkling like red hot coals and inflamed with anger, they attacked the Fathers. They heaped insult on them from head to foot, then pushed and dragged them to Cardelat and locked them up in a castle keep. There in the dungeon they bound them with fetters and chains, as they do to highwaymen, murderers, and other criminals. The noisome prison and the ill-treatment they received caused the three to become seriously sick. This was brought on not a little by the blows on the face, the gashes from knives and daggers and reeds with which they jabbed them. Meanwhile they turned their tongues on them in most impure and horribly blasphemous language.

But the most lamentable result of the imprisonment was that the holy man, Father Martin Gutiérrez, received a fierce wound from a knife, and from that fell in a weak faint. Other ills added to his suffering, and for some days he experienced the full gamut of sorrow, yet with much patience:—the flesh enduring a terrible fever, the bones drying out, as that blessed soul struggled and battled to free itself from the weight of the body.

The students at León got wind of the attack at Cardelat. They were shocked at the news. As they were asked for help Gonzalo de Tapia came forward and offered to ransom the two living Fathers with a large sum from his own purse.[22] Then, after providing care for them in their distress, he sent them safe on the remainder of their journey.

Chivalry was master of his mind even in his twelfth year, foreshadowing the deeds to come two decades afterward.

There is little set down of his daily life at Sanmillán. Gonzalo was undoubtedly a very active boy, full of enthusiasm and energy. His friends noted a kind of magnetism that made others gather round him. He stood high in his studies, and with this combination of qualities he must have been fond of play and the games of youth. Later life found him unusually jovial and witty, adventurous, too, a lover of the wilds and the vast expanse of untamed country. And he became a Tartar for endurance of fatigue and arduous work.

22. De Ponte says 3000 ducats. Note that he errs in making Tapia a Jesuit at this date. Compare scholion of Varela on Albizuri, B, 6: "It appears that Tapia did this as a secular, and that he acted through another person. Cf. De la Puente, folio 119. According to De la Puente he would have entered before 1573, when he was only eleven years old."

He could scarcely have been otherwise in his younger days. In point of fact he was still very young when his life came to an end. It is no stretch of the imagination to see him at swords play with his instructor in fencing or his comrades in school. He often rode through the open country of his patrimony. He knew the thrill of the hunt and the mountain climb. He was a red-blooded, sixteenth century Spanish boy.

His teachers noted that in his actions he showed a certain definiteness and determination,[23] in spite of the light-hearted jollity of boyhood. And they were not surprised when he came one day to unfold a deep resolve to a member of the faculty. For long the thought of the life before him had played over his vision. Rising up in his mind was the idea of the *conquistadores* of the new world. Eddies of ambition surged about his heart. The cost was counted, were his steps to go right or left. There was the place his father would soon vacate, the lordship. There was the law, and university life loomed up with its reputation and social standing. Commerce had no lure, as beneath the outlook of a Leónese nobleman. What if he should follow the path of those who were his teachers? In his eager and gallant heart were dreams of a high design, the service of an otherworldly court. A noble should act his part. Was it not noble to step to the front and offer his sword and his life for this cause? Was there a land to conquer, hostages to ransom, gifts to give his Lady Queen?

The Spanish youth of fifteen is more mature than his American counterpart. At that age he is well on in college, and his mental attitude has a deep seriousness and a living reality. Gonzalo was ahead of his fellows when he came to college, owing to the careful tutelage and elevated atmosphere of a home of the *nobleza*. And when he came to the sixth year of his studies he quite naturally had a settled notion of what his career was to be. He would follow his countryman, Ignatius of Loyola. He asked

---

23. See Albizuri, A, 289 sq.; Ribas, 132. Albizuri has the most diffuse account of Tapia. He must be checked continually by other histories and documents. There is no biography of Tapia known, aside from the brief sketches in Nieremberg and the writers of the menologies (Tanner, Drews, Chandlery, Guilhermy, Cordara, Leroy, Decorme, Palomo, Patrignani— who uses the *Mortes Ilustres* of Alegre).

one of the Fathers if he might enter the Company of Jesus. The Father consulted his colleagues, and all agreed that the boy had an unusual amount of virtue and ability. His ripeness of judgment indicated a fixed intention to carry through on the line of action he proposed. Thereupon he was admitted to the Order[24] on Ascension Day, 1576.

---

24. Ribas, 132; Tanner, Patrignani, l. c. It was the twenty-sixth of May, 1576. The Rector of Leon was P. Jeronimo de Acosta, and the Provincial of Castile, P. Juan Suraez.

CHAPTER IV

The Quest

I

Live pure; speak truth; right wrong; follow the King.
Else, wherefore born?—Idylls of the King.

The Spanish renaissance raised up a captain and a company that were destined to ride chivalrously through the course of future history. This company, the Society of Jesus, can scarcely be called a Spanish Order, yet there is no doubt that its origin and earliest development owe a great deal to the country of its founder.

Ignatius Loyola[1] was a knight of Charles V. In the performance of his gallant duty on the ramparts of Pamplona he fell, his leg shattered by a cannon ball. He passed the succeeding months in bed at the Loyola castle in Azpeitia. Here, as often happens to one who is disabled and forced by circumstances to lie long hours alone, he pondered over the campaign he had been fighting in the service of his king. He remembered his bold grasp of the standard in the stand against the enemy in Navarre.

Ignatius loved his king with the affection of nobility. Many years he had spent at court in the following of royalty, quick to do service or to rise in answer to a call, stepping aside for a better than he, reverential to his lady queen, his sword always ready to protect the honor of the kingly dignity. That king, too, was worthy of such a courtier, great Charles, His Most Catholic Majesty. Charles it was, and Spain, and in particular Navarre, that roused this Basque to volunteer and risk his life in the losing battle of arms.

As these memories coursed through his mind—pardonable pride in one so intrepid—there flashed before him the thought that all this warfare was paltry beside a more furious battle that was waged for and against the King of his king, the King of all the world.

---

1. Biographies: Astrain, Hollis, Thompson, Van Dyke. All are authoritative. Thompson stresses the man, Van Dyke the times, Astrain the organization, Hollis the significance of Ignatius.

His king was only a man, his conquest but of men and lands. There was another conquest, and there was a King of Kings deserving loyalty beyond compare. And He had a cause that was wide as all the universe. Before the mental eye rode the lieutenants of that King, heroic Santiago, and Saint Peter and Saint Paul, at the head of grand divisions in the brilliant army. And surrounded by all the caparisoned warriors was the Fairest Fair, the Son of the Most High. "Cannot I," said Ignatius, "enter into that company? There is none so worthy of a true knight. I shall not be recreant." The clarion of the host sounded in his ear, the call of the King. And when he arose from his convalescence he was determined to enter the line, advance to the front, and give his best service in the affair that now, for the first time in his life, seemed the all-important quest for a true nobleman.[2]

Completely dominated by that philosophy of life, Loyola set out on his career. Step by step the design of his company developed, and his magnetic genius gathered about him a galaxy of rare followers. On the hill of Montmartre in 1534, the feast of Our Lady's Assumption, they plighted their first vows of union in knightly deeds. Six years went by and they knelt before the Father of Christendom to have him dub them a duly constituted Religious Order. And before the death of their master spirit in 1556, they had made a wide campaign throughout Europe, and their outposts reached to the hinterlands of Africa and the distant shores of the Orient. A truly vital force had come into the world.

The writings of Ignatius, most of all the Constitution of his Order and his Spiritual Exercises,[3] portray the cavalier spirit of the *conquistadores*. The military seriousness is there,[4] and the personal devotion to the King. Continually comes the call to follow the Captain, the Lord and Master of all. They must be prepared to live in whatever part of the world they might be stationed. They are to be ready to go at a moment's notice whithersoever

2. See autobiography of Ignatius Loyola, edited by O'Connor.
3. English translation by Mullen; commentaries by Longridge, Meschler, etc. The Spiritual Exercises form the basis of Jesuit preaching and mission work, as they do of Jesuit life.
4. This and the following paragraph are built on the Constitutions of the Order. The motivating ideas of the Constitutions are all found in the Spiritual Exercises.

duty sends them. They will have light equipment, assured by the vow of poverty. The same vow will be the firm wall of defense against the enemy. Obey they must, but in a way far beyond the purely military submission. This obedience in "as to Christ, our Creator and Lord," entirely, readily, and with due humility. All are to strive to observe obedience with special diligence, and to excel in it; and not only in things that are commanded, but in others also at the least sign of the superior, though there be no express order. And they ought to keep before their eyes "God, our Creator and Lord," for whose sake man is obeyed, and take care to advance, not in the perturbation of fear but in the spirit of love; that through this unity of opinion and determination may come a powerful bond of action.

Selfishness is to be shunned. They must seek and desire whatever Christ Our Lord loved and desired. Every advance or retreat must be according to the will of the Captain. His principles must be studied so that the soldiers will know Him more intimately, love Him more ardently, follow Him more closely. With irresistible power Ignatius drives his lesson home. Here is Spain at its highest, the glowing ideals of knighthood infused with deep religious conviction.[5]

The peninsula gave an early welcome to the Jesuits,[6] and poured out its treasures of men and materials in ardent enthusiasm. Father Araoz introduced the Order in October, 1539. Next year Francis Xavier and Simón Rodríguez passed through the country, and in a few months Peter Faber was laboring energetically in Castile and Aragon. In 1542 the first college of the Company arose in Coimbra, magnificently endowed by Portuguese John III. Valencia had the similar priority in Spain two years later. At Gandía, not far to the south, Francis Borgia founded a college as a prelude to adding his princely name to the rolls of the new institute. Twelve months after Araoz was made provincial of all Hispanic lands in 1547, there were six vigorous institutions: Alcalá, Saragossa, Valencia, Gandía, Barcelona, and Madrid. Still the col-

---

5. The ideal is quaintly caricatured by Cervantes with medieval familiarity.
6. See Schmitt, *Synopsis,* and Astrain, *Historia,* passim.

leges multiplied. The professors were gaining renown, and crowds came to hear their lectures or their sermons. Titled nobles asked to join their ranks, so excellent was their fame. And when Charles the king came to die, he left as his executors Philip II and Francis Borgia.

But it is not in things human to enjoy prosperity for long. Within the Order and without, the tooth of ingratitude, the sting of jealousy, discontent and disorderly ambition struck at the nascent organization. Did the Fathers risk their lives for the plague-infested poor? They sought some secret gain in their sacrifices! The Constitutions were published. They must be scrutinized and delated to the Inquisition! "These men are too successful. Some baneful harm lies hidden in their good fortune!" Enemies arose to stay the progress, but in reply a candid frankness quieted the antagonists. Internal dissension met summary trial;[7] the dissidents were dismissed, or amended their intransigency. The struggle past, the line swept onward.

II

Into this company of light cavalry Gonzalo de Tapia brought his youthful vigor. Enlistment must now be followed by the grind of discipline. Mind and heart must undergo formation. Worthy soldiers need the hardening of arduous training. In the Constitutions Ignatius had mapped out an explicit program of long and thorough education. He had a definite ideal to reach.

Tapia entered the novitiate at Medina del Campo. His name appears on the catalogue of that house in the spring of 1577.[8] The place had a great reputation as a trainer of Jesuits. Father Balthásar Álvarez[9] had but lately left the position of master of novices there, to open a new institution at Villa Garcia. His spirit carried on and became traditional in the Order as the model formation for young Jesuits.

---

7. See Astrain, ibid., III, lib. 2, cc. viii, ix, xv.
8. Cf. Archivum Generale Societatis Jesu, catalogi Prov. Hisp.
9. Biography by De la Puente. See also Astrain, III, IV, passim; also Schmitt, op. cit.; for complete works of Alvarez and life data see Sommervogel l. c.

The novice got his initiation in thirty days of retreat.[10] First he scanned the plan and economy of all life, and his own place therein. How far had he gone from the way of rectitude? The soul must be burnished and fixed in a new determination. Quickly, then, he was introduced to the heroic Captain and King, Christ. The Kingdom was spread out before his eyes, and he heard the call of the Leader, the personal invitation to join in the venture, ride close to the head of the column, feel the thrill of combat. He would not be asked to do any deed that was not previously tried by the Captain. They would share the same hardships and joys, and the victory was certain. Following full view of this campaign and all its ramifications, came a study of the enemy and his plans and methods, an added incentive to service and patient toil. Now he must look at the trials of warfare, the scars and bruises he would suffer, as portrayed in the Passion of the King. Last of all, the glorious future was revealed, the reward, the sharing of the honors, the intimate and unending friendship with the Lord who had shown the way through all the clash of arms, the grand adventure of life.

Thirty days were just the entrance into camp. Now Gonzalo had to put on his armor and step into the ranks. He had to live the life he had been contemplating. For two years the novitiate exercises would try his prudent judgment, his solid views, his adamantine courage. Fellowship with his brothers must be woven into a rentless garment. Eagerness for the business of life would have to ferment. Habits would form and mature. Skill in guiding his new-found powers must combine with principles set deeply enough to last a lifetime. After the apprenticeship he was allowed to pronounce his solemn promises, and in the vows[11] bind himself irrevocably to the service.

The vows put him beyond the period of trial, and he proceeded to a course of higher studies in the Medina superior college,[12]

---

10. Taken from the Constitutions, especially Part III.
11. Perpetual vows of poverty, chastity, obedience. Cf. Cotel, *Catechism of Vows;* also on the same subject, works of Thomas Aquinas, Vermeersch, etc.
12. See catalogue of Medina del Campo, in Arch. Gen. S. J. Cf. Astrain, II, passim.

especially adapted for that work. At this time the Ratio Studiorum[13] was going through its first evolution. The General Congregation of 1581 which elected Aquaviva laid down a decree: *"ratio studiorum examini subjiciatur"* (let the system of studies be examined). Five years afterward a finished but tentative model was sent to all the provinces, to get their approval or amendment. The final document appeared in 1599.

In 1578, then, when Tapia began the superior course, the Ratio was still in a state of flux, and one is not surprised to read in the record that the young student deviated from later practice in that his six years of higher study embraced two of arts and four of theology. According to custom he received no degree when he finished his studies in 1584. His success in the eight years since he began his Jesuit training may be seen from the following remark of Father Albizuri:[14] "at the end of theology, Father Juan Suárez, now Provincial of Castile (whom Tapia had ransomed), remembering the great benefit of his rescue by the young noble, offered him the best posts in his province, the first and highest chairs. But the young soldier did not want to be put ahead of his fellows" and he turned down the offer. One reason may have been that he was not yet ordained priest, because at the end of his theology he was still too young to receive that Sacrament. But there was a further reason.

During these years his philosophy of life had taken a higher position than that of his boyhood. He had entered into the Company with an indistinct view of the future, as was natural in one of his age. Now, every year brought news of his brothers and companions who had gone to distant lands. The most brilliant man of his Order, Francis Xavier, had landed in Goa in 1542 to thrill the world with his unique accomplishments. In 1547[15] five

---

13. For a thorough account of the formation of the Ratio Studiorum see Astrain, IV, cc. i-vi; also Duhr, Herman, Schwickerath, Pachtler, *Ratio Studiorum ..... per Germaniam, etc.,* McGucken, *Jesuits and Education.* In the last-named appears the only English translation of the Ratio (part dealing with the lower schools). For various editions and commentaries see Sommervogel sub "Aquaviva." A complete translation of the Ratio Studiorum has recently appeared in Fitzpatrick, *Saint Ignatius and the Ratio Studiorum.*

14. Albizuri, B. 86. Tapia was twenty-three years old, one year under the canonical age for ordination. See p. 52 infra.

15. Cf. Schmitt and the larger general histories.

Jesuits penetrated the Congo region of Africa. Before long a like number sailed away to Brazil, at the time when the pioneer, Xavier, was entering the Land of the Rising Sun. To Abyssinia and Ormuz, China and Peru, they set forth. The martyrdom of Segura in Virginia marked the date of Tapia's matriculation in the college of León. What a wealth of heroic romance to rouse the young heart! To think that members of one's own family were already *conquistadores de Diós,* such a long and glorious front!

The pride of nobility stirred him, and dynamic ideals called up his generosity. Might he make trial of these wildernesses, these strange and far-off strands? Nothing appeared too hard, no journey too long, no forests or savages too untamed, could he but rush ahead in the battle. He began to beg[16] the General, Claudius Aquaviva, to let him go on missionary work, and that in the land his countrymen were winning so rapidly, New Spain.

This same Aquaviva had recently received the report of the valiant death of his nephew, Rudolph Aquaviva, and his companions at Cuncolim in India.[17] Nature shrunk from offering more victims on the altar of zeal. "Must Thou char the wood ere Thou canst limn with it?" Perhaps he quivered before the insistent call of that motto that he saw written before him, A. M. D. G. If so his hesitation did not last. He was not chosen to fail in his trust as commander. He was known to have a special interest in the missionaries and their labors, and the subsequent part of his long generalship shows his intense preoccupation in this work of his brethren. His published correspondence reveals many letters to the entire Society, encouraging, directing, providing material help for the far-flung line in the countries of the heathen. His, too, is the classic expression of the Jesuit attitude toward missions, as the most important work of the Order.[18] "Agitur de re max-

---

16. See Albizuri, B, 8.
17. Biography by Goldie, *First Christian Mission to the Great Mogul.* Cf. Maclagen, *Jesuits and the Great Mogul.*
18. "This is our most serious concern, that these people are bereft of God. For not to recognize God is as much an insult to the Divine Majesty as it is a misfortune to a rational creature." Cf. *Epistola Generalium,* I, 218. Compare letter of Lainez, ibid., 48 sq. On Aquaviva, biography and works, consult Sommervogel sub "Aquaviva."

ima et gravissima, ut illi nempe sint absque Deo, cujus ignoratione, ut nihil divinae majestati est injuriosius, ita nihil rationali creaturae infelicius."

The letters of Tapia to Aquaviva came when the General was receiving urgent calls for men. Philip II lately had a petition from the Archbishop of Mexico, April 24, 1583. That prelate wrote:

> The Company of Jesus goes ahead with large colleges, and with such success in preaching, teaching, and explaining the doctrine, that I am forced to say to Your Majesty that their abilities, joined to their excellent life and example, are worthy of the grace and favor of Your Majesty and your recognition of them as true coadjutors of the bishops. These men, to give us greater assistance, undertake to learn with particular care the more general languages of the natives in the pueblos of this district. In this point they have made such patent progress that they call forth our appreciation and our gratitude to God. They are asked and urged to come to the province of Guatemala and others of this new world. They are too few to meet the needs of all parties. Therefore . . . I beg Your Majesty to be pleased to request of their General that he send another group of them at once and that they continue to come in each fleet.[19]

The king answered in a *cédula real* to the Archbishop, urging him to treat the Company with great consideration. Word had come from the General that the request for more men would be granted.[20] Aquaviva transmitted the message to the Spanish Fathers, and in 1584 an expedition of recruits departed for New Spain.

Tapia was among those chosen to go West.[21] His answer came from Aquaviva in the form of a notice from his provincial to make ready. With the other missionaries he traveled to Cádiz to take ship in the spring fleet. Unfortunately the chronicles tell nothing of his parting from home. There is thus hidden a very human story, of the son and heir leaving his devoted parents, never to return. Did they dream of his early glory? The like has happened before and since. Quite likely he took his leave as be-

---

19. In Astrain, IV, 403.
20. Ibid., 404.
21. Albizuri, A, 226 sq.; Ribas, 130.

came one of that brave troop, stout of heart, calm before others but inwardly torn at the separation. He concealed his grief to shield the tender feelings of his family. He knew the cost of that step to himself and to them, yet he kept a fair face during the ordeal. Perhaps he even showed a bit of joy beside the tightening lips, as he thought of the victory that he would win for the cause he meant to serve with the fullest measure of devotion.

The number of Jesuits in the fleet was twenty-three, five priests. ten scholastics and eight lay Brothers. Their superior was Father Antonio de Mendoza,[22] of equal name and lineage with the first Viceroy of Mexico. He carried letters appointing him Provincial of New Spain upon his arrival. Astrain describes him as a man of the highest nobility, not only respected but actually revered and loved by his subjects, an extraordinary thing in that time which so cherished liberty and independence.

They sailed out of Cádiz on June 25. In spite of contrary winds and a slow pace, they had a happy voyage. They were traveling over the waters that buried treasures of memory. Columbus had cut these waves in his tiny Santa María. Stout Cortés had passed that way in his black ship, carving the wake of destiny. Zumárraga too had plowed that course, and Las Casas long before him. There was place for dreams as they watched the moonlight dance on the boundless expanse of the broad Atlantic. Finally they sighted harbor, and on September 10 the ships arrived at Vera Cruz. Without a halt they took the road to the capital, where they were welcomed and at home in the Colegio de San Pedro y San Pablo.

In the beginning of October Mendoza took office and a new regime began.[23] The Society of Jesus had now been in New Spain for twelve years, but the newcomers found themselves inducted into a situation that was far different from their comfortable ways in the old country. Here they met a fresh, aggressive and vigorous people. Men moved in the stir of adventure and discovery. Bronzed natives, mailed warriors, rich entourages passed them on the streets. Beyond the city lay a country of bright promise. The seething stream of a new civilization was rushing on. It was the new world!

---

22. See Astrain, IV, 404.
23. See Cuevas and Alegre, l. c.

CHAPTER V

Overseas

The contingent of Jesuits that came with Father Mendoza rode into Mexico on the first of October, 1584. The Order had now set up a solidly organized province, and won the assistance of public opinion for the works that were projected or in operation.[1] The number of men was already too small for the extent of their labors. To add to this scarcity, sickness and death[2] were taking their count. The burden of pioneering had exhausted former energies, and a new crowd of enthusiastic young men cheered the hearts of those who were long on the scene.

They stayed at the main house of the capital and awaited orders as to their disposal. Mendoza took up his position with a long experience in government, aided by general esteem for the intelligence and paternal affection which he had shown in previous posts of authority. Such a man won immediate confidence from those who were before him on the ground, and he began to plan for the work of the next six years.

The Colegio Máximo already stood out as the central establishment.[3] The provincial residence was there until in 1592 it was moved permanently to the Casa Profesa. The novitiate, juniorate, and tertianship were there up to 1585. The courses in grammar, arts, philosophy and theology, for Jesuit students and externs, were given there for nearly two hundred years. This alone was a work that had important results.[4] This Colegio de

---

1. See letters of Viceroy, Archbishop, etc., in Cuevas, II, P. ii, c. iii, and in Astrain, IV, Lib. ii, c. i.

2. Cf. Alegre, I, 107, sq., on the plague of 1575, where he quotes P. Sanchez that two-thirds of the Indians died in that year. See also Nieremberg on smallpox in Sinaloa (III, 344 sq.), and the letter of Juan de la Carrera, p. 140 infra.

3. See catalogi Prov. Neohisp., e. g., 1585, 1592 (Arch. Gen. S. J. Mex.); also report to Plaza to Aquaviva, 1583, cited in Cuevas, II, 345-346 and 354; also Avellaneda to Aquaviva, cited in Astrain, IV, 392-417. Note Alegre, I, especially 105-106; also I, 72, 75, 76, 85, 160-161, 171, 181-183, 218-219; II, 95. See Decorme, I, 15-17, 60-63.

4. Until 1625 when they moved to Puebla, the Jesuit scholastics were given the same courses in philosophy and theology as the other students. Cf. Decorme, I, 15-17.

San Pedro y San Pablo was the ordinary dwelling of the teachers in the adjoining seminaries of San Gregorio and San Ildefonso, and of the inchoate seminaries of San Pedro and San Bernardo. Besides all this, it was the focal point for all the ministerial, social and charitable work of the Jesuits. The Casa Profesa had its special character.

The college, according to prevailing custom, had its "villa," eight miles southwest of the city. This farm not only furnished recreation for the weekly holidays of preceptors and pupils, but it produced much of the food and not a little of the clothing of the Fathers.[5]

Alegre describes the college buildings as they were in his day:[6]

Mark out a quadrangle four hundred varas[7] in circuit, and draw a line one hundred and ten varas from end to end. There were four patios. The first and principal patio had on the south side the lecture halls for theology; to the east were the classrooms for philosophy; on the north, the refectory; and at the west, the various storerooms and quarters for the servants. There were, besides, galleries and rooms for each faculty, except that the northern wing housed a beautiful and well-stocked library. Round the second patio were, eastward, the classes of grammar; on the south, the aula for literary functions and the class of rhetoric; at the north, quarters for the young men and the supplies for the haciendas; above were the respective living rooms and halls, though the northern hall was a large decorated chapel of our holy Father Ignatius. The other two patios were used for living rooms on the upper floor, and below were the remaining rooms for sacristy, dispensary, offices, and the like.

At the extreme southeast were the primitive churches and the seminary of San Gregorio. Corresponding to this, at the southwest, was the church of San Pedro y San Pablo. Along the northern border, orchards and shaded walks gave a rustic touch to the property.

With the others who had recently come, Gonzalo de Tapia

---

5. See Astrain, III, 143; Alegre, I, 74.
6. Alegre, I, 105-106.
7. A vara is about 2.8 feet. Hence the building was 308x252 feet over all.

waited here for his assignment. Not yet a priest—he was only twenty-three, one year under the canonical age for Major Orders —he was in an unusual position, though he had high commendation from León and Medina del Campo.[8] A report sent to the General the next year stated that he was able to teach any of the subjects he had studied, and do it with distinction.

One of the professors at the Colegio Máximo had fallen ill.[9] The course of metaphysics, based on Aristotle, and a fundamental subject in the curriculum of superior studies, was thus without a director. Mendoza chose Tapia to take over the lectures. This course was attended by a large group, undergraduates in the college, seminarians, adults who wished to advance their education.

The young scholastic walked into the halls of the college with confidence, though it was his first experience of the kind, as he had been in continual study since childhood. In those days, before the full development of the Society of Jesus, the program of training was quite flexible, and many men went through their entire preparation without the discipline of teaching that forms so important a part of their present education. He was, nevertheless, gifted with that mental attitude that faces and attacks a problem, rather than sits apart in confusion and worries about it. His whole background had made him aggressive and enterprising, his early home life and association as well as the spirit of the times, the times of the *conquistadores*.

How he acquitted himself of the trust shown him is plain in the record he left. He took pains to be clear in his exposition. He exhibited a wide reading, proof of the hours he must have spent in the library during his previous years. And his vigorous personality coupled with a generous and tolerant disposition won the applause of those who heard him. His superiors noted that they had a remarkable man in Tapia.

One day he was called to see his Provincial,[10] Father Mendoza. This able man was on the lookout for those who showed special

---

8. See Albizuri, A, 226, and cf. p. 60 infra. Tapia did particularly well in theological sciences.
9. The next three paragraphs are based on Ribas, 131, and Albizuri, A, 230.
10. Ibid.

talents and would profit by higher and more specialized study. Tapia, entering the room, was greeted kindly, and asked if he would like to apply himself to the further study of theology. His rector had spoken well of his abilities, and the parents of the students had commented on his knowledge and clear and forceful lectures. Would he care to work for the doctorate of theology?

The question startled him and roused his inmost feelings. Never had such a possibility crossed his mind. His studies, his teaching, were but to make him ready for the career he had chosen. His reply was an entreaty from the very heart: "The only reason why I left my home and family, why I put Spain behind me, was my desire to save the souls of the natives of these Indies, and to convert them from their idolatries. If I had wished to teach theology,[11] I would have accepted the chair in Spain where they offered me the best they had in the schools. I have rejected those offers. I want to correspond with the call of Our Lord, who has beckoned to me to step forward from the rear ranks. I ask you, Father, to forget this suggestion, and let me give my whole self honestly and generously to teaching the heathen."

The Provincial, to satisfy his ardor and avoid afflicting his spirit, agreed to grant what he asked. And to carry out the vocation which he saw there present, he assigned him[12] to live at the college in Pátzcuaro, see of the diocese of Michoacán, so that from there he might begin excursions on the missions.

But before he would depart, he had to take a great step.[13] During the springtime he was told to prepare himself for ordination, and at the end of the year the Archbishop raised him to the priesthood. This day of ordination must be marked well, for it is the psychological apex in the career of such a man as the one who is marching through these pages. On that day he is lifted up in heart above the normal things of life, to see with clear vision the unique course that is marked out for him. He feels a power that

---

11. See p. 46 infra.
12. Albizuri, A, 231-232; Ribas, 131-132. Ribas says his documents on Tapia are the *relaciones* of three dependable men who knew Tapia intimately. One of them was Ramirez. Ribas himself is the best historian of the Jesuit missions studied in this work.
13. He is called a priest in the catalogue of the province for 1585, as well as in that of Patzcuaro. See also Albizuri and Ribas, ib.

is superhuman, a trust in eventual success, and a disdain for the obstructions that may try to hinder his advance. From this point, as from the peak of a mountain, he looks down over the canyons and forests and rocky barriers before him. He notes the main objectives that he must reach, and he takes high resolves as with eyes straight ahead he walks forward on the path of life. It is a very real experience, the key experience in the career of a missionary.

Afterward comes the rude shock of mere earthly existence, as he finds himself once more out of the clouds and among men. In this case, the return to mundane things came in the form of an order from his Provincial to leave Mexico and go to the neighboring diocese of Michoacán. In Pátzcuaro three of the four men were down with sickness, and an opportunity was opened for the new recruit to meet the situation.

Michoacán, from its proximity to the capital, very early felt the tread of the armies of Cortés.[14] Abounding in mineral wealth —and rumor enlarged the supply of gold and silver—it had attracted a substantial population of Spaniards who were settled widely over the rich highlands.

This mountainous State, directly west of Mexico, was one of the fairest of all New Spain. The diocese extended over a hundred and thirty leagues from north to south, with its northern limits the Rio Verde, and its southern Point Petatlan. The Guadalajara River, rising in the springs of Tecualoyita, continued on for more than seventy leagues through the fertile valleys. Along the river, the many lakes had such an abundance of fish that they gave the whole province the name of Michoacán, or the place of many fish.

The principal city was then Pátzcuaro, near ancient Tzintzunzán, the court of the former kings of Michoacán. It stood on a plateau 7183 feet above sea level, in the center of an excellent farming country.

---

14. Bancroft, *History of Mexico,* I, II, passim, gives materials for the history. See also Cuevas, I, and Alegre, I, passim. Olid first set up a Spanish colony at Tzintzunzan; from it were developed the cities of Patzcuaro and Valladolid.

Alegre writes:[15]

With such rivers, lakes, and springs to enrich the fields, one does not find it difficult to conceive the admirable fertility of the land. We know that in times close to the conquest a native named Francisco Terrazas sowed four bushels of maiz and reaped six hundred in the harvest. We read that in those same times one of the first pobladores discovered an extremely rich mine in 1525. . . . There are now within the diocese the mines of San Pedro, those of San Luis Potosí, the famous ones of Guanajuato, and some less valuable in the neighborhood of the villa of León. . . . Besides these, there are many copper mines which the natives work with great skill, and there is a foundry a little to the south of Pátzcuaro.

He continues:

In the whole extent of that country they speak four languages; the Mexican, to the south and on the coast of the Pacific Ocean, which is likely the road used by the ancient Mexicans. In the center of the diocese the common tongue is Tarascan, an idiom very like the Greek in its abundance, its harmony, and the frequent and easy combination of one word with another. In many places north of Guanajuato they speak Otomi, a barbarian tongue, almost entirely guttural, and one which yields only to painful study and most serious application. In the remaining large section they speak Chichimeca, which seems to have been in other days the common language of all New Spain, as we relate more at length in another place. Some confound that idiom with the Otomi, the one that the Christians of San Luis de la Paz commonly speak; but many arguments, that would be out of place here, prove that it is not the ancient and proper tongue of those people.

The air is very pure and mild, the climate pleasant and healthful; and many people go there to convalesce and regain their strength. The natives are well built, vigorous, lively in entertaining. They have strong characters and are very dependable workmen.

The country abounds in medicinal roots. Others have written on this point, especially Laet in his general descrip-

---

15. Alegre, I, 87-95. He was a man of culture, observant, widely traveled, and critical. His geographical descriptions are well done. They were not copied, as Bancroft asserts in *History of North Mexican States and Texas*, I, 120, noting the near identity of Alegre's description of Sinaloa with that found in the *Documentos*. In the present author's opinion the charge should be reversed.

tion of America. There is a great variety of birds. Their plumage is used for adornment, according to the custom common to all the new world. The particular art of Michoacán is the painting of these feathers in different colors. This is done with such grace and elegance that the pictures have been admired in Europe, and given as presents worthy of the persons of our kings.

The king of Michoacán, in the time of Cortés, enjoyed a status but little below that of the Aztec Moctezuma. Tributary to the Nahuas, and awed by their prowess, still he ruled a land that was highly cultured. No tribes north of the silver country approached the level of those on the Nahuac plateau, in Michoacán, and Oajaca. Their buildings and temples were notable for their size and proportion. The calendar, too, that index of astronomical and philosophical thought, was well worked out. And their culture showed most in the depth of feeling of which they were capable.

Bernal Díaz is authority[16] for the account of the visit of the king of Michoacán, Tangaxoán, to the court of Cortés, to do homage to the conqueror. When this ruler of a brother nation came to Mexico, and made his way up the steps of the Teocali, he turned to cast his eyes over the immense wreck of the city of Moctezuma. Seeing this woeful end of a mighty dynasty, and the ruin of what had been a beautiful and most expansive capital, he shook with sudden emotion, and burst into tears at thought of the dissolution of that noble confederacy of Tenochitlán. He was no barbarian, this sovereign who could within four days gather an army of a hundred thousand, who could transport three thousand coffers of gold to Cortés, who had the royal nature pictured in these lines. Far from savagery, his spirit—and it mirrors the soul of his people—possessed the noblest refinement of feeling.

The Spanish conquest had now beaten down this race into a servile mind and robbed them of their riches. It had thrust them violently into a new framework of life, the colonial scheme of encomienda. By 1585 the natives were no longer independent in directing their own affairs. They had become charges of an-

---

16. Bancroft, *History of Mexico*, II, 48-50, gives the sources for this story.

other race, and they spent their hours doing the work or fawning on the favors of that race. The newcomers spoiled their temples and threw down their idols, and left their religious feelings blank for want of an object of worship.

It was now the task of the Christian teachers to take this down-trodden people who had fallen from freedom, and put into them a new leaven of life, and lift them back to the place that their human equality demanded. The missionary balked at the idea that the Indian was inferior of soul.[17] The conquest had shat-tered the morale of the natives, as it had beaten down the emblems of their culture. The broken spirits must be stiffened with re-newed vigor and brought back to a full life. And for beginning this program Vasco de Quiroga and his men deserve unqualified praise.

The earliest documents emanating from this territory came from what is called the City of Michoacán, sometimes cited as Pátz-cuaro. About 1576 a new city was organized slightly to the north-west and given the name of Valladolid,[18] (today called Morelia).

Jesuits were in Pátzcuaro within a year[19] after they reached Mexico. It will be recalled that the Bishop of Michoacán, Vasco de Quiroga, had been asking for them three decades before. This prelate was now dead, but in memory of him the *cabildo* had prom-ised to bring the new Order to their city at the first opportunity. Accordingly, in 1573, the *cabildo* and the dean of the chapter con-jointly offered the Provincial, Father Sánchez, a church with an endowment of eight hundred pesos annually. He accepted the proposition, though he had to reject a further yearly rent of four hundred pesos to support a chair of grammar and a preacher.— The Order could not then accept remuneration for such offices.[20]

---

17. The history of Zumárraga, Gante, Vasco de Quiroga, etc., shows the continual pressure put on the officials to permit and encourage the social uplift of the natives. Cf. Cuevas, I, cc. xix, xx, and Icazbalceta, *Obras,* passim; also Mendieta, *Historia Ecclesiastica Indiana,* Lib. IV, c. xv.

18. For the account of the change from Patzcuaro to Valladolid, see Alegre, I, 129, and the documents cited there.

19. Alegre, Astrain, Cuevas, Florencia, 1. c.

20. Cf. Cuevas, II, 342, and Alegre, I, 87, 95. The right to take pay-ment was later granted by Leo XII in 1824. On the history of this school before the Jesuits took it over, see Cuevas, I, 396-400.

—Four Fathers were soon at work there. They took over the church and residence, besides the important Colegio de San Nicolás, founded by the great bishop in 1540 for the education of young Spaniards.

In a short time they began another small enterprise, a seminary, or boarding school, for Indians. In the first days[21] no one had been allowed to educate the natives to the equality of Spaniards, nor was this institution intended to oppose that regulation. The aim was to develop the most promising youths to a point where they might be effective leaders for their own people. They were hard to train in European thought, and were given only the most fundamental bits of instruction aside from the *doctrina,* reading, writing, arithmetic and music.

A more ambitions program was attempted in Mexico, for one house connected with the Colgeio Máximo was reserved for Indians who were following the regular courses.[22] Students who were more talented were educated so that they might pass on to ecclesiastical or professional courses. It was thought necessary to form enlightened caciques and priests of the native races and languages, who were accustomed from birth to live in the difficult country and who were aware of the manners and feelings of the folk. A *cédula* of Philip II finally discouraged this work.[23]

In Pátzcuaro the seminary had as an adjunct a school of Indian languages[24] begun by Father Méndez, where the Fathers assigned to missionary work could learn the native tongues. Tarascan was the chief study, as it was the most common speech among the population. The students used a three-fold method. They worked privately at the grammatical notes made by their predecessors and the dictionary of terms that was being com-

21. See the controversy over San Juan de Letran, in Cuevas, I, c. xix, and Icazbalceta, *Obras,* II, 422 sq. On the seminary of San Nicolas see Astrain, IV, 426.

22. The Jesuits founded these schools or seminaries in Puebla, Tepotzotlan, Patzcuaro, Parras, San Luis de la Paz, Mexico, and Sinaloa, before the year 1594.

23. Cf. Cuevas, II, 373. The Franciscans and Augustinians had been working among the natives at Patzcuaro for many years. See letter of Carrera to Gutierrez in Arch. Gen. S. J. Mex. Hist.

24. See Astrain, IV, 426. Cf. letter of Avellaneda to Philip II (1592) in Astrain, IV, 415.

piled. They spent some time each day in conversing with the Indians who were always about the house for various reasons, some begging, some asking advice, and others studying in the native seminary. And as soon as possible, the beginners were required to deliver a sermon in Tarascan to the Fathers assembled for dinner in the refectory.

Into this regime Tapia made a ready entry. He had a remarkable gift for languages. Some whispered that he must have a supernatural talent, so quickly did he learn to use the native speech.

The very day[25] that he arrived at Pátzcuaro, September 6, he was sent over to Valladolid to begin a series of Spanish sermons at the church there. Undoubtedly he had been forewarned, for the rector, Ramírez, wrote that he showed wonderful fluency and power in his discourse, and he roused the admiring comments of his fellow Jesuits.

Then came the time for his Tarascan sermon before the rector and the Community. The date was September 21, just fifteen days after he entered the place. Pérez de Ribas[26] says "his speech was so ready and his enunciation so correct that the Fathers who understood called the performance a romance, a marvel." This done, he was appointed to go out and teach the scattered Tarascans on the haciendas of the vicinity.

A document of 1585[27] from the rector of this college—who, it must be confessed, liked Father Tapia and had been a friend of his since boyhood—gives a correct sketch of his standing at the time. The report is part of the regular triennial information sent from each house to the General at Rome. Tapia is thus described:

Name: P. Gonzalo de Tapia. Birthplace: León, in the dio-

---

25. Albizuri, A, 233. See Astrain, IV, 392, that Aquaviva approved separate colleges in both cities.

26. See Ribas, 131. One who knows Jesuit life will say that Tapia had begun his study of Tarascan before he came to Patzcuaro.

27. Arch. Gen. S. J. Mex. Hist. This document is part of the triennial information sent to the General from every house in the Order. The informations are taken on the occasion of the provincial congregations every three years. The covering documents omit names to protect the reputations of the men there described.

cese of the same name. Age: 25. Health: good. Entered
S. J.: 1576. Vows: simple. Study: 3 years arts, 4 years theology. Work: taught one year of philosophy; learning Tarascan.

A covering document gives a character sketch of each subject.
The one after his number reads:

> He has great ability, beyond the ordinary, with good judg-
> ment and fine prudence in any matter. He has had but
> little experience because of his youth. He is observant in
> common business affairs, and handles them well. In letters
> he is well advanced, both in arts and in theology, and he
> could teach any class in these branches. By nature he is
> quick-tempered, and a bit inclined to melancholy, yet not
> notably so. He is affable and very kind. He has excellent
> talent for preaching, teaching, or governing, and for any
> other ministry of the Company. He has facility in learning
> Indian languages, and a strong bent for dealing with the In-
> dians. He gives reason to hope that he will soon know the
> language of the other Province (Otomi) which he has already
> begun to study.

It appears that he had hardly come to work with the Tarascans before he took to thinking of the people beyond, the Chichimecos. The truth seems to be that the Tarascans were well
within the faith by that time. Between the lines one might read
that he had been importuned to go outside the borders of Michoacán. This turns out to be the fact.[28] The neighboring Indians
had heard of him, and had asked their governor to have this
new Father come to them. The appointment to the Tarascans
was an emergency measure. He was simply taking the place of
the incapacitated Fathers. For this he had been sent by his
Provincial, as also to prepare himself for future labors in the
same kind of work.

That Tapia found himself at home in the work is clear from
several details that have survived in different narratives. These
same stories reveal the impression that he made on his fellow-
missioners. The man whose ordinary jokes and little personal
traits are remembered for years must have had a striking character.

---

28. The story is carried on in the next chapter.

Ramírez[29] says that Tapia took with the Indians at once. He was jolly, a thing they liked. He made friends with them, with the help of his ready speech in their tongue and his spontaneous interest in their affairs. The little children used to run after him and catch up to him and make him tell them stories, stories, too, about holy things. "The *chicos* loved him," he says.

Older people liked him too, and, as so often happens, esteem brought imitation and docile obedience. Twenty years after his death,[30] the results of his work there survived in full vigor. The bishop, Covarrubias, of Puebla, on a Confirmation tour through the villages where Tapia had given missions, asked the people in astonishment how they were able to preserve themselves from the ugly vice of drunkenness that was so common among those races. They replied that the blessed Father Gonzalo de Tapia had preached so strongly against that evil that on the spot they had resolved to give it up forever, and that they were simply keeping their promise.

One day he was riding from Guanajo to Pátzcuaro with a canon of the cathedral, the rector of the college, other Religious, and a large crowd that had come to celebrate the feast of Our Lady of Pátzcuaro. Of a sudden his mule took fright and dashed for the open, stampeding the crowd and causing mixed feelings of fear and amusement. Tapia held on, for he had plenty of experience in horsemanship. He tamed the beast and rode back amid the applause of the throng.

The Indians became very devoted to the Jesuits, and several of them joined the Order as lay Brothers. Some years previously one of the race, Pedro Caltzonzín,[31] grandson of the last king of Michoacán, had become a lay Brother, and in the terrible plague of 1575 had died a victim of his charity in serving those who were stricken. His memory did much to bind the natives to the Order of which he had been a member.

---

29. In Albizuri, A, 236-237, B, 10-11. Cf. Ribas, 131-132. He quotes Ramirez, that in seventeen days Tapia learned to speak in the Caribe language.

30. See Tarascan letters on the death of Tapia, p. 165 infra. Cf. on Covarrubias the article by Acevedo in Mess. del Sagr. Cor., Jan. 1901, 41-53.

31. Cf. Alegre, I, 110.

Tapia now had to face an unpleasant situation.[32] Others began
to open an attack against him, both within and without his own
circle. Complaints came to his Provincial that he was given too
free rein for a man so little tried: he was too immature for
Indian work, too young to mingle at random in that civilization.
Others pointed out that he was working himself to the point of
exhaustion in his long, hard rides round the many pueblos under
his care. He was restless as Xavier, eager to do his work, and
equally thoughtless of himself as he was devoted to his charges.
The strain of uninterrupted labor was wearing him down.

Whatever were the facts in the matter, it is certain that his
Provincial, on visiting Pátzcuaro, had a long talk with Tapia and
assigned him to a new residence for the following year. He was
moved to the neighboring college of Valladolid, which had split
off from its parent institution at Pátzcuaro seven years before,
when the change took place in the diocesan see.

The fall of 1586 found him at Valladolid. It is quite likely
that for him this year corresponded to what is called in Jesuit
training the tertianship,[33] a year set apart after all the other
studies for the capping of the entire course. Once again the man
returns to the regime of the novitiate. He begins the year with
thirty days in the Spiritual Exercises. The remainder of the
time is spent in the study of the Institute of the Order, and in
mastering ascetical theology both for personal use and for the
care of the neighbor in after years.

The first years of the Mexican Province necessarily caused no
little disruption to the regular course of Jesuit life. The number
of the men was too small for adequate attention to all their works,
—only two hundred at this period.[34] Pioneer life, too, made regular living difficult. The great distances, the poor means of communication, the nature of a ministry among people who did not
understand European standards: all these things made for a re-
laxing of the normal rule. In his memorial as Visitor, Father

---

32. See Albizuri, A, 241, B, 10-11; also letter of Carrera to Gutierrez
cited above.
33. Cf. *Epitome Instituti Societatis Jesu*, nn. 426-438.
34. See Chapter II, note 26.

Avellaneda[35] in 1592 recommended strongly that these matters be put in order, and in particular that no one be allowed to omit his tertianship. For it had often been shortened or passed up altogether.

The inference from these facts is that Tapia was to make his tertianship on the fly. He would live at Valladolid in a more or less secluded existence. His only companion in this duty was Father Bravo of Valencia, who had come over in the same fleet with Tapia to New Spain. This change, somewhat violent for so ardent a young man, was taken without complaint, and the two began their year of solitude, study and prayer. As an incident during these ten months Tapia preached in the cathedral of Valladolid. At the end of the term he was again returned to Pátzcuaro. His course of preparation was ended. When the time came he would pronounce his last solemn vows, on March 19, 1593,[36] after the prescribed seventeen years, and become a full-fledged Jesuit.

---

35. Memorial of Avellaneda to the Province of New Spain. See in Astrain, IV, 408.
36. See scholion of Varela correcting Albizuri, B, 14-15.

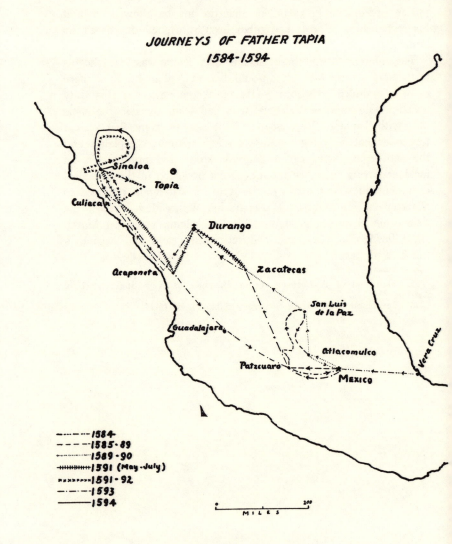

JOURNEYS OF FATHER TAPIA
1584-1594

Sinaloa

Topia

Culiacan

Durango

Zacatecas

Acaponeta

San Luis
de la Paz

Guadalajara

Atlacomulco

Patzcuaro

Mexico

Vera Cruz

- - - - - 1584
- - - - - 1585-89
· · · · · · 1589-90
++++++++ 1591 (May-July)
×××××× 1591-92
- · - · - 1593
———— 1594

0   200
MILES

CHAPTER VI

Skirmishing

The summer of 1587 found Father Tapia back in Pátzcuaro,[1] whose college was still governed by his friend and townsman Father Francisco Ramírez. Ramírez was to remain with the Indians for the rest of sixty years, and at the age of eighty he would still be hearing their confessions and teaching them the *doctrina*. He wrote a lost history of the Colegio de San Nicolás de Pátzcuaro, and also a biography of Gonzalo de Tapia which is known only in citations in Pérez de Ribas and his followers.[2] Ramírez was seven years the senior of Tapia, but they shared one another's counsel and support throughout their lives.

At once the young man returned to his old routine of weekly excursions, through the pueblos in the *partido* assigned to the Jesuits. To Tapia the work in Michoacán was simply an apprenticeship. It was the door opening onto further native labors. The language barrier was leaped. The traits of the barbarians were analyzed. Collegiate prestige and lecture hall atmosphere receded into the remote past. He learned to work for a miserable population, and he developed a character that would be ready to face savages.

As he rode along the mountain paths, the old restlessness took hold of him again.[3] He wanted to go out to those parts so appealing to the conquistadorial mind, *"mas allá,"* the land beyond. He would become an *adelantado,* in a wilderness all his own. These journeys were not hard enough; the Indians were too tame and had too many to care for them. He pointed out to his rector that he felt called to the wild country, to the *"misiones entre infieles."* He said he was wasting his life in the seminary for Indians and the pueblos there, and he asked leave

---

1. Albizuri, A, 248.
2. Perez de Ribas was a source book for Bancroft, Bolton, Chapman, Priestley, as well as for Alegre, Astrain, Kino, Venegas, and many minor writers.
3. Ribas, 132. See Albizuri, A, 253, B, 16.

to go and live among those natives who were abandoned and untouched by other missionaries. This work seemed more urgent to him,—an instance of that individual light and thought that motivates different characters and produces the variety in life and in vocation.

As yet he had not set his mind on his ultimate goal. Like other men he advanced by steps along the way. The entire province of Jesuits had as a common objective to set up missions beyond the sphere of colonization, but they went ahead a little at a time.

The immediate point to attract Tapia was a group of peoples living at the northern angle of a triangle whose base would run from Mexico to Pátzcuaro.[4] In that direction lived the Otomis and Caribes, who were for the most part unaffected by Spanish control. But the great urge was to enter the country of the wild Chichimecos, who lived at the apex of the triangle. Many of these people had heard of Tapia, through that marvelous system of transmitting information that was common to all the aborigines, and they asked their governor to get this Father for them. The request came to Ramírez, who told Tapia what had happened. Within a few days he was on the way.

Chichimecos was the generic name[5] given to all the "wild men" who made such havoc to the adventurers into the north country. The word in its best sense referred to the early race that inhabited the Nahuac plateau, and their history was written by Ixtlilxochitl. This descendant of the royal line says in his introduction:

> The Toltecs, Aculhuas, Mexicans, and all other nations of that territory pretend to be of the Chichimec race,—so-called from their king Chichimecatl, who led them into the new world, and who, according to tradition, had come out of Grand Tartary. He gave his name to his followers and

---

4. Albizuri, A, 253-255, B, 16-18.
5. See Bancroft, *History of Mexico*, I, 96, and II, 395, etc.; Alegre, I, 278-286; Cuevas, II, 390-395 (with interesting documents). Don Fernando D'Alua Ixtlilxochitl wrote in Spanish the *Historia de Chichimecos, o de los antiguos reyes de Tezcuco*. It was translated into French. Another history of these same people was written by Tovar, on which see Beristain and Sommervogel.

descendants, and that custom has been preserved; so that today practically all the provinces and towns bear the name of him who first colonized them.

The country peopled by this race (about 900 A. D.) in their first colonization, formed a circle round Tezcuco about two hundred leagues in circuit. Bancroft says that they were never permanently subjected to the Aztecs.[6]

Cuevas writes[7] that nothing is more indefinite in Mexican history than the classification of those nomadic and fierce tribes that moved over the middle of Mexico, within a circumference of a hundred and seventy kilometers radius and with its center in the north of the State of Guanajuato. The dominant language of the group was Otomi, the most barbarous and rough of all those spoken in New Spain. They included most probably the Huachichiles, Tamaulipecas, Janambres, Pames, and Huestecas.

For sixty years these Chichimecos were the obstruction to any conquest of the northern districts.[8] They formed an unbreakable barricade to commerce and to the full exploitation of the mines. And to the missionary they were a barrier to the winning of that wide territory. They roamed along the highways from Mexico to the mines of Zacatecas and Guanajuato, and the other parts of Nueva Galicia and Nueva Vizcaya. They wrought great damage to property and inflicted many cruelties on the ranchers settled along that frontier. They assaulted and robbed, and often murdered, Spaniards and Indians alike. The mere mention of their name struck terror into travelers. For fear of them many gave up their estancias. Often roads were deserted for months after one of their raids. Trade and the mining business fell much behind early hopes. Sometimes they were so bold as to ride to points within twenty miles of the capital. There was no peace while they were at large.

Thus wrote the royal *audiencia*[9] to the king in 1589. The

---

6. Bancroft, *North Mexican States and Texas,* I, 12.
7. Cuevas, II, 390.
8. See Alegre, Ribas, Cuevas, l. c.
9. The documents in this and the following paragraph are printed in Cuevas, II, 390-392. Luis de Velasco II writes to Philip II, Oct. 8, 1590 (ibid.): "To remedy this difficulty (of the Franciscan attempt to subdue the Chichimecs), our Lord has moved the fathers of the Company of Jesus

same *relacion* urged the point that, with all the garrisons and convoys of soldiers, nothing had been able to pacify these Chichimecos. Alegre notes that ancient injustices had fired their blood to this predatory existence and to resistance to death. The viceroy, the Marques de Villamanrique, saw that the root of all the trouble lay in their grievances over ill treatment by earlier and contemporary Spaniards. Soldiers and land-holders (the *gente de campana*) went far and wide through that territory in their own interest, hunting and enslaving the Indians and taking off their women and children. In retaliation, roused to vengeance, the natives were running riot. Nor could the situation end till they stopped the cause.

This viceroy ordered a cessation of the state of war, removal of *presidios* and soldiers, and a contrary policy for the future. He issued a mandate that only Religious and Christian persons might go among them. In the letter reporting these matters to the king, he added that this new policy was doing wonders; the Indians now treated the whites as friends, and peace had come over the land. The roads were safe once more. In very few places was there any need of escort to travelers.

The taming of these Chichimecos was due in no small measure to the work of Father Tapia. The governor asked for him.[10] The rector of Pátzcuaro approved, and he set out alone on his campaign to overcome these fierce Indians, who could not be checked by sword or armor. He began his *entrada* just across the border of the present State of Guanajuato. During his stay among them he worked steadily northward, till he won a great victory, the settlement of a pueblo where the main body of them would have a permanent home.

He is said to have visited over two hundred groups of them during this expedition which lasted two years.[11] Chief of the centers of these forlorn people were Purbandiro, Yerepuato, Nu-

---

to send four religious (Tapia went first) who knew their (Chichimeco) language, persons approved because they are skilled in that work. In my opinion there will be a betterment of things."

10. Albizuri, A, 253, B, 16.
11. Ibid.

manan, Paqueco, San Felipe, and Panxamo. In these villages
there was not an adult who did not go to Confession to him
during that time. The result was that a nation at war turned
to peace and concord with the Spaniards. For himself there
seems to have been no danger. Some of his friends sent him a
horse for his quick escape if the Indians were to threaten him.
He gave away the horse and suffered no harm.

A young giant of an Indian[12] offered to assist him in his work,
and Tapia appointed him his fiscal, or settler of disturbances.
This representative of the Father at once adopted an important
personal reform, the wearing of clothes; and his example and
urging brought all the tribe to conform to this usage which was
entirely foreign to their previous custom of a breech cloth or
nothing. Tapia endowed his fiscal with a ruff and staff of office,
and sent him about teaching the *doctrina* with authority. If anyone hesitated or proved refractory, this stout fellow would reach
out and take him by main force, without his feet touching the
ground, to the mission chapel.

Tapia then wrote[13] to the Provincial to come and see the good
results of his work, or, if he could not come, to send him a helper.
The answer was a companion to help him with these people,
Father Nicolás Arnaya, the man who later became Provincial.
The two worked on with great success, and the nation that had
been so obstinate and so much feared took on the aspect of good
citizens.

During an interval in 1589, Tapia and Arnaya[14] rode over to
Zacatecas and Durango to give missions to the mining popula-
tions there. On this journey they met the governor of Nueva
Vizcaya, Rodrigo del Rio y Loza, and from this meeting came
the idea that would determine the chief part of the life of Father
Tapia.

While things were prospering, Tapia resolved to try a new
scheme.[15] It was to gain over the Indians to a settled type of

---

12. See Albizuri, B, 21-23.
13. Cf. Albizuri, A, 263-264.
14. Alegre, I, 268.
15. Albizuri, A, B, 1. c.

political life. The first move in the process was to gather them in groups round centers of population, and show them how sensible it was to plant crops and raise stock for their livelihood. He had their confidence in his sincerity and his knowledge, and they watched the maturing of the maiz with the interest of first-born propriety. Then he told them that they were going to build houses round his mission chapel, in the midst of the chief group of their nation. It was at the place now called San Luis de la Paz, the center of the Huachichiles. There he commenced to induct them into actual political life. He gave them governors of their own race, for though they were technically *in encomienda,* they paid no attention to the claims of the Spaniards. He taught them how to elect a *cabildo* for this pueblo, and for the others which they were to incorporate. Their tribal law was to remain in force except for a few of the most important colonial regulations. They could manage their own justice, but it must be in court and not by barbarian torture and death.

To commemorate this event, he decided to found a special pueblo[16] and organize a municipality under viceregal charter. In thanksgiving for their happiness he called it San Luis de la Paz, and the pueblo remains to this day. Their enduring memory of him is there seen in the picture[17] that hangs in the church of San Luis de la Paz, and recalls his dual benefit to them, peace among themselves and with the Spaniards.

At the height of his activity among the Chichimecos, he got a summons to come to Mexico for a conference on the missions.[18] The Provincial wanted him to address the gathering, to explain his methods and success, and to point out the best line of action for the future. He and Father Arnaya left the Indians and traveled south on the main road from the silver country. The council was held, and the Provincial, Mendoza, again noted that he had an unusual man in Tapia.

---

16. Founding a pueblo meant getting viceregal incorporation for the settlement.
17. See Decorme, I, 107.
18. See Albizuri, A, 264, B, 24.

CHAPTER VII

THE SIGNAL TO ADVANCE

The journey from Mexico brought Tapia and Arnaya back to Chichimeco land a month after they had left it.[1] On their return they found that affairs had taken a peculiar turn. They had been making their headquarters at a little pueblo called Atlacomulco.[2] Now when they arrived they found that a party of Franciscan Fathers had set up a convent there. The Franciscans appear to have held a general sort of commission to care for these Indians. They were now at work and laboring hard to continue along the lines begun by their predecessors.

Tapia and Arnaya were faced with a decision. Would they stay on conjointly with the friars, against the accepted code of the day? Would they appeal, and make one of those unsavory cases that brought disfavor on the work of those days? Or would they withdraw absolutely? For reasons of peace and the best interests of the mission they determined to withdraw. They bade goodbye to the Franciscans and wished them well. Their wishes were realized, for that same convent of Santa María was still in full flower when Albizuri wrote his book forty-five years afterward.

They retreated to San Luis de la Paz in Guanajuato beyond the *partido* of the friars, and prepared to carry on that mission. Then the same old uneasiness came over Tapia again. This work was entirely too quiet for him.[3] There was too little danger in it, once the Chichimecos were in a permanent state of peace. Besides, these Indians were now well within the Christian orbit, and could be cared for with small expenditure of effort and

1. Albizuri, A, 264, B, 24.
2. Eighty-eight miles northwest of Mexico. On this episode cf. Albizuri, A, B, ibid. On the Franciscan commission to work these parts, see Cuevas, II, 392.
3. See Ribas, 134. On the intentions of Tapia see Carrera to Gutierrez, Mar. 1, 1600, f. 12. The Franciscans had borne the brunt of Chichimeco work for three decades, on which cf. Mange, 337. Note that the full conquest of the Chichimecos required another whole decade, 1590-1600.

sacrifice. But over the mountains, *mas allá,* was an immense tract where a large population lived in utter ignorance of the truths of the Gospel. Day and night the idea tormented him.

A letter from the Father General at Rome, addressed to Tapia at Pátzcuaro, to which house he was technically attached, tells a large story in its implications. He must have written his thoughts overseas not long before, for in July of 1590 he received the following message from Aquaviva:

17 April, 1590.

You owe much to Our Lord, in that He has so bountifully blessed you and communicated to you this desire, which shows what He intends for you to His greater honor and glory. The matter of the missions is in my mind more important than anything else. Thus I feel now, and I have felt the same for a very long time. And I again commend to your soul that you go into that field. The Lord in His goodness is giving all the brethren such zeal and enthusiasm, in order that by these and their other ministrations they may gain many souls for His Divine Majesty. I trust that with the earnestness and good example of Your Reverence there will come the same abundance of grace to your fellows, so that all as good soldiers will attack the conquest of souls that is so important. I commend myself to your sacrifices and prayers.

Claudius Aquaviva.[4]

The letter of Tapia that prompted this reply is not known today. But it is clear that he wrote to ask the General something special, as there is no ordinary correspondence between individuals in the Society and the General. Evidently he begged to be singled out and sent to the new field that had not yet been opened up, the *"misiones entre infieles."* He had exposed his interior feelings on the matter, and the General answered that he too was of the same mind. Several times Aquaviva had written to the Jesuits in New Spain, to remind them that their prime purpose[5] in coming to that colony had been to occupy themselves with the uncivilized Indians, in the parts not hitherto

---

4. Taken from original journal of Aquaviva, as in Arch. Gen. S. J. Mex. Tapia was an "excurrens missionarius" from Patzcuaro.

5. See infra, e. g., pp. 10, 22, 23, 26, 28.

touched by other religious influences. He had answered the petition to open the Casa Profesa in 1587 by denying the request, on the ground that the first business of the Fathers was the mission to the heathen in those regions.

Albizuri remarks[6] that at this time Tapia importuned his superiors to allow himself to employ himself in farther fields. He also wrote to the viceroy, Don Luis de Velasco II, in the same vein. A short note on the *Patronato Real* later on will show why it was thought necessary to speak to the civil authorities about such matters. Finally the Father Visitor, Diego de Avellaneda, who had lately come over to New Spain, heard his plea. Father Gerónimo Díaz was sent to take his place with Father Arnaya at San Luis de la Paz, and Tapia was summoned to Mexico[7] to talk over the affair with the Visitor.

What now took place in Mexico decided the future history of a large part of New Spain, as it did the next hundred and seventy-seven years of Jesuit activity there. For that reason it needs some detailed explanation.

The Jesuit Order has an interesting Constitution.[8] The General is elected for life. He in turn appoints the rectors of each college, the primary unit of government. Colleges are grouped in provinces, and over each province is a provincial, likewise appointed by the General. The provincials and rectors are each singly independent in their own spheres, and they manage their separate organizations with authority that comes directly from the General.

Whenever an entire province has some pressing problem of moment, or some unusually serious calamity or defect or need, the General sends a Visitor, who may have all the power of the highest authority, that of the General himself. The coming of

---

6. Albizuri, B, 24, note.
7. Ibid. Perez de Ribas says (36) that Tapia and Perez went directly from Mexico to Zacatecas, and then on to Guadiana, in 1590. Thus also Albizuri, B, 27-28.
8. See *Epitome Instituti Societatis Jesu,* Proemium, tit. vii, "De Superioribus in Societate Constitutis"; also n. 538; especially Pars nona, tit. ii, "De Gubernatione Societatis Universae." See Oswald and Fine commenting on the Constitutions.

a Visitor is then an event of great importance, and always marks a decided step in the history of that province. While on the ground he acts as highest executive and judge. He hears evidence and suggestion. He changes men and officers at will. He institutes policies, methods, establishments, as he sees fit. He is, in a word, the powerful force of reform from within.

Now in 1590 the Province of New Spain was at the crossroads. Eighteen years had gone since the Jesuits first reached Vera Cruz and set up their center of operations in the capital. They had expanded their forces and were managing many different works in several cities and towns. They had likewise established contact with the natives within the immediate reach of the chief city. Undoubtedly they thought—all men so think—that they were holding their own, and embracing all the territory they could control.[9]

But contrary to their opinion—and this appears to be a perennial case—the General in Rome was thinking faster and farther than were they on the ground in the new world. Aquaviva[10] was continually impatient for his troops to advance and extend the lines. On the matter of the missions, the reader will notice that he has several times expressed his impetuous ambition. And when the local provincial[11] was unwilling to send his men into the wild lands of the unconquered and heathen Indians, the head of the Order despatched a Visitor.

This man, Diego de Avellaneda,[12] had served for some forty years in positions of trust and honor. Always kept in some official capacity, he had carried on important business in most of the countries of Europe. His personality made for the esteem and respect of all whom he approached, and the Province of New Spain was fortunate in receiving his assistance and direction.

His commission as Visitor singled out two points of em-

---

9. In fact, their letters show that they felt the spirit of the times, and were reaching out for constantly widening opportunities.

10. His regime, 1581-1615, marks a period of great expansion and internal consolidation in the Order. For materials on this point see Sommervogel sub "Aquaviva."

11. Cf. Cuevas, II, 373, and Astrain, IV, 428-429.

12. See Astrain, II, III, IV, passim; also Alegre, esp. I, 226.

phasis.[13] He must see to the manner of living according to the full tenor of the Constitutions of the Order, and he must positively set in motion the *"misiones entre infieles."* The first of these duties was cared for in a kindly but adequate manner, as may be seen in the reports he made to the General and the King of Spain.[14] There was no serious flaw of religious life to be observed, though he did point out several faults that were more or less to be expected in a pioneer country. The superiors were as a rule rather harsh to their subjects, a fact that followed to some extent from their comparative youth. Most of them were in their thirties. The year of tertianship was often shortened or passed by entirely. Some of the men were so occupied in external work that they had no time for prayer and Community life,—a thing that went hard with that close fellowship and solidarity that was much needed in those trying days. But the greater part of his accounts is taken up with the fine story of the brave and effective service in the cause they were prosecuting.

On the score of the missions, however, he differed radically from the man who took office as provincial in 1590, Father Pedro Díaz. Díaz felt that the small number of his men would be compromised in new expeditions that might jeopardize the success of the old establishments. Moreover, as Avellaneda wrote the General, March 11, 1592, the provincial was giving little attention to the study of native languages, and he showed meagre interest in pushing the mission lately begun in Sinaloa. There had come a request for aid in that sector, and it was only after much bother and patience that the Visitor could get the provincial to send on two Fathers and a Brother. "If things go this way while I am on the scene," he wrote, "your Paternity will recognize why I fear that when I go away he will throw the whole business into a corner."[15]

Avellaneda saw the hesitancy of the provincial, and he determined to start things himself. After the previously mentioned

---

13. See Albizuri, Alegre, Astrain, passim.
14. See Avellaneda to Philip II in Astrain, IV, 409-417. Cuevas directs this letter to Aquaviva, II, 345. His references, generally correct, here show some typographical slips.
15. Avellaneda to Aquaviva, Mar. 11, 1592. See Astrain, IV, 428.

conference with Father Tapia, he sent him to assist in the budding Indian seminary in Zacatecas, there to await further orders.[16] Then he watched his chances. He was afforded an excellent opportunity in an offer of aid from an unexpected source.

The work of Tapia in the Chichimeco country had sent its echoes to the furthest northern limits of New Spain.[17] The lands of those Indians ran as far as the mining district of Zacatecas, and now that the formerly wild men were pacified, they came and went to that city regularly.

They say that a white man among Indians quickly acquires a reputation and a name. Tapia was a byword with them, for his vivacity of nature, his generosity, and his goodly speech. Their friends in the silver city handed on the story, and in no time he was a marked man.

Zacatecas was a young city when Tapia arrived in 1590. Only five years before it had received its charter from Philip II. Its origin dated back to 1546, when Juan de Tolosa discovered a rich vein of silver in the mountain there.[18] The same year the pueblo was founded, and it quickly became the mining center of North America, with all the phenomena of a gold rush, the daily strikes, the turbulent mass of men and women, the glamorous tales and the melancholy disappointments. Cristóbal de Oñate, Diego de Ibarra, and Balthásar Treviño, opened up excellent deposits, and they, with Tolosa, were before long the richest men in America.

The city was built in a ravine of the Sierra Madre, at an altitude of 8050 feet over sea level. Today, white, flat-roofed houses of four or five storeys overtop each other along the narrow, crooked streets and climb the steep hillsides. Towering above them all is the Bufa Hill, crowned by the venerable sanctuary of Nuestra Senora de Los Remedios. This city is most important for missionary history. To name but one celebrity, here

16. See Albizuri, Alegre, Ribas, l. c. Cf. Note 6 above.
17. See Ribas, 134.
18. See Bolton and Marshall, *Colonization of North America,"* 55, 58; Priestley, *Coming of the White Man, Mexican Nation,* l. c.

the renowned Padre Antonio Margil was presidente[19] of the Franciscan College of Guadaloupe, of the Propagation of the Faith, the College that sent so many missionaries to the northern frontier in the eighteenth century.

When Tapia reached the Indian seminary, he found a city large in population and varied in the concourse of races. There were Spaniards, Mexicans, Otomis, Tlascaltecans, Tarascans, Chichimecos and others, each occupying its separate quarters in the town.[20] All were interested in mines. Beyond the city extended the large haciendas with their wealthy produce of stock and grain, —for the millionaires of New Spain were more often farmers than miners. The mining rush always subsided in favor of landed settlement, even though the wealth of silver developed in Zacatecas was rivaled only by Potosí in Peru. The silver city was then the financial capital of Nueva Vizcaya, the province governed at Guadiana by Rodrigo del Rio y Loza.

A Jesuit Father, Hernando Suárez de la Concha, had preached there during Lent in the years 1574 and 1575, and had received proffers of financial aid for a residence when the Fathers could come permanently.[21] Again in 1589 Fathers Pedro and Mercado carried on the same devotional exercises. On that occasion they were given a piece of property near the hermitage of San Sebastián, and a small sum to maintain a house where the priests could stay when they came to give missions. The establishment was fixed the following year by the visitor, Father Avellaneda, who sent there Fathers Augustín Cano, Juan Cajina and Gerónimo Ramírez, with Brother Vicente Beltran. One Father was to preach to the Spaniards, and the other two to the Tarascans who had come to work in the silver mines. The Brother managed the house. Many a time they quelled the miniature wars that broke out among drunken men, white as well as natives. The civil officers were entirely unable to keep the peace among them on festive days when they set to stoning and knifing each other.

---

19. On Margil see *Cath. Ency.*, l. c.; Bolton, *Spanish Borderlands* (Texas), *Texas in the Middle Eighteenth Century*.
20. See Albizuri, B, 24.
21. Alegre, I, 83-84, 225-229; Decorme, I, 42. Cf. Avellaneda to Philip II in Cuevas, II, 351.

This little college was the point of departure for the first missioners who went out to Sinaloa, Tepehuanes, Laguna and, after
Tapia had made the foundation, to San Luis de la Paz.[22] Two
Fathers,[23] one of them Gonzalo de Tapia, were added to the staff
in 1591, one, as the catalogue says, as a teacher of reading and
writing, the other for the rudiments of grammar. The philosophy
lecturer came some years afterward.

The exploits of Tapia were well known to the governor of the
province, Rodrigo del Rio y Loza, and the two became quite
friendly. This was a fortunate circumstance, for the distinctly
missionary character of the Jesuit work in New Spain owes much
of its impetus to the aid of this remarkable man.

A distinguished cavalier and a companion of Francisco de
Ibarra, in the conquests and discoveries of that notable pioneer
and millionaire miner and ranchero, Rio y Loza[24] was one of the
heroic characters in the early history of Mexico. He was a native
of Arganzón in the diocese of Calahorra on the Ebro in Castile,
at the edge of the farthest Moorish conquest of the tenth century.
He came to New Spain as a soldier of the king. Advancing in
command, he was captain of the skirmishing cavalry under Ibarra,
on the famous *entrada* that carried all over the northwest of contemporary Mexico. For his services he was made a Knight of
the Order of Santiago. Like Ibarra, he invested carefully in
mining stock, and on his retirement from active service he had
accumulated a goodly fortune. His rancho bordered the road
from Zacatecas to Durango. So broad was his estancia, and so
great his herds of cattle, that he is said to have branded 24,000
calves during one springtime.

Hospitality was his chief virtue. His home was a refuge and

---

22. Cf. Decorme, Alegre, l. c.
23. Decorme, I, 42, following Alegre, says it was in 1591; that is, the
winter of 1590-1591. Albizuri, B, 24, says the sermons of Tapia did much
to straighten out widespread marital difficulties.
24. See Ribas, 35, for short biography; also Albizuri, A, 91; B, 26.
Alegre and Astrain follow Ribas, apparently not knowing Albizuri. Ribas
tells of the large herds. Rio y Loza gave a large sum to found the college
of Durango (Guadiana). (Thus Bancroft, *North Mexican States,* I, 124).
He wrote the viceroy and king to encourage the Sinaloa work. See Astrain,
IV, 436. Durango was the political and ecclesiastical head of Nueva
Vizcaya. Thus Albizuri, B, 40.

a halting place for all who made that hard journey in the early days. "In 1604," writes Ribas, "I was traveling that road to Cinaloa. With me were a captain and a party of gentile Indians who had gone to Mexico to ask the viceroy for *padres* and the *doctrina*. And I saw with my own eyes the liberality and magnificence of that caballero, Rio y Loza, and also the practical exercise of Christianity that he exhibited. And it struck me that here was a replica of the old patriarch Abraham, whom God kept in these fields for a refuge and an aid to travelers."

This dashing hidalgo had settled down after his wide roamings in the governorship of the northwestern province. His territory was divided into Zacatecas and Sinaloa; it embraced the present State of Durango, and extended up until it was lost in the Northern Mystery. He took a special interest in Sinaloa, where he and his illustrious companions in the list of *conquistadores* had begun or ended most of their expeditions. His youth gone, his pastures grazing more cattle than any rancho of his time, his reputation made, Rio y Loza gave thought to the larger things of life. He wanted to see the province of Sinaloa a flourishing civilization, and its Indians brought to the true Faith. From 1585 onward he appealed to the Provincial of the Jesuits,[25] Father Mendoza, to send him some missionaries. Now that the Fathers were in his capital, he saw them in action and he liked their work. He had spoken to one of their number about going far north in his country, even to New Mexico.

Albizuri[26] tells that Father Tapia actually wanted to go to the distant land of New Mexico, of which he had heard from the lips of the explorers returning to Zacatecas. This new "Otro México" was very much in the air in those days. The populace of the mining town was continually stirred by the stories of the northland. Plans for colonization were afoot. Tapia also heard that the natives of those parts were idolaters, and he "asked his superiors and begged the saints to intercede for him that he might be sent there." He likewise communicated his wishes to "Comendador Rodrigo del Rio y Loza, Caballero del habito de

---

25. Cf. Albizuri, A, 91; Alegre, I, 241; Mange, 337.
26. Albizuri, A, 91-94; B, 25-26.

Santiago, Gobernador y Capitán General de la Nueva Vizcaya."
Between them they agreed that the project was highly worth
while.

But the governor knew the country better than Tapia, and the
distances. He recognized the problem of proper support from
the rear in such a hazardous adventure. One can well see the
venerable bearded grandfather in audience with the young and
ambitious pioneer padre, experience countering the audacity of
twenty-eight years, foresight and prudence encouraging dynamic
power yet restraining it to channels that were within the range
of intelligent possibility. Their conversation is reported in the
following lines:

"Consider, Father, the thought of Sinaloa. It is close to Guadiana, (Durango), and there are other white men and priests
within a few days' ride. Cíbola is far beyond,— (and he makes
that beautiful sweeping gesture of the grand old days). The Sinaloa Indians have many tribes and languages; they are very wild,
and their numbers are too great for a few men. But New
Mexico is impossible, so vast, so strange, so far, over 1200 miles
from civilization. Could you not go first to Sinaloa? Win them
over to the Gospel, and then you can go on to the lands beyond.
For Sinaloa is on the road to New Mexico. The Lord is offering you a vast field for your young soul. Think it over."

Tapia replied: "You speak well, Don Rodrigo. I shall go to
Sinaloa, and convert the native peoples there, and then go on to
New Mexico. If I can do both I shall be happy, but if only
Sinaloa, I shall be satisfied. The glory of martyrdom will be
equal either way."[27]

It is interesting to wonder what would have happened if the
Jesuits had accompanied Onate[28] to New Mexico instead of the
Franciscans. Onate in Zacatecas was under Governor Rio y
Loza, but as *adelantado* he could choose his own missionaries.
It is well that things went as they did, to make a glorious history
for New Mexico, a history of trial, suffering and death, and re-

---

27. Speech reported in Albizuri, A, 93. His authority may have been
Ribas, a good friend of Rodrigo del Rio y Loza.
28. On Onate see Hammond, *Don Juan de Onate and the Founding of
New Mexico.*

newed life. But after 1680[29] and the rebellion, the Moqui Indians never returned to Franciscan control, unwilling for some reason to live on the missions. Later on, when Kino was in Pimería Alta, and during the time of his successor Keller, and even to this day, the Moquis have a tradition that the blackrobes will one day convert all their tribe.[30]

The conversation reported above took place at the very time that the petitions of Rio y Loza and the demands of Father Avellaneda converged and brought the decision. The news came in a letter[31] to Tapia at Zacatecas. He was ordered to place himself at the disposal of Rio y Loza, and to go wherever the governor thought best. That loyal companion, Father Martín Pérez, who was then in Zacatecas, and whose biography is still to be written, would be his partner.[32] The two were to devote the rest of their lives to the *"misiones entre infieles."* They should accordingly make all arrangements with the governor, pack their supplies, and set out at once for the lands beyond.

The governor was at Guadiana. Tapia and Pérez started immediately for that city, encouraged by the orders and *beneplacitum* of the viceroy sent to them at Zacatecas. Rio y Loza gave them a hearty welcome, and repeated his counsel as to starting the great drive in Sinaloa. Full of joy and enthusiasm at the wonderful experience before them, the Fathers arranged their goods, and in mid-May of 1591 they said goodbye to the governor and their friends. Astride their mules,[33] with an extra beast for the packs, they rode out westward to the great unknown.

---

29. See the Leonard Edition of the *Mercurio Volante* of Siguenza; also Hackett, *The Revolt of the Pueblo Indians of New Mexico* and *The Retreat of the Spaniards from New Mexico in 1680.*
30. Bancroft, *North Mexican States,* I, 536. The continuing tradition was reported to the author by an Arizona missionary, Father Robert S. Burns, S.J., during Christmas week of 1931.
31. Albizuri, A, 94; B, 26-27; Alegre, I, 242.
32. Cf. Tapia to Aquaviva, Aug. 1, 1592, printed on p. 132 sq. infra. According to Tapia, the former Provincial, Father Mendoza, had assigned Perez to accompany him when he would go to Rio y Loza. But Avellaneda gave the final impulse to the move. For biographical data on Martin Perez see the Anua of 1625, noted in bibliography. Cf. Bancroft, *North Mexican States,* I, 227; note Cuevas, II, 435; Ribas, 341.
33. They did not walk. In speaking of missionaries, many writers translate "andar" as "walking" rather than "going." Pérez says in two places that they had horses, but otherwise the records refer to mules. The point is moot and is not worth pressing.

SPANISH JESUIT MISSIONS
IN
NORTH AMERICA
1566-1767

AXACAN X

BAJA CALIFORNIA

PIMERIA
† ALTA

Santa
Elena †

GUALE

FLORIDA

† San Augustin

TARAHUMARA
† SONORA †
CHINIPAS
† SINALOA † TEPEHUANES
† TOPIA PARRAS
ŏ Durango

† NAYARIT

San Luis
† de la
Paz

Habana

CUBA

⚓ MEXICO

† CAMPECHE

† Denotes headquarters
of each mission group
ŏ Durango - general
headquarters after 1594

† GUATEMALA

SCALE
500 MILES

W.E.S.
S.J.

CHAPTER VIII

THE JESUITS ON THE PACIFIC SLOPE

These two Jesuits who rode out over the mountains west of Guadiana were embarking on a historic journey. Their campaign on the Pacific slope was to mark the opening of the Jesuit missions of North America.

The Society of Jesus threw large numbers into the field of the Spanish colonial domain. In 1767 at the suppression there were 2897 men engaged in the territory south of the Rio Grande.[1] Of these, 678 were in New Spain, while the remainder served in the districts of New Granada, Ecuador, Peru, Chile, Maranao, Brazil and Paraguay.

For approximately two hundred years the Order gave this important group to the diverse religious operations of Hispanic America. In city and pueblo, and in the distant wilds where the missions were situated, they carried on their institutions. At times under bishops, at others under the direct control of Rome, they knew the full gamut of success and failure, friendship and strife, esteem and final dispersion. Their influence was wide, so much so that the two noted investigators, Santacilia and Ulloa, declared that "the continuance of this Order in America would have prevented the subsequent revolution, or at least have retarded it for another hundred years."[2] The closing of their schools in 1767 had a direct bearing on the end of Spanish rule.[3]

The two most important tasks of these men were the educa-

---

1. In 1749 the catalogue lists of the entire Order (see Astrain, VII, "Conclusion," and Schmitt, *Synopsis*) showed 22,589 Jesuits throughout the world. There were in the Province of Mexico 572; in Peru 526; Chile 242; Novi Regni (Bogota) 193; Paraguay 303; Quito 209; Brazil 445; Maranao 145; 2635 in all Hispanic America. An increase of 361 up to 1767 (see Campbell, *The Jesuits,* 425) shows the enduring enthusiasm and expansion of the field right up to the end. Cf. Cretineau-Joly, op. cit., for the Tree of the Society of Jesus institutions in 1773.

2. Cited from their posthumous "Noticias Secretas" in Bertrand, *Histoire de l'Amerique Espagnole,* I, 327.

3. See on the real results of their suppression, Moses, *Spain's Declining Power in South America,* and Williams, *People and Politics of Latin America.*

tion of leaders among the creoles, and the civilization of the native tribes. It was the latter work that claimed most of their man power, as it did their interest.[4]　The records, too, show that many more individuals came under their influence in this work of the missions.　Paraguay reports cite over 700,000 baptisms during the years of the Reductions.[5]　Sinaloa—meaning most of Nueva Vizcaya—during the first forty years of the mission operations there, had 151,621 persons individually named in the books that kept the baptismal records.[6]　Evidently well over a million, possibly millions, of natives, had lived under their regime.

In South America the historical importance of their missions is clear.　In New Spain the point is not so plain[7]—nor so well known—, for much less than half of the land fell to their care. The eastern section lying beyond the Sierra Madre, and the northern provinces now lost to Mexico, were chiefly the field of the sons of St. Francis, working out of Guadaloupe in Zacatecas, Santa Cruz in Querétaro, Santo Evangelio or San Fernando in Mexico.　Not till these padres got beyond the limits of eastern Texas at Los Adaes did they again meet the blackrobes, the men who were making the southern story of the French Jesuit *Relations*.

There was nevertheless an immense range of territory allotted to the Jesuits.[8]　They held the line along the entire Pacific slope, from Guatemala to modern Arizona.　In the middle section of this long country they leaped the mountain barrier, in the center of that wild and savage people called the Chichimecos.　Far to the northwest, their outposts reached beyond the Pimas on the

---

4. See letters of Aquaviva "Inter multa," May 12, 1590, and "Dum apud me," Aug. 1, 1594, in *Epistolae Generalium*, I, 214-247.

5. Cf. Bertrand, 1. c.　Schmitt gives the figures on the mission Reductions in 1763: in Mexico 122,001 natives; in Paraguay 113,716; Chaco 6,000; Chile 7,718; Novi Regni 6,594; Quito 7,586; Peru 55,000: in all 318,615.

6. See Heredia, *Bibliografia de Sinaloa*, on Arch. Gen. Mex., 25, concerning the missions 1622-1642; also Bancroft, "North Mexican States," I, 236, citing Ribas to show 300,000 baptisms before 1645 in the Sinaloa mission.

7. Note the figures for the Reductions given above.　The largest number belongs to Mexico or New Spain, which seems to have been the most important mission of the Order in those days.

8. Bolton, *Spanish Borderlands,* chapter on Jesuits on the Pacific Slope. See Alegre, Ribas, Venegas, Kino, Clavigero, passim.

Gila, and all over the California peninsula; and at the time of their expulsion they were on their way up the coast and into the beautiful land of contemporary California.[9] It was their sad mischance and his hard duty that made José de Gálvez,[10] the Visitor sent out by Charles III to wind up their affairs, the very man who sent the expeditions that terminated in San Diego, Santa Barbara, Monterey and San Francisco.[11]

No one has better characterized the missions of the colonial period than the outstanding authority on the Spanish borderlands, Herbert E. Bolton. They were, he writes,[12] specifically a frontier institution. To hold the frontier, to extend the frontier, to gather the discordant elements of the outpost country and bring into the refining medium the groups that lived *"mas allá"*: such was the function of the mission. He conceives the mission operating primarily as a religious factor. He recognizes, too, the Spanish psychology—common to Catholic culture wherever it is found—in the notion that Christianity is the elemental civilizing force.[13]

In this light the mission was the frontier of Christianity. The fringe of the folk who already lived the Christian life was likewise the rim of paganism, and the dividing shell could only be pierced effectively by that force that reaches to the division of spirits. And it is no coincidence that the Society of Jesus aimed to be the light cavalry of the Father of Christendom, ready to be sent to any part of the world where danger threatened, or new country must be explored and opened up. They were specially adapted to this kind of life.

The mission was also the advance post of civilization. Mining

---

9. See e. g., the biography of Father Consag (Konscak) by Krmpotic; also Clinch, *Missions of Lower California;* Englehardt, *Missions and Missionaries of California,* I; Venegas, *Noticias de California;* Clavigero, *Storia de California;* Pockstaller, *Salvatierra;* Chapman, *Founding of Spanish California.* The *California Historical Review,* July 1931, has a list of the latest books on California history.

10. See Priestley, *Jose de Galvez, Visitor-General of New Spain, 1765-1771.*

11. See Bolton's editions of the magnificent diaries of Crespi, Font, Garces, Anza, and of Palou's *Noticias de California.*

12. Bolton "Mission as a Frontier Institution," in *A. H. R.,* 1917, Oct.

13. Compare Chateaubriand, *Genius of Christianity.*

prospectors and encomenderos with vast stock ranges were in continual embroilments, through their thinly veiled enslavement of the native. This policy brought constant reprisal from the outraged tribes who dwelt beyond the reach of military control. And no wonder. The Indian saw his liberty checked, his hunting and fishing ground overrun, his women and children in virtual captivity. For the evils of the *encomienda* system were as patent to the sixteenth century observer[14] as they are today; and many an innocent victim of this hostility[15] passed into the number of the martyrs when his single-hearted charity deserved a better recompense.

The economic exploiter was finally checked in this unfair advantage over a weaker race. Philip II ordered[16] his viceroys to hold the leash over the employers of native labor. And the mind of the sovereign did not stop at mere negation. As an intelligent ruler, he understood that some ferment of gentility and high ideal must be worked into the sterile mass of border morality. The upshot was an emphatic patronage of the missions, as the force that would supplant the *encomienda* on the frontier.[17]

The great rub came in the fact that now the native races were exposed to competition with the whites; and for humanitarian purposes, as well as to protect their legitimate interests against the base greed that would attack the weakling, insistence was laid on teaching them the art of life as practiced by the newcomers. Both the royalty and responsible leaders were at one on this matter, against the schemes of men who would make unfair profit by the *repartimiento,* and its child, the *encomienda.* Accordingly, a system was devised that would fit the savage to live a parallel existence with the creole.

A mission means something more than itinerant preaching and

---

14. The point made by Las Casas, though overdrawn, was a familiar fact to writers and rulers and missionaries.

15. Undoubtedly many a missioner was put to death in New Spain because he was a Spaniard, a "Yoris" as the Sinaloans called them. Such seems to have been the case on the first military entrada. Cf. infra, pp. 104, 122, 123.

16. See Simpson, *Encomienda in New Spain in the Sixteenth Century.*

17. See Bancroft, *History of Mexico,* II, and *North Mexican States,* I, passim.

sacred ministry. It is a fixed residence in Indian country, independent of urban assistance. Here the missionaries make their headquarters. They have the residence, the mission church, the school of agriculture and rudimentary letters. From this center the priests travel in all directions, visiting the native pueblos or rancherias. They try to bring to this location as many as possible of the Indian families, inducing them to settle round the mission compound and build a little municipium.[18]

In a land where the Indians had not already found a settled habitation, where they roamed winter and summer in search of food or war, such a fixed home was the first step in their civilization and conversion. It was unthinkable to try to teach them solid Christian ways of living when they were ever on the go. But where the native had already advanced to village life, supported by agriculture and industry, the central pueblo was not so much of a necessity; and its development was rather the result of the economic urge than of the insistence of the Fathers. These missionaries were intelligent, sometimes the finest scholars in the European colleges, and they knew it was better to keep the Indian in his natural habitat than to try to teach him a new kind of living, if they wished for the fruits of Christianity in a permanent and rapidly maturing form.

The natives needed to be taught many lessons. Rarely did they live a political life, and then the prime concern of the mission was to bring them to a settled and regular mode of public association. This was the more urgent as they were now in contact with a superior race, which by its very superiority would

18. Bancroft, in *North Mexican States,* I, 430-435, gives a description of the mission system as seen under the direction of Salvatierra in Lower California. The reader may be unaware that the last quarter of the nineteenth century saw the introduction of a new science called "missiology." The whole complex of missionary work, in its various phases, is now being treated with proper scientific method. The Pontifical Institute of Missiology deserves special mention. Its publications, under the able and energetic direction of Dr. Joseph Schmidlin—co-worker on the history of Ludwig Pastor—, are considerable and of great value. See, e. g., the work of Schmidlin, *Catholic Mission Theory.* At Louvain, Rome, Milan, Lille, Paris, Nymegen, Vienna, and Marquette University in Milwaukee, regular graduate and undergraduate courses are given in the departments of missiology. For a brief account of this new study see Ahaus in the *Clergy Review* for May, 1932.

be certain to take advantage of the unprotected rights of the inferior people.

Another vital need was the improvement in domestic economy. Outside of the Nahuac region the Indians lived on scanty fare,[19] and their mortality then—as today—was very high on account of the ravages of tuberculosis and other diseases caused by exposure and undernourishment. Of education one hesitates to speak. Grave professors have been heard to say that the lore of these peoples and the training given their offspring fitted them quite well for the needs of their lives. In morality there was a wide divergence. For even barbarous tribes have been known to keep as high a standard of conduct as much of so-called civilization, while on the other hand there were some very bad men and tribes among those mountains along the Pacific slope.

Such, in brief, was the system employed in the early missions. The matter is hardly subject to generalities. Often the Fathers came to people who were called savages, but who really had a comparatively fine civilization. The annual letter of 1593, printed further on,[20] sketches the rudiments of their life in some detail. There one sees the pueblo of well-constructed little houses, the fields planted and bringing rich harvests, the wicker work and blanket manufacture. They were, however, small as a tribe, and hence they lacked the outlook and the ambition that would mean larger developments. Their language differed from river to river, as many as four distinct tongues being found within the space of the Four Rivers. That this divergence of language was a real one we can infer from the known varieties of our contemporary Indian tongues in the northwest of the United States, where in some States as many as five languages are spoken, and to a man who knows only one of the five all the rest are absolutely unintelligible.[21]

---

19. Bancroft, *Native Races,* passim.
20. See p. 109 infra.
21. This is the judgment of missionaries with long experience and marked linguistic ability, such as the late Father Joseph Cataldo, who spent over sixty years among the Northwest Indians, and who wrote a grammar and a dictionary besides numerous shorter pieces on the remarkable Nez Perces language. This experience may be contrasted with the report of an Alaskan missionary who found an Arizona tribe speaking the

The language question introduces a discussion of several features of mission methods which will become more concrete in the following chapters. The Jesuits pursued a singular policy. They renounced the objective of making the Indians into Spaniards, and countered with the plan to bring out the best that lay in the potentialities of the native culture. They learned the native language themselves,[22] and the indigenous religious thought.

From the first entrance into New Spain this study of native languages was a matter of first importance. The Colegio Máximo had a permanent chair for lectures in the Mexican language, "as this was the most common and hence the most necessary." "Every Jesuit student attended these lectures," the provincial wrote to the General in 1585.[23] The previous year he had noted eighteen linguists in the province, of whom ten knew Mexican (Nahua), four Otomi, and seven Tarascan.[24] In 1592 the visitor Avellaneda wrote[25] to the king that enthusiasm for this study was widespread: seven Indian languages were being used "among the Mexicans, Otomies, Tarascans, Zapotecas, Huichichiles, Mazahuas, and now at last among the Cinaloas." He said that the men seemed interested in nothing else, and that in each of the houses and colleges there were always some two or three who attended on the aforementioned Indians.

Avellaneda in this same letter told the King that he had left orders, "as has the General, that hereafter no priest is to be ordained until he has mastered the first language. So far ten have been ordained, and of these seven know Mexican and can thus take their full part in the ministry. The rest are studying. Each year more come up and labor to acquire the proper style of writing and speaking these languages. Thus we shall have

---

same language as his people in Alaska, and who encountered a fellow workman from Argentina who understood him perfectly when he used the same tongue as his Northern natives. See, on Sinaloa, Orozco y Berra, *Carta Etnografica de Mexico.*

22. Later on the government insisted that the natives in California be taught Spanish. See Slosson, *American Spirit in Education,* 187, following Bancroft and Engelhardt.

23. Mendoza to Aquaviva, Jan. 12, 1585, in Astrain, IV, 426.

24. The entry for each man in the catalogue, e. g., Patzcuaro 1585, includes the languages he knew.

25. Avellaneda to Philip II, 1592, in Astrain, IV, 414.

correct models in these tongues, to help us attack what we so desire, preaching and the *doctrina*." And the viceroy, the Conde de Monterey, wrote[26] to the King in 1596 that "the Fathers of the Company use a different approach; for they give themselves to the study of the languages and learn them with ease; and they deal with the Indians most kindly, with the sole desire of their improvement, and very disinterestedly in everything else."

This linguistic control led directly to a policy of isolation. From the first the Fathers tried to have their mission Indians cut off from contact with white soldiers and traders.[27] The reasons for this move have been repeated so often as to preempt iteration here. The idea had been first suggested in the Virginia and Florida episode.[28] In Sinaloa it will be seen shortly. Later on, in California, Father Salvatierra[29] got permission from the government to try the method again—it had been given up because of the martyrdom of many missioners—but a short attempt decided him to abandon it. Only in Paraguay, and under the Franciscans in Upper California, did it work perfectly, in the two examples of mission experience that most nearly approach ideal conditions.

Along with this effort was a similar movement that succeeded in greater measure, the separation of the converted Indians from those who were still pagans. So long as the converts remained in contact with the heathen population of the native villages, they could not be kept constant in the requirements of the new life. The power of the medicine man counteracted the persuasion of the priest. Thus it will be seen in Sinaloa that the pioneer missionary built a new pueblo for his converts. He set up the native dwellings round the square in which were the church and seminary, and he forbade communication with the Indians of other villages.

Once the languages were mastered, and the Indians set apart,

---

26. Monterey to Philip II, 1596, in Astrain, IV, 439. See ibid., IV, 627.
27. This was achieved completely and successfully only in Paraguay, during approximately 160 years of Jesuit direction in the Reductions. See Cunningham-Graham, *Vanished Arcadia*.
28. See p. 20 supra.
29. See his biography by Pockstaller, and by Venegas; also Taraval, *Indian Uprising in Lower California, 1734-1737*.

the mission began to show its positive contribution to the civilization of the natives. Scholars and the general public are familiar
with the almost unbelievable utopia of Paraguay, where they see
the mission in its fullest success. The main lines of the Paraguay system were followed elsewhere in the Jesuit efforts; in
fact, there is some likelihood that the Paraguay Reductions were
modeled on the primary efforts in New Spain.[30] In this latter
country, the Fathers and Brothers of the missions gave much
time and thought to improving the native agriculture. They
guided the sports and amusements, the art and architecture,[31]
the political development. The talent for music was carefully
nurtured. The primitive economic method of barter was retained.
In every point they tried to nourish indigenous culture, for in
this way they could instill Christianity more effectively into a
natural race.

Their success? Better for the reader to judge as he may.
For historians, the worth of the work is likely never to be fully
known. These missionaries were taken away from the scene
before the tremendous change of the revolutions, that paved the
way for the situation of today.[32]

Some few of their names have come down to us in the annals
of Sinaloa. Many more are buried in manuscripts that await the
patient eye of the historian.[33] Spanish Fathers furnished the first
complement of sacerdotal troops. At the turn of the sixteenth
century volunteers from Italy and other Southern States were
introduced into the ranks of the veterans. Then, as the seventeenth century began to wane, the great German reserve[34] was

---

30. Paraguay mission work began in 1589, two years before Tapia entered Sinaloa. Only in 1610 was Paraguay given a definite system by the
missionaries and the government. By that time the Sinaloa work was well
on the way. See Ribas, op. cit., and Astrain, V, passim.

31. See, e. g., Duell, *San Xavier del Bac* on Jesuit mission architecture.
Also see Buelna, *Compendio*, 58; Bancroft, *North Mexican States*, I, 231.

32. It takes considerable sang froid to esteem the present social and
economic condition of the Mexican Indian as more desirable than his state
one hundred and fifty years ago.

33. The Bancroft Library of the University of California is a rich mine
of treasures for that history. See also the Brown, Ayer, and Garcia Collections.

34. See Duhr, *Deutsche Auslandsehnsucht im 17 Jahrhundert. Aus der
uberseeischen Missionsarbeit deutscher Jesuiten.* Cf. also the *Neue Welt*

thrown into the battle, in the days made notable by that son of the Tyrol, Eusebio Francisco Kino, who was preferred by his governor to a whole army of militia. These missions were the cause of a tremendous burst of enthusiasm in the Jesuit provinces of Europe, where the heroism of martyrs and the large number of converts inspired the rising groups of young men in the Order.

Bott of which a fine appreciation is given in HISTORICAL RECORDS AND STUDIES, VIII. On Kino see especially Bolton's edition of the autobiography known as *Favores Celestiales,* and his *Padre on Horseback* and *Rim of Christendom;* also Mange *Diario,* 211-341. Supplementary to these are the works noted in *A. H. S. I.,* 1932, 350-351.

CHAPTER IX

On the Way

The ride from Guadiana took the Fathers through some of the wildest mountain country in the world. The Sierra de Nayarit, a fringe of the Sierra Madre, rises high and rugged west of Durango. Here and there in the folds of the mountains dwell peoples who even today are a scourge to travelers, and the way is not safe without a military escort. Barren and dry, with no alleviation for hunger and thirst, and plagued with insects and wild animals, the road, if such it may be called, is most uninviting. It was not the shortest way at the time. A better route lay through Topia and straight to the Northwest, but the Valle de Topía at that time[1] was a maelstrom of tribal wars, and it would have been absolutely foolish for Tapia to choose that trail.

They made their way southwesterly over the range to the Rio San Pedro, and thence on down to Acaponeta[2] in Nayarit. Martín Pérez wrote[3] to the provincial that they went "through all the jungle and wild passes and over the high mountain, with double labor for many days." Purchas, in *His Pilgrimes,* continues the story in his quaint translation of the same *relacion*:

> We came into this Province of Cinaloa, being guided by Governor Rodrigo del Rio. We passed and travelled through divers Castles, Countrie Villages, Mines of Metall, Shepherds Houses, Townes of Spaniards, and certain Seignories,

1. See Alegre, I, 242-243; Albizuri, A, 84 sq.; B, 28-31.
2. Thus Ribas, 36; Mange "Diario," 337.
3. Half of this letter is translated, crudely and sometimes erroneously, and printed in *Purchas His Pilgrimes,* IV, 1552-1555. Purchas says it was written on Dec. 1, 1591. The same letter is incorporated with slight variations into the Anua of 1593. Perez had written a letter on the day he and Tapia arrived at San Felipe, July 6. 1591, according to Purchas, ibid. This letter is unknown to the author. The same letter of Dec. 1 is cited in Streit, and appears to have been printed in many European languages. The Anua is the first of many similar documents that make up the volumes of records called *Memorias* and *Documentos para la historia de Sinaloa,* on which see Bibliographical Note. These *Documentos* are the basis for the remaining chapters of this book. Purchas built his *Pilgrimes* on Hakluyt's *Voyages,* on Antonio Herrara's *Historia general de Indias* and other histories, besides various accounts of famous journeys throughout the world up to 1625.

helping our neighbors by our accustomed duties, so that we were always full of business. We crossed over in eight days the rough and hard and painfull Mountains Tepesnan, seeing no living creature, save certain Fowles. The cause Whereof is, the force of certain Muskitos, which trouble Horses, whereof is exceeding abundance in all the Mountaine, which were most noisome to our Horses. There met us certain Cuemechi, which are warlike Indians, which offered us bountifully such as they had, without doing us any harme. There are almost an infinite number of these, which wander dispersed up and downe, doing nothing else but hunt and seek their food. And it was told us that three thousand of them were assembled in a part of the hill, which besought the Governour, that he cause them to be taught and instructed in the Christian Faith. Their Minister, which was but onely one, came to visit us. There met us also a certain Spanish Captaine, which had the government of six Castles or Countrie Villages in a part of the Mountaine, who, knowing well enough what the Society meant to the Missions, wrote unto the Father Visitor, requesting him to grant him one of the Fathers, by whose Travell twenty thousand Soules might be instructed, which He would recommend to Him.

They were now skirting the line of effective colonization (the 24th parallel in 1591). Scattered expeditions of soldiers, or explorers and discoverers, had penetrated many parts of this region, only to return in most cases much the worse for their trouble. Isolated mines or ranches were located over the border, and hardy adventurers continually sought to locate in the still unopened parts that were thought to promise wealth and peace. Still, in general, this land was considered by the colonists as the *"mas allá,"* or, as many put it, the Northern Mystery. Glorious tales of mythical gold and of the seven cities had come back with each penetration of the wilds. A glamor hung over it all to lure the brave and the enterprising, even though to conquer this immense *estrecho,* which was thought to extend to the Strait of Anian,[4] was recognized as a most dangerous and doubtful affair.

The Fathers reached Acaponeta on Pentecost, May 30, 1591.[5]

---

4. The mythical northern passage from Pacific to Atlantic, sought by sailors down to the eighteenth century.

5. Ribas, 36. It was the "vesperas de las pascuas del Espiritu Santo."

Next day they set out toward the Northwest, and followed the coast-line trail to San Miguel de Culiacán, the modern San Lorenzo at the mouth of the Rio Navito,[6] or as it was then called, the Rio de Mugeres. This town lay in the ancient province of Culiacán, or Ciguatán,[7] the Land of Women, where fable had it that a tribe made up only of women with a queen to rule kept their independence. The mysterious nation of the Amazons had been one of the strongest incentives to northwestern exploration in the minds of both Cortés and Guzmán. The Amazon bubble finally burst, but the soldiers who had made *entradas* there were not inclined to forget the marvels on which their imaginations had so long feasted. They continued to talk long after they returned to Mexico of the wonderful City of Women.

At San Miguel the travelers stopped to rest.[8] The colonists were overjoyed to see them, and soon became so attached to them that they would not hear of their going further. To influence the Fathers to stay, they urged the fierce inhumanity of the barbarians. They told stories of Indian cruelty, of the deaths of the first Franciscans, the destitution of the few Spaniards they would meet, the obstinate vice and idolatry of the Chichimecos, or bad Indians. They begged Tapia not to be his own executioner, for he would no sooner get there than he would be killed. But all this had been thought out beforehand. Tapia, to tell the truth, refers in several places to a desire of martyrdom that was extraordinary. Pérez adds: "these and other villages we passed by, not without grief, because it was resolved already among us that we should stay in no other place but in this Province."

The settlers decided that someone should accompany the missioners, and prevailed on them to write ahead of their coming. Pérez continues: "a few days before our coming thither we wrote to six or seven Spaniards, which dwelt there without any Priest, and heard Mass only once a Yeare, to wit, when a Priest, dwell-

---

Bancroft, *History of Mexico,* II, 203, says Acaponeta may mean the modern Rosario.

6. Albizuri, B, 31.
7. See Bancroft, *North Mexican States,* I, 33-34.
8. Ribas, Albizuri, Mange, Alegre, Purchas, Anua of 1593, ll. cit. These are the basic sources for this chapter.

ing thirty or forty leagues off, came unto them, to confess and absolve them being penitent; who, being accompanied with most of the chief Indians, met us with exceeding joy and gladness, about twenty leagues distant from their dwellings, and accompanied us into the second River of this Province, where the town of Saint Philip and Jacob standeth." The two leaders of this native escort, Juan del Castillo and Antonio Ruiz, rode down with their troop to Capirato, ten leagues north of the next stop at Culiacán, chief pueblo of the district of that name.

Antonio Ruiz[9] was the alcalde mayor of the farthest settlement, San Felipe. In December of the previous year, he had been chosen by his fellows to go down to Chiametla to greet the new governor, Rodrigo del Rio. It was his talk with the governor that apparently moved that man to his final decision to send Father Tapia out on this frontier.

Culiacán was the last Spanish outpost[10] that had a resident padre and an organized government. There the Fathers found an old Indian woman named María, a Christian, who was very much interested in seeing the northern tribes converted. She and her son at once attached themselves to the cavalcade as permanent helpers for the mission. She told them a great deal about the manners and lives of the Sinaloa Indians. She spoke Mexican, and thus Tapia understood her. With her little boy she became his tutor in the Sinaloa tongue. These two natives went with him when he left Culiacán, to be his faithful servants for the rest of his life. And they were helpless witnesses of his death.

On to Capirato they went, where they met the frontiersmen and the Indian caciques who had come to conduct them safely for the rest of their journey. Ruiz,[11] who witnessed that meeting, and whose *relacion* is a valuable document for this mission history, says that the Indians received the Fathers with rejoic-

9. Alegre, I, 241.
10. See letter of the Tarascans from Culiacan, printed on p. 165 infra.
11. Alegre and Ribas quote copiously from this relacion. It was lately found by Dr. Sauer, head of geographical research at the University of California, in tom. 316 of the Arch. Gen. Mex. Hist.

ing. They knelt on the ground and begged to be baptized, though this had to be put off until they could be instructed.

Next day they went to Palmar, four leagues from Mocorito. The cacique of Mocorito, a Christian, when he heard from one of his children that the Fathers were approaching, gave orders for all the unbaptized children[12] of the pueblo to come together. He and all that innocent caravan marched out, and in the middle of the night came to Palmar where the missionaries were sleeping. Needless to say, they roused themselves to receive this happy augury of future success. At dawn the little folk formed a circle within which the Fathers said Mass. Then the children were baptized.

After two days in Palmar, they passed on to Orobatu where there was an old church, built of mud with a thatch covering. By means of an interpreter, probably María, Tapia spoke to the crowd of Indians who had come together. "We have not come," he said, "to seek gold or silver in your lands, nor to make slaves of your women and children. We come to you alone, few in number and unarmed; and we come only to give you the knowledge of the Creator of heaven and earth, for without this knowledge and faith you will be unhappy forever." The Indians, in spite of their barbarity, seemed to appreciate this proof of sincerity. They showed themselves pleased and promised to be docile to the precepts of the Fathers.

The following day they rode with their escorting delegation into the villa of San Felipe, the end of the journey. It was July 6, 1591. On this ride they must have covered close to six hundred miles. San Felipe de Sinaloa was the remnant of an early settlement founded on the Fuerte River by Ibarra in 1564[13] and named San Juan Bautista de Carapoa. At the time of the Jesuit entrance just nine borderlanders were left there. Albizuri names them:[14] Juan Martínez del Castillo, Juan Caballero, Juan Pablo, Francisco Martín Redondo, Antonio Ruiz, Bartolomé de Mon-

---

12. They were fourscore. See Perez in Purchas, 1. c.
13. Cf. Mange, 336.
14. Albizuri, B, 41. Five of those men, according to Mange, had been in the original foundation of Carapoa: Mondragon, Castillo, Soberanes, Ruiz, and Caballero.

dragón, Tomas de Soberanes, Juan Órtiz, and one Belmar. Two of these, Castillo and Ruiz, had already decided to pull up stakes, and the rest were in utter destitution, when the coming of the Fathers revived their courage and gave them hope for future peace and success. The villa—it was not an organized pueblo till the death of Tapia induced the authorities to send a colony of Tlascaltecans and Aztecs and a *presidio*—was built on the north bank of the Rio de Sinaloa,[15] about fifteen miles above the junction of this stream with the Ocoroni. Old Carapoa had come to an end with the rout of Pedro de Montoya and his men, the last of seven fatal *entradas* attempted in this difficult sector of the frontier.[16] Its successor, San Felipe, some thirty miles[17] south of the old site, was now nothing but a miserable group of huts and ready to be abandoned when the two Jesuits came. They took for themselves a little dwelling made of mud and sticks, and the mission of Sinaloa was begun.

---

15. The Sinaloa was earlier called the Petatlan, sometimes the Tamazula.

16. Alegre, Mange, and Ribas, all sketch the previous history of San Felipe. The compiler of the *Documentos* does the same, copying for his introduction of seventeen pages the passage of Alegre, I, 230-241.

17. Twelve leagues, according to Mange, 336.

CHAPTER X

Sinaloa

The keystone of the arch of colonial expansion to the north-west was Sinaloa.[1] There the historic cavalcade, that rode the long trail of fifteen hundred miles to settle San Francisco, was organized by the frontier captain, Juan Bautista de Anza. There the earlier opening of Lower California had its base, and took its personnel and its inspiration. And the movement that conquered the immense tract from Chihuahua to the gulf, from Culiacán to the Gila River, began in the center of mission activity now to be opened by the pioneers.

The name Sinaloa[2] was used for a century to denote the Jesuit missions on the Pacific slope down to the coming of Father Kino. Today it is a long and narrow State along the Gulf of California, just below the border state of Sonora. In the time of Father Tapia the province was restricted to the region of the five rivers, so often mentioned in the documents illustrating this chapter and those that follow. The geographical account here reproduced is borrowed from the history of Alegre,[3] and represents the district as it stood at the suppression of 1767:

> The province of Sinaloa is about three hundred leagues northwest of Mexico, and extends some hundred and thirty leagues[4] along the east coast of the Gulf of Cortés or Bay of California. Its northern limit is Sonora; the southern, the province of Culiacán and a part of the Bermejo Sea or Bay of California which bounds it on the west. The eastern

1. On this chapter see in general Bancroft, *History of Mexico,* II; *North Mexican States,* I, passim; Buelna, *Compendio historico geografico y estadistico del Estado de Sinaloa*; Bolton, *Spanish Exploration in the Southwest* and *Anza Expeditions*; Sauer, *Aztatlan* and *Road to Cibola*; Venegas, *Noticias de California;* Clavigero, *Storia de California;* Ortega, *Apostolicos Afanes*; Kino, *Favores Celestiales*; the Anuas, as in *Documentos para la historia de Sinaloa;* Ribas, Alegre, Mange, op. cit.

2. Cf. passim, letters in *Documentos* cited above.

3. Alegre acknowledges his indebtedness to Perez de Ribas, in I, 229-230, where he gives a brief resume of Ribas' long discussion of Sinaloa.

4. A Spanish league in those days was 2.63 miles.

border is Taraumara, and a part of the province of Tepe-
huana. . . . The latest maps of our missionaries give Sinaloa
an extension of four degrees along the coast, from 24°, 20′
to 28°, 15′.

The whole province, from southeast to northwest, is cut
by a cordillera of very high mountains called the Sierra
Madre. This ridge with but few interruptions runs along
the whole coast of both Americas down to the Straits of
Magellan. This line of division is the reason for that saying
among the Chinipas, who live to the east of the ridge, that
sometimes they wonder to see themselves a province separ-
ated from their city, leaving the name only to some valleys
that run between the sea and the sierra. These valleys are
watered by the five rivers into which all those nations are
divided. Each of the streams takes its origin at the fall of
the mountains, and all alike empty into the Gulf of California.

The most northern and rambling of all these is the Yaqui.
It rises east of the sierra, and, enriched by the waters of
other rivers, empties through Sinaloa at 27°, 20′. The next
toward the south is the Mayo, which comes to the sea at
27°, augmented by many smaller streams. The third is the
Zuaque,[5] on the southern bank of which stood long ago the
villa of San Juan Bautista de Carapoa. It got the name of
the Rio del Fuerte when Fort Montesclaros was built there.
Father Andrés Pérez de Ribas calls this by antonomasia the
Sinaloa River (as does Martín Pérez in his *relacion* of the
death of Tapia.) Into it from the south flows the Ocoroni
River,[6] and the enlarged stream empties at 25° and 20′.
Fourth comes the Petatlan, today commonly known among
geographers as the Sinaloa, because beside it was built the
capital of the province, with the name of San Felipe y Santiago,[7] after the ruin of Carapoa. Some call it the River of
the Villa, and of old it had the name of Tamotchala, as Laet
calls it, or Tamazuela, a tiny pueblo past which it flows to
the sea at 24°, 38′. The fifth is the small Mocorito River,
so called because of the pueblo of that name that is located
a few leagues from its source. Once it was known as the

5. The Zuaqui was also written Suaqui; it later became the Fuerte
when the Fuerte de Montesclaros was built on the river in 1610. The fort
was named for the preceding viceroy.

6. This is a geographical difficulty. The Ocoroni today runs southwest
into the Sinaloa. Probably the name was then given to a stream running
northwest from a point near the town of Ocoroni to the Fuerte. Compare
p. 120 infra.

Sebastián de Evora, and some have confounded it with the Petatlan, and also with the Piaztla, many leagues distant. The Mocorito forms the boundary of Topia and Sinaloa, and it reaches the sea at 24°, 20′.

These rivers, during the rainy season—although rain is not copious along the coast—are swollen from the watershed of the sierra. Like the Nile they have their periodic floods, and they water and fertilize the neighboring land for two or three leagues.

For the rest, the terrain, though level, is at the same time dry, and the atmosphere is warm, as on most of the coasts of America. In the river valleys there are forests and woods from three to six leagues wide, where one meets the Brazil wood, and not infrequently the ebony. Wild game abounds. The rivers are full of fish, especially where they approach the sea. Father Ribas affirms that he saw the Indians draw out more than fifty arrobas[8] of fish in less than two hours. The ground, both in the rocky heights and in the meadows, shows the riches that are concealed in the mines, a fact that was noticed even in the beginnings of the discovery. But the poverty of the inhabitants has thus far prevented their reaching this wealth.

Father Martín Pérez, in his letter to the Provincial on December 1, 1591, adds:

They measure and divide the province of Cinaloa by the eight great rivers which run through the land. The reason of that division is this, because all the Castles and Villages of the inhabitants are settled near the banks and brinkes of the Rivers, which are replenished with fish, and which in a short space do fall into the Mediterrane Sea or the Gulf of California.

The soyle is apt for tillage and fruitful, and bringeth forth such things as are sown in it. The air is clear and wholesome. The Peasants and husbandmen reap twice a year, and among other things store of Beans, Gourds and Maiz, and such kinds of Pulse whereof we and they eat so plentifully that there is no speech of the rising of the price of things or of Famine. Nay, rather, a great part of the old crop perisheth sometimes and they cast away their old Maiz, to make room for the new. They have a great store of Cotton Wooll,

---

7. It was first called Petatlan, then San Felipe y Santiago de Sinaloa, and finally Sinaloa, the capital city of the province.
8. An arroba is twenty-five pounds.

whereof they make excellent clothes, wherewith they are appareled. Their apparel is a piece of cloth tied upon their shoulders, wherewith as a cloak they cover their whole body, after the manner of the Mexicans.

It was the rumor of the mineral deposits, and the generally glamorous story of the Northern Mystery, that drew the conquistadores to attempt the conquest of Sinaloa from the first days.[9] Through what seemed an almost miraculous escape, Alvar Núñez Cabeza de Vaca had come this way, when he returned from his wondrous journey, after the wreck of Narváez on the coast of Texas.[10] That was in the years 1529-36, and the romantic traveler carried such stories to Mexico, about the wonderful things to be met in the regions *"mas allá,"* that the whole province turned eager eyes in the directions of his adventures. The Indians, too, sensing the situation and the dangers to their own lands and people, gladly told the Spaniards tales that would urge them beyond the native villages, and thus save themselves the fate of those who had wealth of any kind. In this way Sinaloa quickly became the highway to the famed Seven Cities and the Gran Quivera and the mythical Strait of Anian.

While Núñez was toiling across the wild land from El Paso to Sonora, trouble in Mexican affairs forced Governor Nuno de Guzmán into a military expedition[11] that would save his name and very likely his life. His regime during the absence of Cortés, who was then on trial in Spain, had merited for him an official *residencia* and a prosecution for his crimes and long injustices. Accordingly he equipped a large force, and with a corps of Indian auxiliaries he began his infamous *entrada* on the north Pacific coast. Going straight west through Michoacán and Jalisco, he turned northward, and his advance guard reached the Sinaloa country. Franciscans with the expedition baptized a considerable

9. Lummis, *Spanish Pioneers,* is a delightful story of these roamings. More scholarly and with excellent literary form is Bolton, *Spanish Borderlands.*

10. For materials on Cabeza de Vaca see Bancroft, *North Mexican States,* I, 59-70. Also Sauer, *Road to Cibola,* and Bandelier, *Journey of Alvar Nunez Cabeza de Vaca.*

11. See Bancroft, ibid, c. ii.

number of Indians. *Encomiendas*[12] were distributed to several captains. Others went in search of the fabled Seven Cities. However, the supplies ran out, and the natives resisted the savage deeds of the soldiers. Soon the whole affair had to be given up, and Guzmán returned to his downfall in the capital.

Next to strike that way in search of the ethereal conquests, was the party of Fray Marcos de Nisa, with the Moor Estefanico as his guide. They pushed their way far on toward[13] the pueblo country of the Rio Grande del Norte; and in true conquistadorial fashion returned with a wealth of narrative that made the eyes of the public large and round with anticipation when the turn of the next should come. It booted little that their show of copper and gold and precious stones was meager. Any tale in those days was enough to draw on credulous fortune hunters to find their place in the sun.

Coronado now came on the scene. The reader should be dissuaded from identifying these marches over the vast spaces of the north, with the lives of the ordinary colonials of those days. The black lines left on the map by these explorers represent only the unusual and extraordinary tramping about of the few rich and blustering adventurers. Back of the picture is the framework of an agricultural and urban civilization that forms the main story of the settlement of New Spain. The voyages and expeditions, while extremely useful, were little more than incidents in the regular, persistent transplantation of the old world into the new.

---

12. Ruiz in his relacion has copious data on attempted early encomiendas in Sinaloa. Simpson, op. cit., treats the encomienda from the administrative point of view, in its evolution under governmental direction. See also Fiske, op. cit., II; Priestley, *Coming of the White Man.* The Encomienda "is a right granted by Royal Favor to the deserving of the Indies, to receive and collect for themselves the tributes of the Indians that shall be given them in trust, for their life and the life of one heir . . . . with the charge of looking after the spiritual and temporal welfare of the Indians, and of dwelling in and defending the Provinces where they are given them in trust, and of doing homage and making personal oath to fulfill all these duties." This definition is taken from the cedula of Philip II, 1571, as given in Solorzano, *Politica Indiana,* I, 237.

13. Sauer, *Road to Cibola,* concludes that Fray Marcos got no farther than the present southern boundary of New Mexico . See on the same point Alegre, I, 237.

The sweep of Coronado,[14] following the route of Guzmán and far on to the cultured tribes of Arizona and New Mexico, rouses the imagination of the lover of romance. Historians trace his farthest advance into the south of contemporary Kansas. His was the great geographical exploration. He passed through many nations of American Indians, the country of the cimarron cow or buffalo, the plains and mountains that in a future day would harbor a new race and a new culture.

His going out and returning led him through the province of Sinaloa. Following in his wake, other *adelantados* attempted similar or greater feats of conquest. Ulloa sailed up the gulf to a point near the mouth of the Colorado. Alarcon outdid him on a similar voyage, and his men in their small boats actually went some distance up that stream. Francisco de Ibarra,[15] in a privately financed trip of discovery, crossed over from Guadiana into the Sinaloa country, and founded the ill-fated town of San Juan de Sinaloa, or, as the documents call it, San Juan Bautista de Carapoa. That was in 1564.

On this expedition two Franciscan padres, Acebedo and Herrera,[16] were left with a small garrison, to attempt the Christianization of the natives. In an unfortunate battle with the Indians, who were evidently incensed at a theft of grain, fifteen Spaniards were put to death, and the friars with them, and the villa was burned. In 1583 Pedro de Montoya refounded the villa, but the Suaqui Indians, determined that no Spaniard should possess their country, swooped down and killed Montoya and twelve of his men.

One of their number, Bartolomé Mondragón, was appointed commandante by Governor Monroy in 1589. They had led a precarious existence.[17] The Indians were at war with them con-

---

14. See Winship, *The Coronado Expedition*, 1540-1542; Sauer, op. cit.
15. See Mecham, *Francisco de Ibarra*; Hammond and Rey *Obregon's History*. In general see Bolton, *Spanish Exploration in the Southwest*.
16. Mange says there were three Franciscans, op. cit., 335-337. He says the Franciscans left off in Sinaloa because the New Mexico opportunities were more inviting.
17. Alegre, I, 241, following Ribas, says the sole interest of these colonists was a couple of entradas in search of mines in the province of Chinipas, a search that furnished little profit though much risk and danger.

stantly. These savages would have none of the white men, who came to take away their lands, their maiz, their women and children. And in 1591 the little group was ready to give up the frontier post, when the coming of the Jesuits changed the whole complexion of the country.

CHAPTER XI

"The Most Savage Men"

A Jesuit, Father Mathias Tanner, writing in Prague in the late seventeenth century, said that

> In ferocity and cruelty, the natives of America surpass those of any region known to man. For the most part they are more like beasts than human beings. They are ignorant of political organization. They have no laws or bonds of social life. In Florida, Virginia, Canada and the country of the Iroquois, they are cannibals and barbarians more cruel than have ever been heard of. . . The most loathsome and repulsive idolatry has full sway. Nowhere are the magic arts held in higher esteem. Magicians, and demons, appearing visibly under the most horrible shapes, are frequently given divine honors.
>
> There the Society has had to use methods of action that were entirely new and different from any that had hitherto been employed in her apostolic work. The barbarians had to be taught the elemental usages of civilized society, before they could be instructed in the truths of Christianity. Hence the missionary was occupied at first almost entirely in drawing them away from their normally wild life in the woods and mountains, and bringing them into villages and towns. Thus it was necessary for the Fathers to build them huts with their own hands, and teach them agriculture and all the mechanical arts.[1]

Such was the traditional picture given in Europe in those days, and with proper exceptions, it expresses the sober truth. Of course the more highly developed nations had a complete civil polity and an astounding scientific knowledge.[2] Evidence of this becomes increasingly clearer today, in the study of the Aztecs, Mayas, Chibchas and Quichuas.

Another exception must be made with the less favored tribes.

---

1. Tanner, *Societas Jesu Militans*, 434 sq.
2. See Bancroft, *Native Races*, passim; also Brinton, *American Race;* Wissler, *American Indian;* Joyce, *Mexican Archiology;* Bertrand, *Histoire de l'Amerique Espagnole*, I. Buelna, *Compendio,* is useful for data on peoples and early history of Sinaloa; so is Sauer, *Aztatlan.*

When first the European met them, he was kindly received; and this attitude was continued wherever he did not abuse their goodness or interfere with their rights. But with the missionary an entirely new factor came in. It was the medicine man, the native priest, and the power of these potentates over their people.

More than is realized, the deaths of many missionaries were due to the activity of these sacerdotal rulers, who resented or feared or were jealous of the Christian clergy. The appeal to nationalism is not a new one, and often enough the khiva or the temple would ring with the call to patriotic resistance, where the true reason for hostility was veiled under the semblance of natural rights and liberty. A good case of this is that of Nacabeba, who will appear in Chapter XVII. His personal licentiousness was rebuked, and his religious power broken. The result was a murderous plot, and an uprising that nearly wrecked the mission for all time. These native priests were always calling in the "secular arm" to enforce their dictates after the best old world manner, little realizing in their barbarism that the psychological reaction to persecution is persistence in the thing persecuted. They claimed that preaching Christianity was a civil crime, as the Inquisition had done, *mutatis mutandis,* about heresy. This is history, and it is only fair to recognize it.

Cuevas holds[3] that all these Indians were of a civilization much inferior to that of the Mexicans, the Tarascans, the Mayas and Mixtecos. They really had not even the rudiments of culture. They had no fixed homes, often no fixed lands to till. They were excessively inquiet and mobile, and they had no notion of what social life meant nor anything like it.

A short sketch of the Sinaloa type of Indian, as he was found in 1591, is given in the letter of Father Pérez which has already been quoted in part. It is somewhat facetious in the old translation of Purchas:[4]

True it is that, though they be all workmen, yet for the moste part of the year they are not covered but go naked;

3. Cuevas, II, 379. See Beals, *Comparative Ethnology of North Mexico before 1750*; Sauer, *Aztatlan.*
4. See Purchas, IV, 1552-1555.

yet all of them wear a broad girdle of the said cotton cloth, cunningly and artificially wrought, with figures of divers colors in the same, which the shells of Cockles and Oysters joined artificially with bones doe make. Moreover they thrust many threads through their ears whereon they hang earrings; for which purpose they bore the ears of their children as soon as they are born, in many places, and hang earrings, round stones, and coral in them, so that each ear is laden with fifty of these ornaments at least, for which cause they always sleep not lying on their sides but with their face upward. The women are decently covered from the waist downward, being all the rest naked. The men as well as the women wear long hair; the women have it hanging down their shoulders, the men often bound up and tied in divers knots; they thrust Corals in it, adorned with divers feathers and cockle shells, which add a certain beauty and ornament to the head. They wear many Beads of divers colors about their necks.

They are of great Stature, and higher than the Spaniards by a handful, so that as we sat upright on our horses, without standing on tiptoe they could easily embrace us.[5] They are valiant and strong, which the wars which they had with the Spaniards doe easily show, wherein though they sustained no small damage yet were they not unrevenged nor without the blood of their adversaries. When they would fight resolutely for their Uttermost Liberty, they denounced and appointed the Day of Battle. Their weapons are Bows and Poisoned Arrows, and a kind of Club of hard wood, wherewith they need not to strike twice to brain a man. They use also certain short javelins made of red wood, so sharpe and hard that they are not inferior to our armed spears. And as fearful and terrible as they be to their enemies, so quiet and peaceable are they among themselves and their neighbors, and you shall seldom find a quarrelor or a contentious person. The Spaniards after certain conflicts at length made friendship with them, leaving their country to them; but those eight Spaniards whom I mentioned before live quietly among them; and though they be called Lords, yet are they contented with such things as the Indians give them, offering no violence nor molestation to any man.

Fathers Tapia and Pérez wrote a better description of this

---

5. In most of the relaciones the animals are called mules, and the picture here suggested connotes the same. Still we know that by 1590 there were plenty of horses and cattle roaming wild over North Mexico. Cf. Priestley, *Coming of the White Man.*

people in 1593, after two years of life among them had given the
missioners a good knowledge of their ways:[6]

The province of Cinaloa is 300 leagues west of Mexico, and
runs in a northerly direction. It is situated at twenty-three
or twenty-four degrees north latitude. The settlements are
built near the coast of the South Sea, on the banks of copious
rivers. These descend from the grand sierra called after the
Tepehuanes, the nation of warlike Indians who live in these
high mountains. On the shores of the rivers, according to the
information that we have received, there dwell more than a
hundred thousand souls. Besides that, this province gives
an entry to the fine valleys made by the rivers, and to the
mountain region, and to New Mexico of which there is so
much stir, and to another infinity of barbaric peoples of whom
we also have information.

The whole nation has no king or lord except in times of
war. Then the most valiant among them takes the captaincy,
and they all obey him. But in times of peace, each one does
what he wishes; and they think highly of these peace times,
for there are many wars of nation against nation.

They have no idols. But they do not understand that there
is a Providence in Cinaloa, nor do they hope for happiness
in another life. They simply believe that the dead go to a
place under the earth called Darkness, whose prince they call
Yoris. There, they say, those who lived righteously or evilly
on earth will all be equally cared for, and whatever they will
wish to do will be allowed.

The rivers are so placed that the lands at the slope of the
sierra produce fine maiz; but it is cold there, and the lack of
cotton for clothing is supplied by abundant vigor and spirit.
The parts nearer the sea are more sterile since it does not rain
there. Midway lie the plains where we are now. The people
here enjoy great temporal blessings. They have maiz, cotton, calabashes, beans and other legumes.

The first river, which they call the Sebastián Evora, has
three languages, but very few people in each tongue. The second, the Petatlan, has six distinct languages and is thick with

6. It is in the Anua of 1593. The Provincial sent this annual letter
to the General. It was made up of letters sent to headquarters by the
missionaries. The author prefers to quote this and the following lengthy
descriptions from the sources, rather than try to better the story. There
is in these accounts the authority of first hand information, as well as the
flavor of age. Ribas gives a much more complete discussion, and a better
differentiation of tribes, in his *Historia de los Triunfos*.

inhabitants. The third, the Ocoroni, has two languages. The fourth, the Cinaloa, is all of one tongue, and has a large population. The fifth, the Mayo, has the same language with some slight variations, and a much more dense population that the fourth. The sixth, the Yaqui, has one language. From there onward we have no definite information.

On all these rivers, they live in pueblos and communal settlements. This means no little good for our teaching them the *doctrina*. They have their gardens in the lowlands along the rivers. They are great farmers, sowing twice a year, and they generally have abundant crops. Hence they are well supplied, in such abundance that there is no beggar among them who asks for alms. Still, they have few native fruits except some cantaloupes and melons. And if these bear as well as they have begun to do, everything will go very well.

At the door of each house they have their porch. This serves for shade and for keeping their maiz above in the manner of a trophy. On the porches they sleep in summertime, when it is quite warm. In the winters, which are four months long, and cold, they sleep in their houses. These get the light through a large opening in the middle of the roof. The mattress is a mat, the pillow a chunk or log of a tree.

Their ordinary eating times are twice a day, morning and sunset. Their foods are maiz, boiled beans, squashes, either boiled or baked, and fish, of which there is plenty in the rivers. They also hunt Simarron Cows, deer and rabbits. Their drinks are made in several ways. Sometimes they take maiz or flour of maiz in water, and from that they make a fresh beverage. They also make wine of the same maiz, and at times they have their very solemn carouses. Then the whole pueblo gathers together, though they do not allow drink to the new race and the youths. As all the tribe is present at these bouts, and we know some days before that they are going to have them, they are easy to control. We have already begun to check this practice, and we hope in God to end the whole thing.

During the hot weather the whole tribe goes almost naked. In the cold, they cover all the body with a blanket. They make fine, closely woven, cotton garments.

Men and women both cultivate a great head of hair. The women always have it hanging down. The men braid and arrange it, making it up in a variety of fashions, and adorning it with much plumage. For this, they raise different birds with beautiful feathers in their homes. On the neck they hang great strings of beads.

When someone dies, in their heathen way they cremate the body. Sometimes, however, they inter a branch of a tree with all his blankets, plumes, beads, bow, quiver of arrows, and much food, and a gourd full of water. They intend these to be of some assistance for the long journey he has to take. On that occasion they customarily solemnize their drinking bouts, and they likewise put a great quantity of wine on the sepulchral fire. They kill the dogs and other animals of the dead man, so that nothing of his possessions remains alive. And at the very moment that they see he is dying, they rush to deck him up in the garb that he used to wear in war.

In their marriages they make no account of the degrees[7] of affinity, but are very rigorous in the law of consanguinity. The manner of marrying is this. At the time that they go to their dances, they first dance with the relatives. Then the spouses give their hands to each other, and when they have finished this each one goes to his own home. If they are too young they remain without seeing each other for months and years. Then in due time the father of the girl gives a house and the bridal furniture to his daughter and son-in-law. Meanwhile they arm the newly married man according to their ceremonial. They give him a bow shaped to his body, for he will use it for three years. This bow is a mark of dignity among them. Then they send him out to use his arms in some deed. This is ordinarily to kill a lion, the beast that infests all the land.

The ceremonies of adoption are so attractive to them and so prized, that in exchange for a promise of no ill treatment they permit their adoption into other families. Among these ceremonies the chief act is to insert a stick into the mouth and down to the throat. This almost chokes the man. When he frees the stick, and disgorges what he has eaten, he becomes adopted. Then he is allowed to play a game like our dice, with some small pointed reeds, having different signs that come up according to chance.

They play continuously from sunrise to sunet, and they lose their blankets and beads and everything they have in these games. They go the limit with great calmness, and run home without their clothes with no word of anger or affliction. In that game they spend much of their hot summer. In winter they often challenge one pueblo to run against another, run-

---

7. Perez adds to this in his earlier letter of 1591: "a man marries quite complacently the mother, sister, or daughter of his other wife—two or more wives were no handicap—, thinking thus to enhance the atmosphere of domestic peace."

ning, as they say, to the tree. As they run they use their feet to
throw along a chuck of wood about a span in length. They go
with their log to one pueblo or another that has been chal-
lenged, and then they proceed in their game, throwing and
running a league or more. Those who first come with their
block to the assigned place get the prize. It may be blankets,
bows, arrows, and other weapons which they call *macanas,*
as also strings of beads, feathers, and other similar objects.

They are a very docile people, naturally good, and it is easy
to impress anything on them, particularly the younger folks
of twenty-five and under. They do not swear, but say simply
"yes" or "no"; and for more assurance they add "I swear that
it is true," or *"Juma"* which means the same thing. The
parents do not whip their children. For all that, these are
reverent and respectful, so much, in fact, that when daughters
of a family are asked to become wives of young braves, even
though the girls wish none of it, they give in, just to keep
the good will of their mother. Each man has as many wives
as he can provide for, and thus they do not care to solicit the
unmarried. Therefore adultery is rare.

The young maids behave very modestly during the games,
and they put off the time to meet with men, for it is a matter
of great shame to have lost virginity before marriage. This is
a wonderful thing for so barbarous a tribe. When a man has
two or three wives he plants a field for each to harvest. And
the penalty a husband gives his wife, when she will not get
on in harmony or does not please him, is to repudiate her and
marry another. This practice causes these women great
hardship, for they do not find another who wants to marry
them. Lastly they have something of the nefarious sin, but of
such sort that the one who thus falls from virtue no more
takes bow or arrow, but goes from there dressed like a woman
and does the chores which the women have to do. Still, in
the place where the Fathers are working there is none of this
vice.

There are few thieves among them. When they go from
the pueblo they leave no other lock on the house than a mat
at the door and the maiz on the flat porch-roof, and nothing at
all is taken.

They are great merry-makers, and they speak of each other
with laughter and mirth, not sparing anyone. However, their
conversation runs very short.

When they get sick, they make little use of doctors and medi-
cines, and much use of simples.

This sober and detailed picture exhibits the ordinary lives of the Sinaloa barbarians. It was made from notes and roughly thrown together for the provincial report to the General in 1593.

Forty years later Father Albizuri composed a more graphic account of these Indians.[8] He wrote from the viewpoint of the sixth river, the Yaqui, the northern boundary of his district of San Ignacio. At first sight his narrative seems to be overdrawn—and it is highly rhetorical. But its veracity is vouched for by his rector and another censor. They were quite rigorous in annotating and correcting the manuscript, a thing that can be seen by the added *scholia* and the lines crossed out in the original:

> To come to the inhabitants, they are true children of their land, matching its pattern in everything. They are as poor in intelligence as the soil is in resources. Generally speaking they are barbarians, uncultured, ungrateful, and bestial in their habits. So fierce and uncouth are these enemies of the human race, that the continual exercise of their lives is to spill human blood, and more, to drink it. They engage in continuous and sanguinary wars, and even for trivial causes they will eat up one another in bits. They are so subject to their horrible appetites that they give themselves day and night to drunkenness and sensualities; so alien to the ordinary ways of humanity, that they prowl about the dark and dense forests as wild beasts in their dens. They frequently change their mud houses and move away,—and this is the chief impediment to our planting the Gospel among them. They are as lacking in humanity as in clothes, for they use only those which nature has given them. They make much of their fine hair, and they let it grow long to fall flying over their shoulders. With them, the sign of conversion to the Faith is to cut the hair.
>
> As a general thing they are tall, with the bodies of giants, well built for violent deeds, and bronzed by the sun from their life in the open. Their skin is hard and baked by the inclemencies of the weather, their faces wrinkled from the changes in temperature. Though they are large bodied, they are agile and clever in warfare, and from their jumping and continual exercise they are able to dodge the darts thrown at them by their enemies.

---

8. See Albizuri, B, 46-52. The "A" copy is signed personally by Juan de Albiçuri, at San Ignacio, Vamopa, 1633. It is dedicated to his superior, Father Varela, who also signs his name in approbation, along with Fathers Villafane and Mendez.

The ordinary arms are bow and arrow. At the point of the arrow they fix sharp flints or fire-hardened shafts touched with poison. Up to this time we have found no remedy for this poison, which is so deathly that only by a miracle could one recover from a wound. They make this poison from a certain herb and other drugs. The cooking of it they leave to the old women who have already had enough of this world; and if in the preparation they are touched by the vapors that fume up, their lives are over in a few hours.

They are so accurate with the bow and arrow that it is rare for them to miss their target. With equal success they shoot the birds that fly through the air and the fish that swim in the water. They defend themselves from their enemies with a gilded head dress covered with plumage of various colors: white, purple, fiery red, green, and other hues; and when they adorn their heads with these helmets, they make a beautiful sight. They show marvelous dexterity in warding off the arrows of their enemy with the bow. In close engagement they come hand to hand with the enemy, and then they use the *macana,* a rounded stick with a spike at the end.

They seem timid to meet. Yet in battle they rush in desperation at the lances and spears of their foes, without order or unity, as though they had no fear of death or esteem of life;—a curious apology which the Licentiate Gerónimo Ramírez makes in defense of the talent and bravery of these Indians of New Spain, so you will pardon me if I follow the same trend of thought. Still, it is known that these Indians are more courageous than all the others of the viceroyalty. Finally, in celebrating the victory, they are inhuman and cruel, and will not even spare the children who are clasped to the breasts of their mothers.

It is incredible what a variety of language they have, and this makes no little extra labor for the ministers of the Gospel. All the languages are poor in vocabulary, and the words are as barbarous as their masters, so that it is difficult to pronounce any of them.

Their ordinary games and entertainments are these: The first consists in running a stick for two or three leagues without stopping. They work it along with the feet, with no assistance from the hands; and the side of the person who first brings his stick to the goal and drives it into the ground is declared the winner and gets the prize. They have another game not unlike our Oca and Dados.[9] It is played with four

---

9. I. e., Royal Goose, and Dice.

split reeds, formed with as poor shaping as their makers. But they show their greatest dexterity in playing pelota—though the game is not so widely used. They make a big ball out of rubber, and then divide into opposite sides. They throw the ball high, in large open spaces which they have cleared for the sport, and then begin the game under almost the same conditions as we do pelota among our people. But there is this difference, that no one is allowed to touch it either with the foot or hand. They impel the ball with the haunch, and less often with the rest of the trunk of the body, from the chest to the waist; and to play it in any other way loses the game.[10]

They also have their dances; but these are none too modest, so that not only the sight but even the description would offend a Christian. Later on it will be our place to touch lightly on them in a necessary connection.

They have no need of governmental thrones, with silks, brocades, taburettes, gold fastenings, and the decorum that makes one sit with the left foot arched for long hours before royalty. In council they sit without any of these aids, unwearied, and for a long time. Each one carries his chair and equipment in the natural state. Their houses are huts or hovels of straw and branches, or a mat covered with palms. The food they eat is not only coarse and vile, but rather the food of beasts than of men. They do not spare lizards, snakes, rats, grasshoppers, worms, and a thousand other loathsome things. But their greatest delicacy, their most tasty plate, is human flesh, and particularly if it is a good Christian; so cruel and base are they, so gross and vile in their appetites. They keep a marvelous watch over their food till hunger strikes them. Then without any thought for the future they eat up the whole store in a day. Living as they do in a country of extreme poverty and misery, when they get something from someone, they do not stop at a little, but act as if all belongs to them in justice. If they are displeased with what they get, at once they cry out "I want this, or that."

They have no arts or trade, because their life is one continual idleness. Well may the new laws and the domination of the Gospel move them for the better in their customs. Still, experience shows that if their untamed and wild natures be cultivated, they will acquire any trade or any art.

In the matter of religion, though they are totally ignorant of the one only God, to whose justice is due supreme reverence

---

10. They still play this game in Sinaloa and other places along the Sierra Madre.

and adoration, they seem extravagant in their hallucinations and find gods blindly among creatures. Some adore the famous wizards, who are the worst of men in their vices. Others, more deceived, make images of senseless creatures, the sun, rivers, mountains, or radiant stones. Others fabricate imaginary objects, horrible monsters with vivid colors and shapes, which one cannot see without a shudder, such as one with the head of a lion, or tiger, or stag, or other wild beast, something like the ancient Egyptians and Greeks with their sphinxes, tritons, centaurs, satyrs, fauns and the like. I do not think they lack atheists who recognize no god and live like brutes.

With all this variety of manufactured gods, the community is scarcely devoted or religious in its cults and worships. Some of them, both men and women, act as priests and ministers of the superstitions, and hold conversation and make express pacts with the demons that appear in various forms. Out of this school they come forth skilled in every kind of vice and abomination, and they lay fearful threats and laws on the people. They are venerated and obeyed for this, but more from fear of what they can wreak on their victims than for any good faith. They think it proper to see a god in everything to get his greater protection for their welfare. And so one god is invoked for rain, another of the mountains, or the chase, the river, the seed time, and so for all their concerns. They have innumerable rites, ceremonies, uses and bestial customs. But we must leave these to go on with their history.

SINALOA MISSIONS
1591 - 1594

CHAPTER XII

MISSION SAN FELIPE

The sixth of July in 1591 marks the beginning of the permanent Jesuit missions of North America. And the little house of mud and branches at San Felipe became the mother of them all.[1]

Fathers Tapia and Pérez sat down together that first night, after the busy events of the reception day were over. Like generals planning a campaign, they bent over a table on which were some rough charts. Before anything else, they made a joint resolution:[2] they consecrated their lives to the conversion of these heathen and the spiritual conquest of the province; they would not move from that resolution till they had finished the work or ended their lives in it. And they put the mission under the patronage of Nuestra Senora de los Ángeles de Sinaloa.

Before them they had a sketch of the territory, as it was described for them by the Spaniards and old María.[3] The rivers were the highways along which they would work, for all the natives lived on the banks of one or other of the many streams in that country. Chief of these for the present were the Sinaloa and its tributary, the Ocoroni. Their headwaters tumbled down the slopes of the sierras where a large number of Indians, the hill people, had their homes. These were of the more aggressive type, and Tapia assigned them to himself.[4] Pérez took the lower tribes down the river, to its mouth on the Gulf of California.

The bother of caring for the house was readily solved. María and her little son wanted to do that for the Fathers. The white

---

1. This was the first permanent Jesuit mission in North America. The mission at San Luis de la Paz, where Tapia worked from 1589 to 1590, had no organized establishment until 1594. Meanwhile the Sinaloa foundation was being expanded into the great mission system along the Pacific Slope.
2. Albizuri, B, 59.
3. The record calls Maria "vieja" in spite of the youth of her son.
4. Thus the Anua of 1593, and Alegre, I, 258. Alegre, the last historian of the Jesuits in New Spain before their suppression in 1767, is an excellent guide to this chapter. Besides using the dependable and copious Ribas, he had before him all the store of documents collected in his province since the beginning. See, e. g., I, 235, 241.

settlers volunteered to help construct a small chapel, where the Indians might be gathered to hear Mass and learn the *doctrina*. They, too, would provide food and other necessaries of life as well as they could, so that the missioners might be free to give their full time to their work.

Their equipment must begin with a mastery of the native speech. María was invaluable there. She had been teaching Tapia on the way up from Culiacán, translating from the Mexican, which both spoke, into her own Sinaloa dialect. This was continued at San Felipe, and the Spaniards aided in the process, so that in a few days Tapia felt that he could make his way alone among the savages.[5] He formed a sort of grammar to simplify the study, and to be a guide for others who might come to join him. He also put into Sinaloan a short catechetical system. When he became more adept at the speech he composed couplets illustrating the chief teachings of the Faith, and had the Indians sing them in church. As time went on, he learned all four languages of his immediate environment, the Cahita, Ocoroni, Baturoques, and the Tepehuanes, which the whole region seemed to understand. He is continually singled out by his contemporaries for his remarkable gift for languages,[6] and it was a large factor in his rapid rise to ascendency among the Indians.

His experience with the Tarascans and Chichimecos had taught him the approach to the Indian mind. Now, as he surveyed the

---

5. The rapidity with which Tapia learned languages astounds most readers. Yet other men have been known to possess similar talents. There is at present a missionary (Galvan) among the Tarahumara Indians, who is reliably reported to have learned to speak that tongue readily within fifteen days, though of course he could not have the facility of a native for years. On Tapia's ability, see, e. g., Albizuri, A, 98-99; B, 118-119; also the Anuas in and after his time as noted later on; Ribas, 134.

6. Albizuri, in the last named pages, says that before his death Tapia had learned to speak in Mexican, Tarascan, Huachichile, Acaxee, Baboria, Ocoroni, Bamoa, Sinaloa (Cahita), and that he learned all eight within nine years. Perez gives another striking indication of this prodigy of memory, in his word that Tapia knew by name all the Indians in the pueblos he visited. Albizuri cites in attestation of his statement Fathers Ramirez and Ferro; and his censors, Varela, Villafane and Mendez, gave it their approval. Tapia was a remarkable man. "Had he lived," says Albizuri, "he would have taken Christianity not only to all Sinaloa, but to California and New Mexico and would even have penetrated to Florida, as he himself desired."

situation, he could set down just what points to emphasize, what examples to use in expressing notions that would be new to these pagans. He and Pérez discussed the general program of enlightening and bettering the condition of the natives. Theirs was the task of taking a raw people, with few ideas of political or economic life, and building among them the structure of a race that would stand on the same footing as its rulers. Law and order, dress, and the end of idols, were their cardinal aims as they set out to remake these nations on the fringe of the world.[7]

The first trip of exploration took him northward along the Ocoroni, to the pueblos that were reported to be kindly disposed.[8] He visited Baboria, Tovoropa, Lopoche, Matapan, and Ocoroni, the last a considerable village at the head of a stream that flowed into the Zuaque or Fuerte. At Ocoroni he heard a strange tale. Before ever the Fathers had come, a beautiful blue lady[9] had appeared to the Indians, and told them to go and find teachers who would tell them about the Christian religion. This blue lady, whose apparition was told by nearly every tribe from the Hasinais in Texas to the Colorado River of the West, and on upward into California, was sometimes said to be a Spanish nun named María de Agreda. The story is a charming one, and to this day it is in the lore of the old frontier. Similar appearances have been re-

---

7. See his program in Albizuri, B, 64.
8. See Alegre, I, 258-269; Albizuri, A, c. x; B, 58-65; Anua of 1593; Ruiz, fol. 29-30.
9. On the story of the Blue Lady see Hallenbeck, *Spanish Missions of the Old Southwest*, 143, 157-164. In the latter passage is a brief philosophical examination of the facts, but it is unsatisfactory, due to the author's lack of training in such matters. Mange gives a longer biography of the nun, Maria Coronel (1602-1665), in religion Mother Mary de Agreda, in his *Luz de Tierra Incognita*, 183-201, i. e., cc. xxvi, xxvii. From these two accounts the expanded story may be developed. It is certain that a "Blue Lady" went among the tribes in question, teaching them the faith and baptizing them. But note, she was born in 1602, and Tapia heard of the Lady at Ocoroni in 1592. No connection, then, can be made here with the pious Spanish nun.
The statement in the text rests on the authority of Albizuri, B, 73. He cites in corroboration the alcalde mayor of Sinaloa, Antonio Ruiz (who also tells the facts in his Relacion cited herein), as also the then Rector of Sinaloa, Father Figueroa, and Captain Miguel de Leon, in Tamazula. Campbell, in the *Cath. Ency.*, I, 209 sq., writes a succinct account of "Agreda, Mary de."

corded in connection with the Lily of the Mohawks, and the Flat-head nation told the same to Father De Smet in 1841.

Father Pérez in his turn made a trip down the river to the aldeas and pueblos that began with Bamoa and Cubiri. Tapia seems to have accompanied him to the latter place,[10] for it is said that during their first days they found a pagan sanctuary on a hill near Cubiri. A large crowd was gathered there round an idol. Tapia fearlessly entered the group during the ceremony. He told them of the folly of worshipping an idol, and explained the truth about God. He had the idol taken down, and a cross erected in its place.

Bamoa was a friendly pueblo, six leagues southwest of San Felipe. A group of Indians there traced their descent from the escort who had come down from the north with Alvar Núñez on his famous journey.[11] Now they were faithful allies of the Spaniards and most docile to the Fathers.

Pérez wrote to his Provincial at the end of the year:[12]

> We are learning the first two languages very rapidly, and we have advanced so much in three months that we can easily understand the Indians when they speak to us. And so we are beginning to instruct them in the catechism. We exhort them with goodly speeches to keep within the limits of the commandments, and to put aside all fear of us. On their part, they are glad to see that they receive the *doctrina* in their own language, and not in a strange tongue. They learn the prayers and catechism exactly and in a very short time.
>
> So far we have baptized about sixteen hundred adults and young people. We found four hundred Christians who had been baptized by the Franciscan Fathers who came here twelve years ago. When these latter were slain by the savages, the Christians were left without teachers.

One wonders how it was that these Indians took to the Fathers and their teaching so easily in those days. Perhaps there is an untold story, that would reveal a strong survival of the Franciscan influence which seemingly passed away with the deaths of those

---

10. Albizuri, B, 59.
11. See the Anua of 1593. They still maintain the tradition in Bamoa.
12. See Purchas, 1. c. The same matter is incorporated into the Auna of 1593.

first intrepid missionaries, but which secretly lived long after them. Pérez continues:

> We ourselves cannot instruct all those who wish it, unless some help come to us. For besides the great numbers of these people, they also differ in language and dialect.—There are, however, two chief languages among these races.—The four hundred baptized by the aforesaid Franciscans have now been neglected for twelve years and have scarcely any appearance of Christianity, for they were baptized in infancy. They married pagans, as one would expect. We separated many of them from their concubines,—you know they take as many wives as they can keep—and these were fixed up in new marriages.

> At the end of November just passed I visited the people of this river (Sinaloa), and in the space of twelve or thirteen miles I found at least four thousand warriors, besides women and children. Some among them have bad reputations, for they keep company with the devil, with whom they commit abominable sins. Many of them fled away to the mountains with their children so these would not be baptized, for the devil had spread abroad that they should die if they were baptized. Still in seven or eight days we baptized two hundred and forty children. I had to leave off then and go to another place that was calling for me. But I am anxious to return to them, for I see them much possessed of the devil and utterly without knowledge of the Faith.

> There are now thirteen churches in all three rivers,[13] besides those which are being erected little by little. We have no vestments and furnishings for them other than what we carry about with us, and no altar except the one that belongs to the Spaniards. There is not a single bell in all the churches. We did set up one rough altar, with a cross and some paper images that we brought from Culiacán. But we look to your reverence[14] for other furnishings. And these will be very helpful, for this nation is delighted with outward ornament.

> On the day of the conception of the Mother of God we celebrated the dedication of the church at Petatlan.[15] We set up a small image there in honor of her conception. We had a fine procession. A large crowd of pagans came to see

---

13. The first three rivers were the Mocorito, Sinaloa, and Ocoroni.
14. Father Provincial.
15. Pe' 'lan stands for Sinaloa, or San Felipe.

the ceremonies, and afterward they stayed and listened to our *doctrina*.

The natives here kept a reserved attitude toward us from the first, as they thought we were the same kind of men as the soldiers who came here in past times. But when they noticed our disinterestedness and anxiety for their happiness, the report spread all over the country that some men had come who appeared to be Spaniards,—Yoris, their name for demons—and were not what they seemed to be. For they did not carry the arcabuz, nor demand maiz and meat. They came alone without any escort. And their sole business was to speak of *Virigeva*, which in their language is the word for God.

With this rumor abroad, they commenced to come in troops of twenty or thirty. It was a task to meet them and explain things in their language, but with the help of the catechism which he had written, Tapia made the chief truths of the Faith clear to them. He said, in a letter the following year, that "these people know no more religion than a Turk."

During this period of six months, Tapia made a trip as far as the fourth river, the Fuerte. There he was very kindly received among the Suaqui tribe. They were moved by his words, and many asked to be baptized. But as he had no home among them at the time, he decided to put off that ceremony to a later occasion, after he could instruct them thoroughly. At his departure they showed deep feeling. Many went with him plying him with questions about God, where He was, what went on in the future life. One of them said: "truly this man is not like the others. He must be a brother or a son of *Virigeva*."[16] These Suaquis had the name of being a very fierce tribe, but, as on many other occasions, the Indians returned the same treatment they were given.

Christmas of 1591 found the Fathers and the Spaniards in a reunion at the pueblo of Lopoche. Lopoche had the largest church in all the territory, and Tapia chose that place because it was central and could accommodate a numerous gathering. He avoided calling the council at San Felipe, out of respect for the

---

16. Thus Alegre, I, 259, relying on Ribas and the letters of the missionaries. See Avellaneda to Philip II in Astrain, IV, 417. Ruiz has a long account of these Suaquis. Cf. also Anua of 1593.

susceptibilities of the Indians. Many of the natives came to the celebration, the converts bringing their pagan friends to witness the ceremonies. The singing of the Christian Indians was the special feature that attracted the admiration of the pagans, and the happy spirit of union among Fathers, Spaniards and converts exerted great force in winning the interest of those who had not yet been baptized and taught the *doctrina*.[17]

Father Pérez remarks of his people:

As far as we have been able to find out, the inhabitants of these and the neighboring pueblos are quick and ready in mind, tractable, and easier of conversion than any I have hitherto known.[18] I often wish that I might be alone with myself, but the crowd of visitors is so insistent that they give me no rest. Although I sit silently, still they go on with their talking, asking about our personal affairs and rehearsing their own, even in the night when I want to pray. They are ingenious and docile, though they have no teacher whose instructions could develop their natural powers. They live in groups of villages. Their houses are closely joined to each other. These are built of clay and timber. Ornamental mats decorate the interior. The roof is a covering of reeds.

Such were the occupations of the Fathers during their first year in Sinaloa, as far as the meagre outlines of the documents reveal their actions. They were making a beginning. They had to learn to know the different tribes, their manner of life, their languages. A friendly spirit must be created, particularly with the children, for this won the older folks. It was hard labor to change their dislike for Spaniards into trust and respect, and this was the first victory. The second was the baptism of many children and some among the very old.

Tapia meanwhile wrote several times,[19] to his Provincial and to friends, to tell of the immense number of the natives and the

---

17. Ribas, 44.
18. Martin Perez knew whereof he spoke. He was born in Nueva Galicia at San Martin. The letters sometimes disagree on the point of native conversational ability. The explanation of the divergences is that different peoples are under discussion.
19. The frequency of his writing will be gathered from statements in subsequent chapters. See also Ribas, 44.

diversity of languages and customs. His purpose was to get more men to enter this field. He knew that the whole Jesuit province was watching the success of this effort, and that the instructions of the Visitor were to follow up the advantage and put all possible power into the drive. For it was the first *"misión entre infieles."*

CHAPTER XIII

Expansion

In the winter of 1591-92 Tapia decided to build a permanent center for the mission.[1] This house would be the main station in all the Sinaloa territory. It would be the resting place for tired workers, after their excursions to the pueblos along the rivers. The superior would make it his regular residence, where from time to time he would call his men into conference on the difficulties of the work or the consideration of new projects. The Brothers would live here, and maintain a steady support for the needs of the far flung operations.

The place chosen was the aldea of Cubiri,[2] or Santiago de Cubiri, as they named it. With the help of the Spaniards and those Indians who were well disposed, material was gathered and a substantial rustic house was erected. Tapia himself took the lead in the building. He went with his men into the forests, and personally directed the cutting of timbers for the structure. And he carried the logs on his own shoulders, working along with his primitive assistants.

Connected with the residence was another domicile, the home of the Indian boys who now came to begin their education in his seminary. He had gathered together a number of the most promising youths, and he proposed to instruct them in the first steps of reading and writing. This seminary, or boarding school, was his special delight, and he had hopes that it would be the foundation of a new era for his savages.

The work was scarcely completed when he was forced to become the first patient in this house of rest. The hot malarial atmosphere began to wear him out, and he fell sick as he had done before at Pátzcuaro.[3] He was brought by his friends to Cubiri. A burning fever kept him on his back for many days. Besides

---

1. Albizuri, B, 73 sq. This work was begun before he went to Topia.
2. Cubiri was some six miles southwest of Sinaloa, on the lower bank of the river.
3. See Albizuri, B, 74.

this, his eyes were affected by the disease that almost made him blind. In this state, Father Pérez prevailed on him to go away somewhere for a change in climate until he should improve, and he suggested the cool summits of the sierra near the mining town of Topia. The proposal timed well with a letter from that very place.

Topia was a settlement up over the crest of the mountains in the southeasterly direction of Guadiana. Francisco Ibarra[4] had worked the mines there to a point where they turned out large quantities of silver, and the rush brought Spaniards and Indians from all directions. The prosperity was now enjoying its usual concomitant, a period of lawlessness and crime, and the officials looked about for someone to check this chaos and put some order into the life of the villa. They heard of the fine success of Tapia with the natives down in Sinaloa, and they sent a messenger over the mountain road to ask the Father to leave his work for a time and come to them.

Tapia thus had a double reason for the trip. And there was a doctor at Topia. Besides, an old friend of his, Father Gerónimo López, was there. This aged man had come up from the college of Guadalajara to regain his health, and his company was sure to be a benefit to Tapia.

With the messenger, and a convoy composed of stalwart neophytes, Tapia mounted his mule and rode the hundred leagues to Topia. His letter had told him of many pueblos of Indians along the way. Probably he broke his journey with several stops among these natives. In Holy Week of 1592 he reached his destination.

The doctor did his best to cure him, but what helped him most was the meeting with his old Indians, the Tarascans,[5] who had come there to work in the mines, moved by the chance to make their fortunes. He had an excellent command of their language, and he gave them all the help he could in their troubles. As it was a special season of devotion, he also conducted religious services for the Europeans, preaching, hearing Confessions, celebrat-

---

4. On Ibarra see Mecham; also Hammond and Rey.
5. See p. 165 infra.

ing the Masses of these days of Holy Week. How he settled the disturbances is not recorded. But in a short time he left, with the good wishes and gratitude of the officials. At his parting the Spaniards and Tarascans gave him a large alms for his personal needs and for his missions.

On the return ride, he stopped for some time among the Acaxees Indians.[6] These savages were related to the Tepehaunes, and were a warlike tribe. They had made havoc for Ibarra, and beaten him badly in a pitched battle. They were reckoned among the worst of all the bad Indians of Nueva Vizcaya. Their home was along the upper waters of the Rio de Tamazula del Culiacán, the Rio de San Lorenzo, and the Piaztla. The country is very cold in the high places, while the canyons are hot. The roads today are incredibly difficult because of the deep arroyos, the cliffs and the very rugged mountains. All the ridges were inhabited by these cannibal Acaxees who worshipped demons and were no strangers to drinking human blood.

Tapia must have been well over his illness when he attempted this terrain. It is said that even with one who knows the way you risk your life among the crags and dangerous passes. But he was adventurous and agile in body. He went boldly into their strongholds, where, as Albizuri writes, they were hidden like crouching animals.

Someone must be found who knew their language and could teach him. Tapia discovered a mulatto who had been born and brought up among this race. He took this fellow for his master, and in fifteen days felt confident enough to address the Indians in their difficult language. He aroused his vigorous spirit, and began going about the sierra as though he were playing a game.

As he approached their haunts—they dwelt under trees or in caves in the rock—he shouted a greeting to them. They told him to come among them, and he began to tell them stories and witty sayings. They marked his ability to speak in their language, and his courage in coming alone to them, and they commenced to admire

6. See extended account in Albizuri, B, 73-82; also Astrain, IV, 443; Alegre, I, 259; Anua of 1593; letter of Carrera to Gutierrez; letter of Armano to Aquaviva; Tanner, 451 sq.

him and listen to his message. He showed them constant courtesy. Kindly he explained the Faith, and with a bare beginning
of the catechism he baptized a large group of them.

Then he told them that they ought to live in houses and pueblos,
as do the rest of wise men. He also exhorted them to be at peace
with the white man. These people had long been an impossible
obstacle to Spanish soldiery, and Albizuri remarks[7] that Juan de
Onate left in writing his story of humiliation at their hands.

Nearby, in the Valle de Topía, were other rancherias of Indians. This valley has long been noted for its beauty, its fertility
and its strategic situation. Inaccessible against resolute defenders,
it is rich in products of the soil, and is said to afford the finest
views in all the Sierra Madre. The thick forests, the mar-
velously colored hills, the rivers and canyons, are a fit subject for
those artists who are brave enough to conquer the terrain and
win the favor of the inhabitants.

On this expedition Tapia founded the first organized pueblo
of the Acaxees, and called it Santa Cruz del Valle. Late in the
same year, 1592, the Franciscans moved in and continued the work
among the newly made Christians. The name Santa Cruz com-
memorates the prime factor in their conversion.[8] Part of the race
lived high up on the sierra, where they worshipped with frank
superstition a stone idol called Topia. Tapia made his way to this
group. With his persuasion he so convinced them of the futility
of their worship that they decided to break up their old idol and
put in its place a great wooden cross. Then he arranged a solemn
procession to confirm their final rejection of demon worship, and
the naming of their new pueblo Santa Cruz del Valle. In time
the Jesuits developed this mission into the *partido* that cared for
much of Durango and eastern Sinaloa, Misión de San Andrés de
Topia.[9]

While this good work was going on, some of the old chiefs
held a powwow to deliberate about expelling him from their lands.
Tapia found out about this. He went to their meeting and spoke

7. Albizuri, l.c.
8. Ibid.
9. See Decorme, I, 131-151; Alegre, I, lib. iv.

to them. He demanded freedom of conscience for the converts. They listened to his pleas and gave him their promise not to break the peace. As he was leaving for Sinaloa, he told them that he would get missionaries for them as soon as he was able. In 1599 the mission became permanent, under the sterling priest and martyr, Father Hernando de Santarén.[10]

With this strenuous work over, Tapia summoned his Sinaloa escort and together they rode back home. They cut through the sierras to the Mocorito River and on down to the pueblo of that name.[11]   From there to San Felipe the way was frequently stopped by welcoming Indians, who were glad to see their Father come back in good health. At the headquarters glad news was waiting. Pérez had extended his work to the villas of Ures, Guazave, and Sisimicari.[12] His efforts at conversion were meeting increasing success, and he was teaching the Indians how to use new tools for the better development of their crops.

Other good news was the coming of two Fathers to assist him.[13] They were Alonzo de Santiago and Juan Bautista de Velasco, and they arrived in the Lent of 1592 while Tapia was away in Topia. Their entry had been marked by signs of extraordinary joy on the part of the Indians. Entire pueblos came out to the road in procession singing the *doctrina*. Triumphal arches greeted them. Tanner has a description of one of these arches that may well have been taken from some document that is now lost. More true of Paraguay, it fits this scene quite well:

> Of course in these arches no one should expect to find Parian marble, or the deeds of heroes skillfully carved in stone. Still, from the novelty of the work, and the heartfelt intentions that produced it, you would not here envy even Rome with all her mighty palaces and amphitheatres. Out of their poverty they build their arches of the interwoven branches of trees and shrubs. They hang on them all kinds of things—like the horn of Amalthea—: fish, both fresh and roasted, wild flesh, roosters and hens hung up by the neck,

---

10. See Decorme, I, 126, 132, and passim; also Alegre, Astrain, Cuevas, Bancroft, *North Mexican States,* I, l. c.; also p. 151 infra.
11. Anua of 1593.
12. Ibid., and Alegre, I, 260.
13. Anua of 1593; Albizuri and Alegre, ibid.

ostrich eggs, partridges, and the many-colored birds with
which these regions abound. Foxes, also, and dogs, are suspended in various ways from the arches. The bases and col-
umns are adorned with the skins of lions and serpents and
other wild creatures, stuffed with straw to give a life-like
appearance. Interspersed between these decorations are sacks
filled with foodstuffs and small baskets of cotton, maiz, and
vegetables. Lest anything be wanting to this array they heap
round the imposing structure wooden shields, garments, bows
and quivers of arrows, even prayer-garlands. By all this
elaborate display they make known to their welcome guest
that they dedicate all their goods to his welfare and happiness.[14]

Tapia assigned Velasco[15] to take care of the first river, the
Mocorito, with the pueblos of Bacoburitu and Orobatu and a few
smaller ones. His residence was to be at Mocorito. Pérez was
to keep those of the second river, his first conquest. To Santiago
he gave the pueblo of Lopoche and those beyond, as well as the
places he himself had opened up along the upper Ocoroni and
Sinaloa. The Superior took no definite district. His mind was
undecided. He planned to go to wider fields, but for the present
he would wait and see how things turned out.

---

14. Tanner, 435-436.
15. The program of the superior may be seen in the Anua of 1593,
the groundwork of which is formed from the notes of Tapia and of Perez.
This letter is most valuable material for the first two years of the Sinaloa
mission. It is to be supplemented by the manuscript material cited in this
chapter, and by the writings mentioned in the general notice of sources
on Tapia.

CHAPTER XIV

Back to Headquarters

Father Tapia was a very young superior to put in charge of this most important enterprise of the company, their first *"misión entre infieles."* That he gave a fine personal example is evident from the recital of his work. His planning of the attack was also quite correct, and matters went on at a rapid pace during their first year in Sinaloa.

But he had a consuming desire to see this labor a success, and he felt that all possible material and man power should be thrown into the campaign. To this end he importuned the Provincial to give him more men. When the answer did not come quickly, he wrote to the Father General, Aquaviva, at Rome.[1]

This letter, the only one of his that is preserved complete, is a precious document. Here the character of the man stands out better than in the fragmentary narrative of his deeds. His intense zeal, his thoughtfulness for others, his energy and tireless labor, become clear in this very personal and frankly intimate account of his initial experience as a superior. And the tendency noted in 1585, that in moments of depression he might look too sadly at the seamy side of things, crops out here in lamentation over the indifferent attitude that others take towards his mission. Undoubtedly he was writing in a period of weariness, when the magnitude of the task before him, and the comparatively small success, made this electric spirit grieve beyond measure.

> To our Father Claudius Aquaviva, Prepositus General of the Company:
> Father Diego de Avellaneda, Visitor of the Province of New Spain, sent me with one companion to the mission among the heathen. I was to go wherever it seemed most

---

1. Tapia to Aquaviva, Aug. 1, 1592, in Arch. Gen. S. J. Hist. Mex. This letter is printed in part by Astrain and Cuevas, but they overlooked some important sections. It is the first extant report of Tapia in his new position as organizer of a great system of mission work. He was the founder. He realized it, and he appears to have acted so as to ensure permanent solidity and expansive power.

necessary. I communicated with the Governor of Nueva Vizcaya, and in his judgment our best field lay in Sinaloa. We
set out, and arrived here July 6, 1591.

This province runs from the South Sea to the northward.
There is a great mountain region extending through almost
all New Spain, but it seems to break in this province.

The men of this territory wear no clothes; but the women
cover themselves, though with a very short cloth,—a sign
that modesty is a natural virtue with them. Now, however,
they take pride in dressing themselves quite carefully. They
live in groups on the banks of rivers. They have no ruler,
and recognize no superior; yet with all this they get along
very peacefully with those who speak their language,—a
matter in which there is wide variation.

In their wars they choose a captain, but outside of war
times they are all equal. Thus they admit the principle of
obedience, but only in conflict. During these periods they
take orders without any forcing or violence.

Their land abounds in ordinary food products, and they
gather their grain twice a year.[2] They know nothing about
religion in general, and they have no idols. They believe in
a creator, but they do not invoke or honor Him. They say
His abode is over the sierra. They also believe in a future
life, though one bereft of happiness, an unescapable misery
for all the dead.

They are a vivacious race, curious and quite talkative.
They have intelligence enough to understand most anything.
In the matter of habits, they are as Saint Paul pictures them
in the first chapter of the Romans, those who are not idolaters. They make no resistance to the Gospel. Still, obedience to its precepts is not to be looked for except in those
seemingly predestined to eternal life,[3] who are in the main
those under thirty years of age. Those above this age appear
without question a reprobate nation, though even of these
some have responded well.

The number of these people is so great[4] that, though we
be four, we cannot give our message to the first three rivers.
Following these there are three other rivers with countless
peoples, and then the province of Tenaberi, and beyond that

---

2. That is, in July and October. It is a fertile country.

3. This phrase is a commonplace in the Spanish language. It might
be rendered: "those who are well-disposed."

4. They estimated over a hundred thousand between the Mocorito and
the Fuerte. See Sauer, *Aztatlan,* for careful views on this point; also his
Linguistic Stocks in Sinaloa.

to the north is Cíbola and to the northeast New Mexico, with an opportunity for the Company to open up the portal to all the infidelity of these Indians. Of their diverse languages which I have learned thus far, I can preach in three without an interpreter. This year the number of baptisms, including children and old people, will come near to five thousand, and each day we are baptizing.

A large part of this province is in *encomienda*[5] to the Spaniards, which was an important factor in that it kept them without a leader. But as they are a race brought up in so much freedom, our government ought not to be too oppressive, but rather persuasive, to put some order and system into things that need fixing badly. For there were many Spaniards and Religious of St. Francis killed here. And in other years they feared us too, both Ours and the seculars. But now they show us love and obedience in whatever we demand.

Now, understanding that this mission is to go on permanently, I wish to represent to your Paternity some matters in reference to those who may have to come to this mission, as appears best in the sight of Our Lord.[6] Those who are sent here without any interior movement of Our Lord, and more for their own mortification than devotion, live here under great strain. And they seek reasons to justify their return to the colleges, in a way that cools and disheartens those who came from pure zeal. Those who from temperament or a lack of self-denial are a burden to the colleges, do not correct themselves when they come to the mission, and they become a greater charge on their co-workers than all the rest of the mission labor. Those who are pleased only with Spanish things, and expect to find a well-made, comfortable house, with everything ready on time and all things in becoming condition, without any thought of fervor or a desire to bear discomforts and solitude and the abandonment

5. See Bancroft, *History of Mexico,* II, c. viii; also Simpson, Fiske, l. c. Bancroft says in *North Mexican States,* I, 15: "many of the northern pueblos were distributed as encomiendas at this time (1524), but it does not appear that either encomenderos or garrisons were left in the country." See Ruiz on the point.

6. Tapia was a man of very high ideals, but his youth and inexperience made him somewhat severe in his judgments of other men. As a matter of fact, the two men here alluded to, Santiago and Velasco, served with success on the mission, the latter for many years; and with a certain dramatic irony they wrote beautiful eulogies of Tapia after his death. See thus in *"Documentos."* Santiago got sick and had to return to Mexico later on. Thus Ribas, 53.

of men: these, I say, live very disconsolate lives here. For the people with whom we deal are wild, crude and uncultured. There is no change of clothing, no house in which to live, no cooked food, and often no food at all, nothing for small diversions and much to tire the spirit. One gets very little time for prayer and retirement, nor such as can furnish even honest recreation. The superiors are far off. A letter reaches them in three months, and three more are required for the answer.

I have felt myself bound to bring this to the notice of Your Paternity. During eight years I have not known what it is to live in a college, and I have learned what I need to be able to live away from home, as obedience has always carried me along. In the second place, they now send me two companions, men born in this territory, one of whom his superior requested to have moved from his college; and the other never dreamed in the wildest lapses of his imagination of such things as mission work. This latter told me he wanted to see how things go here before he was willing to give himself to do any work. This mission is the first that the Company has had among the heathen, and the Christian rulers and the other Religious Orders are on the lookout.

For my part, I recognize my own little zeal and prudence. I had expected companions and I had begged for them as a favor of charity. But they send me sons who cause me more care than all the rest of the mission. I know by experience that those who come from Spain consider more the soul of the Indians and the conversion of the heathen, while those born here and raised among Indians are more impatient of hardship. But Martín Pérez, my first companion whom Father Mendoza assigned to me,[7] is in no way like the rest who are born here.

May Your Paternity provide what you judge proper. May Our Lord guard Your Paternity for many years.

GONZALO DE TAPIA.

From Cinaloa, August 1, 1592.

The superior of the mission spent the summer of 1592 in supervising the three *partidos* of his mission. During the fall he felt

---

7. This settles several mooted points for the biographer. Mendoza chose the pair for the "misiones entre infieles," but he gave them no definite assignment. Avellaneda, as Tapia says above, sent them to organize the Sinaloa mission.

that affairs were in such shape that he could make a further move. He called a consultation of his assistants, and the decision was that he go down to Mexico to see the authorities. He would interview the viceroy and the *audiencia*. He would meet the Father Provincial and other men of moment in the colleges. And he was sure that he would return to Sinaloa with the help that he knew was so much needed; for in Mexico he had a great reputation as a missionary.[8]

Accordingly he bade goodbye to his companions and rode out on the long journey.[9] It was at least eight hundred miles to the capital. He chose a troop of strong young men whom he had won over to Christianity, boys who could stand the trip, to ride along with him. Tapia wanted the company of these natives for protection on the long road, and he had a further objective in view. He would show them as his first and splendid conquest, to the viceregal officers and to all his Jesuit friends along the way. They would be an object lesson, a powerful stimulus to gain him the support that he desired. And they would enthuse, by their mere presence, many of his brethren to volunteer to be his fellow soldiers in that fruitful mission.

They retraced the route of the year before to Culiacán, where Tapia stopped to beg supplies for the trip from his prosperous friends. On down the coast past Acaponeta they went. They were now following what was to them a new trail,—though an old one since Guzmán,—cutting across Nayarit to the Rio Grande de Santiago and along the river road to Guadalajara in Jalisco.[10] Then they made over the high country to the scene of his early work in Michoacán, and they got a grand reception at the college of Pátzcuaro. The rector, his special friend Father Ramírez, welcomed him. The college showed its hospitality and devotion to the brave young missioner, and saw to it that his com-

8. See *Documentos,* fol. 49; Alegre, I, 261.

9. See Albizuri, B, 66-71; Alegre, Ribas, Astrain, Cuevas, l. c. The best document on the entire journey is the long letter of Brother Carrera to Father Gutierrez, the Spanish assistant to the General in Rome, 1600. Cf. also Armano to Aquaviva, 1594, and Ramirez' lost biography of Tapia, used by Albizuri and by Ribas (Ribas, 131).

10. See Carrera to Gutierrez.

pany was well cared for. To Tapia the rector gave a new outfit of clothing, to replace his worn and ragged garb. He in return offered souvenirs of Sinaloa to Ramírez and the Community. It was a happy reunion. But one detail marred their joy, for the rector, according to Albizuri, foretold that Tapia was soon to die a martyr, and he outlined in detail the attack and death stroke of the *macana* that would snuff out this valiant young life.[11]

For Tapia this thought was no deterrent. Many contemporaries write that he lived in constant sight, even wish, of martyrdom. He said as much to Rio y Loza at Zacatecas. And his conduct in approaching the savages of the sierra and in Sinaloa makes it clear that he had no fear of a violent death.

From Pátzcuaro the cavalcade rode across the high plateau to the capital. At once Tapia went to the viceregal palace and paraded his braves before the crowds that gathered to see this strange caravan. At the palace Don Luis de Velasco II received him tenderly and heard him tell the experiences he had met on the frontier. He listened intently as Tapia presented his petitions.

The first request was to commission more Fathers to work in the mission.[12] In those days of the *Patronato Real,* the viceroy had a great deal to say and much influence in furthering establishments of religion. This was his duty, as clearly as that of setting up new *presidios* or opening new colonies. Tapia represented the immense number of the natives along his frontier, and the variety of languages that was bound to put a large obstacle in the way of easy conquest.

Then there was the matter of a *presidio* and a garrison, and funds for his Indian seminary. Tapia did not want soldiers in his mission environs, but he felt the need of a guardian of the peace in the event of war or insurrection, and he had history to back him up in that point. The garrison would be a great help in setting up legal government, in sanctioning the laws, furnishing a civilized ideal to the natives, and protecting the missionaries who would attempt to go farther north. He himself had

---

11. Thus Albizuri, B, 68. Carrera mentions a similar idea. Cuevas says the fixed idea of the danger of death haunted the missionaries in the early days. (II, 380).
12. See "Note on the Patronato Real," p. 172 *infra.*

often been escorted by Antonio Ruiz or Bartolomé Mondragón. This garrison would not be close to his headquarters at Cubiri, but it would be at the central villa of the province in readiness for any lawlessness. The shadow of the king would always have a settling effect on ardent spirits along the frontier.

Velasco granted both these petitions in principle. He sent word to the Provincial of the Jesuits, that it was his wish that more men be despatched to the Sinaloa front. He promised, too, to set up a garrison at San Felipe at the first opportunity. This promise was kept too late.[13] The *presidio* was not established until the sad lesson of the death of Tapia forced the viceroy into action.

In addition Velasco issued an order that a regular supply be granted to the mission.[14] Tapia wanted the Fathers to be absolutely independent of the Indians in material things, to avoid belittling the Fathers in the eyes of those who would otherwise look down upon them. It was unbecoming to beg of the very ones whom he was leading up to civilization. He and his brethren must always keep their dignity and the respect of the natives.

This subsidy was granted. Albizuri says it amounted to three hundred pesos. A royal order of 1594 records that the viceroy supplied Tapia with money, though the amount is not given. Very likely it was the same as that afterward given to missionaries, two hundred and fifty pesos annually to each, and after 1608 three hundred pesos silver.[15]

The viceroy gave more on his own account.[16] He was devoted to the Jesuits and wished their work to prosper. With his help Tapia procured presents for the Indians, ornaments for the churches, and musical instruments which he intended the natives should learn to play.

After this audience, Tapia must next meet the dignitary second in rank, the Archbishop of Mexico, the primate and ecclesi-

---

13. See pp. 143, 164, infra.
14. Astrain, IV, 432.
15. Ibid., citing Velasco to Philip II.
16. See, on Velasco and the Jesuits, Astrain, IV, 438; Cuevas, II, 391. For details here mentioned see Carrera to Gutierrez.

astical superior of all New Spain.[17] The record of this visit is
confined to a mere mention in one document. Without a doubt
Bonilla, or his vice-gerent Cervantes—for the Archbishop seems
to have been away as Visitador in Peru—received the group
kindly and admired the native converts. But there is no sign
of any practical results from the visit.

Tapia now turned to call on the man in whom he was most
interested, his Father Provincial, Pedro Díaz.[18] The reputation
of the missioner had been widely known for some time. His
patron, Rodrigo del Rio y Loza, had written of his mission success to officials in Mexico, and Tapia himself had kept up a fine
correspondence in the midst of his active life in Sinaloa. Father
Díaz met him with paternal joy. He asked him many questions
about his work and his governing, questions that could be answered
better in a personal conversation than in the cold formality of
letters. The show of native converts gave the higher superior
a concrete illustration of the claims of Sinaloa on the province.

As things turned out, the chief gift of the Provincial to Tapia
was the excellent lay Brother, Francisco de Castro.[19] The Brother
was told to get ready and go back with the group when they
returned home. Díaz also gave his word to send more priests,
and his word was good. From this visit dated the constant
stream of missionaries that entered Sinaloa down to the last
days of the Jesuits in New Spain. As a final word, the Provincial
told Tapia to go back to Michoacán, there to prepare to pronounce his last vows in Valladolid with his former rector, Father
Francisco Ramírez. He himself would follow in a few days.

Farewells were taken, and the cavalcade rode out of the city in
high spirits. All the essential aims of the expedition were
achieved. Brother Castro was told to meet Tapia in Zacatecas,[20]
and more priests were promised at the first feasible moment. The
supplies, the money, and the church goods, would put the mission
on a solid economic basis, and enable Tapia to begin things that he
had planned a long time.

---

17. See Albizuri, B, 69; Nieremberg *Varones Illustres,* III, 325-331.
18. Ibid. See, too, the cited letter of Juan de la Carrera.
19. On Castro in Sinaloa, 1593-1627, see Albizuri, B, 68; Ribas 231-235;
Alegre, II, 173-174; Nieremberg, III, 341 sq.; letter of Juan de la Carrera.
20. See letter of Juan de la Carrera.

The trip now took them back along the same road to Michoacán, and within a few days they arrived at Valladolid. Tapia took up his quarters at the Jesuit college. The Indians were safely housed, and the military escort of his pack train bivouaced for the time of their stay.

One great sadness now came to Father Tapia. The Indians whom he had brought with him, strong young men who were used to hardship, found themselves unable to stand the altitude and the cold of winter in the city. One by one they weakened and fell ill, apparently with smallpox,[21] and before the visit was over all but one of them had died. The chagrin of the Father must have been very great, as he saw his first fruits thus taken from him at the very time when they were doing so much good for themselves and for his work. And what would he say to their parents, for Indian parents are fond of their children to an extraordinary degree! Probably he had other thoughts. For himself, he was accustomed to parting with things that were dear to him.

Tapia now made ready for the final step in the Jesuit Order. He had spent seventeen years thus far, from the time when he entered the novitiate in 1576. He had been successful in every stage of study and trial, and his character met the approval of superiors. Accordingly, on Saint Joseph's Day, March 19, 1593,[22] he knelt before his Provincial, Father Pedro Díaz, and with his friend Ramírez pronounced the four solemn vows that bound him forever to the highest service in the ranks of the Company.

Brother Juan de la Carrera has a letter[23] about this event and the subsequent incidents that carries on the story quite well:

> Among all the burdens borne by the Father (Tapia) in the course of his journey, he felt none more than having Our

---

21. This small pox worked havoc with the Indians. It is often mentioned in Jesuit documents, particularly the terrible plague of 1575 in which two-thirds of the Indians near Mexico died, according to Sanchez. See Alegre, I, 107, and passim. The best description of the malady as it was found there is given by Nieremberg, on Castro, l. c. Cf. also Velasco as quoted by Alegre, I, 263, and in *Documents,* fol. 122 sq. See also the letter of Juan de la Carrera.

22. Albizuri, B, 14-15; also Carrera.

23. The letter is really written to answer a demand for information on the dead Tapia. Carrera, as is clear from his own words, was a close friend of Tapia.

Lord take to Himself the Indians whom he had brought to Mexico, as the first fruits of that mission. They were his companions and his helpers and they made his hard work easy to carry on. Only one escaped death, and he was left so weak that he could not be of any assistance to Tapia. After he recovered he set out with the pack train that carried the many things the viceroy gave for that country, and he got there in safety.

On the return from Mexico the Father waited for the Provincial to come to Michoacán to receive his profession. With him was the Father Rector of the college of Valladolid where I was then stationed. At the profession a Brother met me and said that he saw Father Tapia come out wearing a red stole, and the other Father a white one, and that the former would be a martyr and the latter a confessor.

After the ceremony, Tapia met me, and the good Father begged me to ask the Rector and the Provincial to send me with him. He said that my petition must be granted: he had treated with them on the same matter, and the Provincial had not given his consent, even though I had been the companion of Tapia in his early journies.

I am, I said, ready to go gladly if I am told to go, and I shall make the Provincial understand this clearly, for that is my way of dealing with him. But he said it was necessary to urge him on the point. I then went to the Provincial and proposed the need of someone accompanying the Father, who was so poorly assisted in so important a work. I said that if I had done anything for the Company and he wanted to reward me, it would be to send me with Father Tapia to die in that country. He heard my plea, and after thinking a while he yielded to my request, and gave orders that it be so done.

And I took charge of the goods in the pack train, the statues, instruments, clothes, and all other things which the viceroy had given. And with the one surviving Indian, and with the others, (a captain and six Spanish soldiers, sent by the viceroy to Sinaloa, and an alcalde mayor who would look out for the interests of the natives and protect them from any abuse; he was also to assist the poor Spaniards who lived there, and if anyone broke the peace he would correct him and demand reparation according to the duty of an alcalde) I set out for Sinaloa by way of Guadalajara. Father Tapia went to Guadiana, which is the other way through Zacatecas.

In Guadalajara I got a message from Father Provincial

to the effect that floods would make it necessary for me to
go to Zacatecas and stay there, to avoid disaster on the road.
He said there was a providence in this. And so it fell out,
for from my visit to Zacatecas resulted many deeds that re-
dounded to the glory of God.

We came to the City of Zacatecas, where our house was being
just begun. During my stay of several months, I helped in
the building of it. Between times I accompanied a certain
Father, who knew the Indian languages, to a mission among
some Indian charcoal workers who lived in the mountains
nearby. They received the *doctrina* very well.

While there I wrote to Father Tapia about my situation,
my work, and my detention there. He replied in the following words: (Letter,—[24] which, as it is from so Holy a
Father, ought to be esteemed highly, for in it he shows very
well his spirit and zeal and sanctity—transferred by me
from a chapter of a letter to Brother Juan de la Carrera,
which Father Tapia wrote from Cinaloa, which says that:)

"I received the long letter of the Brother from the charcoal works, and there are with that one three others which he
has written. You say very truly, dear friend, that in many
places people are criticizing this mission of Cinaloa. And
yet that does not make me feel badly, for those far away
do not understand. I pass it over, as there is no use in saying anything. Better take it patiently. Impatience gains no
conquests. Where is the good ground that has no weeds or
rocks? But against all the carping, you, my Brother, might
answer that your coming here is deferred because of the bad
weather, and you are not abandoning us to remain there.
I can do little at this distance to quiet rumors. They say all
the brethren are against this mission. If the superiors do
not send me any more men, then I have got to get along as
well as I can.

"We have all been very busy in baptizing all the dying and
burying them, for the pestilence which took those who died
in Michoacán is widespread here. Two-thirds of the children
whom I baptized in this province are now in heaven.

"In the last letter, I wrote you that after I returned here I
learned the Tepeguan language, because there is a pueblo of
that language in this province. Now all their children are
baptized, and two dozen adults, and almost all of these are se-

---

24. Translated exactly as in the letter of Carrera. Luckily Carrera
had saved this letter, thus helping to reconstruct the life of Tapia. Note
that Sinaloa was spelled Cinaloa in the sixteenth century.

cure in the next world. For that reason I may not rest from baptizing. Today I baptized some and I do not know if they will see tomorrow come.

"We have not advanced because we cannot leave the sick. The alcalde mayor has not arrived. Where he is we do not know, because no letters have come except those from you, my Brother.

"GONZALO DE TAPIA."

These are the words of the blessed Father. Therein one may find what kind of man he was, what were his ambitions, and how content he was with his lot and his vocation.[25]

Tapia, then, had returned to Sinaloa without the company of the brave young converts who came down with him in the preceding winter. But a surprise was waiting for him. He wrote ahead to Father Pérez as to the time of his arrival. As he was riding along the road near his destination, he saw the dust of a large crowd of horsemen. Drawing near, he found that it was a group of his Indians, coming to welcome him and escort him in procession to the villa of San Felipe.

---

25. Juan de la Carrera was a veteran. He had come from Spain with Segura in 1568, and was with Rogel at Havana when the martyrdoms of Virginia occurred. See Alegre, I, 17, 33; also Florencia, passim.

CHAPTER XV

The Light of Full Day

The letter of Juan de la Carrera noted that Tapia left Valladolid to hurry back to Sinaloa. He rode northward through his old tramping grounds in Chichimeco land to Zacatecas and Guadiana. From this town he might have taken the shorter route across the high country near Topia, where he had spent so useful a period in 1592. His entire journey seemed to be, at least in part, a visiting of old friends and old country. And now that he had made himself so well known to the Acaxees, he would surely have stopped to see them on his return. But rumor of wars near Topia changed his route, and he went down from Durango over the Sierra de Panuco to San Sebastián, whence he followed the coastline road northward.

The journey from Zacatecas to San Felipe was made with but one companion, but he was more welcome than any he could have chosen. It was Brother Francisco de Castro, whose life has been so beautifully sketched in the short account of Nieremberg.[1] Castro was a Sevillan. His father managed the domain of the Marques of Villamanrique. When the marques came to Mexico as viceroy in 1585, he brought Francisco with him to be his secretary. This service merited the gift of a hacienda and a title of honor. But suddenly, in the next year, the promising young man decided to give up his wealth and position, and to take instead the humble estate of a lay Brother in the Jesuit Order.

Brother Castro spent two years in the novitiate, and five more as cook in one of the colleges of Mexico. He was working at that assignment when Tapia came to Mexico in 1593 to rally men and material help for his mission. Tapia made a great effort to rouse as many as possible to go back with him to Sinaloa, and he wanted in particular a devoted and able lay Brother. It fell out that Castro had been longing to do that very thing. Their meeting, then, was fortunate, and they quickly decided to ask the Provincial to make

---

1. See note 19 on Chapter Fourteen; also Relacion of Ruiz.

the appointment. Father Díaz consented, and Brother Castro joined the mission staff.

Thirty leagues down the road from San Felipe, near Mocorito, they encountered the welcoming band of Indians.[2] Tapia gathered them in a crowd and spoke to them. He first told them the sad news, the death of their young men who had shown such personal devotion to him. Then he turned to the children, and he praised the little folk. He addressed the braves in his customary cheerful way, and informed them that he had taken counsel with the viceroy for their welfare and improvement. New Fathers were coming to teach them. Then he introduced the Brother to them. They crowded about Brother Castro, these bronzed sons of the forests and mountains, and shouted their greetings to their guest. Then the whole cavalcade turned and rode fast to San Felipe.

The Brother now proved to be an invaluable asset to the mission.[3] He found to his surprise that the Fathers had in Cubiri nothing but a miserable shack of logs and mud. The food was in a similar bad state, dry squashes, maiz, and dried fish. There was no wine except for the Mass, no bread beyond the hosts. The clothing of the settlement was so bad that the Spaniards went about covered with the tanned hides of animals. Castro saw opportunity in every direction, and with the help of the most intelligent of the young Indians, he began the management of all domestic concerns.

He at once took the office of cook, and gathered and prepared all the food. As sacristan he kept the altar in shape and all the articles for religious services. He made and repaired the clothing. He was the doctor for the sick. He planted and irrigated a garden. Then he dug ditches and guided the small streams into a channel for a water wheel to grind the grain of the settlement. But his greatest delight was in the carpenter work, for he at once set himself to build a church and a decent house for the Fathers.[4] He went with the Indians to the mountains to cut timber, and with

---

2. See Nieremberg, III, 341 sq.; Albizuri, B, 71.
3. This account of Castro depends chiefly on Nieremberg l. c., supported by materials cited above in note 1.
4. This building was an enlargement of the beginnings at Cubiri noted in Chapter Thirteen.

his tools he trimmed the logs and even did some carving. Gathering clay, working and molding it into bricks in the hot sun, he led his little band of youthful workmen in their first industrial school.

When the Indians were weary and perspiring he cheered them by his wit and lively speech, and they kept on indefatigably till they had finished the entire mission compound. This done, the boys got a short rest. Then the troop set off to build another church and house for Tapia; and in turn each of the mission stations had its full equipment, thanks to the labor and ability of this unusual man. To see him work did much to win converts, for the natives admired a man who could do manual labor better than they could, who could work longer than they, carry heavier loads, keep more jolly under the trials of heat and fatigue. This type of mission Brother has not died out, and today many a visitor marvels at the skill and capacity for getting things done that are displayed by these quiet-mannered, talented men.[5]

When he had time in the intervals between his building operations, Castro often accompanied Father Tapia on his missionary tours. His fame spread all over the province. Particularly when trouble arose, he became the man of the hour. Soon after he arrived in Sinaloa smallpox broke out among the Indians, and many of them died. The contagion was so bad that it seemed to be in the very air, and there was not a home without its suffering. Many of the natives lay dying in the open fields and on the hills, without medicine or doctors, and the Brother had an opportunity of showing all his talent and energy. The four priests went the rounds of the ranchos and pueblos, curing the souls and caring for the bodies of the aborigines. Castro remained in the center at Cubiri, which became a hospital for all who could be brought there. He took personal charge of the sick, preparing their food and what medicine he could make, consoling them, even acting as surgeon and bleeding them. He had great success in bringing many back to health. The dying children he baptized, and for many he performed the last human mercy of burial.

When that fatal day of the death of Tapia came to sadden his

---

5. They may be met in many of the missions in the United States from Dakota westward.

heart, this faithful companion wept with manly tears that he could not have shared the same death as his martyred brother. After thirty-three yars of this noble life in Sinaloa his own time came. He was one of the foundation stones of that historic mission.

Brother Castro was intimately connected with the seminary that Tapia had begun at Cubiri. To this school the Fathers brought the young men among their converts. Here, as Ribas writes,[6] they learned to read and write, to practice good manners, to sing, and to recite the *doctrina*. This author, whose book is one of the truly great works on all that country, devotes an entire chapter to the work of this seminary, in improving the education and refinement of the youth of Sinaloa. Another familiar character in this story, Rodrigo del Rio y Loza, wrote long letters to the viceroy on the same subject, and Monterey in turn sent highly laudatory reports of this foundation to Philip II. The rapid and wide success of the mission began to thrill the mind of official New Spain, and the Jesuits were spoken of with enthusiastic approval.

The success of this school impelled Father Tapia to a larger scheme. He envisioned the conquest of all the tribes of the Sierra Madre, and he foresaw that a general seminary for the youths of these nations would be most useful for the missions and the development of the Indians. The ideal location for this school would be Guadiana, the city that soon became the general headquarters for all the missions of the Pacific slope. To this school the Fathers could send the young hopefuls of the mission seminaries from all points of the compass, and form a kind of university for Indians. There they could train leaders, men of broadened mind and mature character, with some ideals of refinement and a solid knowledge of religious truth. The superior sent Father Pérez to go to Guadiana and stir up interest in the project. Tapia himself did not live to see this foundation materialize. It was opened just seven weeks after his death, on August 31, 1594.[7]

A paucity of documents prevents the presentation of a complete

6. Ribas, especially 99, 110, and c. xxvi. Rodrigo del Rio y Loza wrote long letters to the viceroy in praise of this school. Cf. Astrain, IV, 439.
7. Cf. *Memorias para la historia de Sinaloa,* fol. 817; Alegre, I, 268-269; Cuevas, II, 378; Astrain, IV, 441; Bancroft, *North Mexican States,* I, 124.

picture of the material side of the mission work.[8]   Only from in-
dications can it be conjectured.   It is a commonplace that the
Jesuits built beautiful and permanent churches for the Indians.
The nature of their "reductions," so often mentioned but never
described until Pfefferkorn wrote late in the eighteenth century,
may be suggested from the story of the Paraguay reductions begun
in the next decade.   For Sinaloa was a pioneer in all America, in the
method of dealing with the savages.   Stray notices in the records
tell of establishing pueblos, setting up political life among the Indians, teaching them the trades, music, the rudiments of learning,
the religious ceremonies.   In cases of crime or infractions of the
peace the word of the missionary was law.

Ribas[9] gives a list of eighteen rules drawn up to guide the missionary.   They were written by the Father Visitor Cabredo, and
their model was the first conduct of the pioneers.   They refer to
the policy of isolation, a policy that is clear in the plan of Tapia
to build the center of the mission away from the whites at San
Felipe.   In some way then, one can find here all the elements
of the system that was developed and enlarged throughout the
entire range of the missions on the Pacific slope.

The plague of smallpox put a severe strain on the reputation
of the Fathers among the Indians.   During the epidemic it was
impossible for any new work to be undertaken.   And, what was
worse, the superstitious minds of these primitive people began to
lose confidence in the priests and to return to their old ways of
idol worship.   They were grounded in these ways for centuries
past, and their fathers from time forgotten had prayed to the river,
the mountain, the sun, to avert these awful visitations of nature.
The childlike savage lives very close to nature, and his chief con-

---

8.   This is the first biography of Tapia since the lost account of Ramirez
written in the sixteenth century, and naturally it will be found incomplete.
The documentary remains are not very full for this earliest period of the
missions, and only by piecing separate records can anything like a connected narrative be formed.   The author hopes that this study will form the
basis on which a full account of the origin of this great mission system
will be built.

9.   Ribas, 447 sq.   The rules were put into final form in 1610, six years
after Ribas himself reached New Spain.   See Astrain, IV, 339, on Cabredo.   On the mission system as a whole a fine study may be found in
Pfefferkorn, *Beschreibung der Landschaft Sonora.*

cerns are the material welfare of himself and his family. Now these new teachers had been unable to stave off the deathly pest.

Tapia recognized these facts, and at the first moment he moved to offset their devastating force. Leaving the three Fathers to operate round the center at Cubiri, he decided to go farther on into the wild places, through the mountains and along the upper tributaries of the Fuerte. Ocoroni would be his new headquarters, and he took Brother Castro with him to help him build a house and a church at that place.[10]

The largest people to the north and east of Ocoroni was the Suaqui tribe. These Indians were gross pagans, and often confused religion with superstition. It was a hard task to teach them the Faith. Christian truth often seemed less powerful than their gods, and they hesitated to accept it. At the slightest provocation they turned away from the priest to their idols, if ever they failed to find in him the superhuman powers that they associated with their notion of priesthood.

The smallpox had hardly passed when an earthquake in their country terrified them.[11] They had taken to their idols, but now they thought that they were being punished by this Father, who, some said, was the son of *Virigeva*. They sent messengers to beg him to come to them.

These revolutions of nature, storms and temblors and pestilence, thus opened the way for him into their wild and savage tribe. He left Castro at Ocoroni, and went alone to visit him. He agreed with them that these natural disasters might be a sign of divine displeasure. He told them of the true God, and that all men are His children. He encouraged them to come and live like their brothers down at San Felipe. And he left them with his promise to come and live among them as soon as this was possible.

At Ocoroni another work was waiting for him.[12] Some Spaniards were in the country, recently landed on the lower Sinaloa,

---

10. See notes on Castro above, 1, 2, 3; also Albizuri, B, 83.
11. Albizuri, B, 82. He quotes the informe of Martinez to the viceroy (1603-1604) that on this entrada Tapia baptized 600 infants between the Sinaloa and Suaqui confines. See Alegre, I, 263-264.
12. Albizuri, B, 73; also Ruiz, ff. 30-31. Ruiz notes that Tapia built a seminary at his new headquarters, Ocoroni.

intending to enslave the natives for work in their mines and haciendas. Against all the laws[13] these traffickers in human beings
sought out stray Indians whom they could capture and sell or
indenture. Tapia set himself firmly against this practice that would
in its rank injustice do so much harm to his work and make the
Indians lose their confidence in all white men. And he succeeded
in keeping them out of the province of Sinaloa by his defiance of
them and his threat of punishment to anyone of them whom he
found in his mission territory.

Christmas of 1593[14] was the occasion for the last reunion of
the Fathers and the Brother before the terrible events of the next
year. They met at Lopoche, a league or so north of San Felipe, as
they had done in former years. It was a quiet but happy celebration for these men, weary from the wear of journeys in that
rough country and from continual contact with an inferior race.
The mind craves occasional company with its equals. But they
were light of heart at their successes and the prospect of a rich
future.

These little assemblies, which they were able to hold only once
a year because of their busy lives, were an extraordinary source
of relief and comfort to these men. The superior gave an exact
account of all that he had done and of his plans. The others did
likewise. They conferred on a uniform method of procedure in
the work of the mission. They renewed their vows and refreshed
their spirits.

Besides the Jesuits, the Spaniards of the villa and all the
Christian Indians of the first three rivers came together for this
celebration. These in turn invited all the pagans of the nearby
pueblos for a feast in which they gave many presents. It was a
spectacle to move hearts, these hundreds of savages gathered in
true brotherhood and joy, with no feeling of war and hatred. One
venerable old Indian gave a speech on this occasion:[15]

13. Especially the New Laws of Charles V, 1541-1542. On the New
Laws see Bancroft, Fiske, Simpson, Cuevas, l. c.
14. See letter of Santiago quoted in Alegre, I, 265; also Anua of 1593;
Astrain, IV, 399. On the Christmastide of 1596 see Anua of 1596 and
Cuevas, II, 384.
15. Alegre, ibid.

We have worked anxiously, my sons and brothers, to prepare this grand feast. Now all enmities and wars are ended. We are like the Spaniards here, and we have but one heart in mutual friendship. Our beloved Fathers have made this for us by holy baptism. They have taken away our evil hearts. They have given us all the one same blessing. We ought to be thankful to these men. They have no aim but our own good. They have left their lands, their great houses, their refined friends, to come to teach us the way to heaven.

But one Indian named Alonso Sobota, an apostate from his old baptism by the Franciscans, knowing that the Suaquis were congregated on that same night for a great celebration, went to them and tried to stir them up against the Fathers, and Father Tapia in particular, as the leader of this new mission.[16] He had taken their young men to their death in Michoacán. He wanted to make them all slaves. The cacique of the Suaquis answered that they were all satisfied with the intentions of the Fathers. Sobota in rage went to the house of Tapia and tried to set fire to it and the church nearby. But a friendly Indian put out the blaze and saved everything. The evildoer escaped to the mountains.

Once again Tapia went into the land of the Suaquis. He entered their country from the sources of the Fuerte and moved on down through their pueblos to the site of old Carapoa. There he got a message[17] that two new Fathers were coming to the mission, Hernando de Santarén and Pedro Méndez. They were at San Miguel, on their way to San Felipe. He despatched Brother Castro to go back and meet them, and he remained alone among the Indians. Late in the spring he returned to his headquarters at Ocoroni. Indefatigable in his love of his fellow man, his mind and body were straining every nerve to plant the Faith deep in that virgin soil.

There is a letter from the General dated Rome, March 5, 1594, which shows that Tapia must have written Aquaviva a long account of the work being done in Sinaloa. A marginal note in the journal of the General says that "after writing this and sending it the first time, I received his letter sent March 13, and I saw there the

---

16. Alegre, I, 266.
17. Albizuri, B, 83.

same things that he had said of Zacatecas, and that he had written in similar terms to the provincial."[18] The answering letter reads:

The joy that God takes in the fruitful labors of Your Reverence does not confine itself to Mexico. Now it comes sailing over to me with the good news, and gives me no small occasion to praise and adore the divine mercy, which will be communicated with such liberality to the mass of the gentiles. Be sure that I feel the great sufferings which Your Reverence and your companions must necessarily bear in such a land and among such people.

Still, I believe that I am more envious than compassionate. For most happy is the lot of those whom God uses as instruments to discover that poor and abandoned race. Likewise it is undoubtedly His merciful goodness that His workers live so lonely and deprived of the human enjoyments that are wanting in such an occupation. However, He supports them and produces the divine helps that are most useful and comforting to make their labor bearable.

I have charged the superiors and do now again charge them that they aid your mission. For it strikes me that it is the opening of a grand gateway to the many parts beyond, where hitherto God has not been known. Nor shall I fail to aid always with my prayers, Your Reverence, in remembrance of which I beg you to place me in yours, and to give my kindest wishes to all your companions.
Rome, March 9, 1594.

CLAUDIUS AQUAVIVA.

18. Fully transcribed from journal of Aquaviva, entry Mar. 9, 1594, in Arch. Gen. S. J. Hist. Mex.

CHAPTER XVI

The Storm Gathers and Breaks

Things now began to move fast for Father Tapia.[1] The epidemic that brought death and dismay to hundreds caused uneasiness in native circles. The terrifying earthquake revived the hopes of the opposition. Trusted before, he now found the medicine men stirring up the people against the "false teachers." The missionary was equal to the attack, and his lack of concern for his personal safety made a profound impression on his converts.

But other forces, subtle and powerful, were gathering to destroy him. The remote cause of his death arose in this way. The pagan Indians in their heathen ceremonies engaged in very lascivious dances, in which every instinct of decency and honor was outraged.[2] Native drink played an important part in the revelries. The outcome was an impossible situation for morality. No civilization, no religion, could grow in such an atmosphere.

Tapia hated every kind of vice, but his heart trembled at the demoniac bestiality of these rites, and he decided to check them, even if it cost him his life. He often warned the new converts to avoid these carousals, especially the older folk.[3] Some complied and stayed away. Others pretended that the rites were good and useful customs, come down from their ancestors of old. The elderly men failed most in this matter.

The Father worked long and hard to win them over. He warned them in public, in private, with all possible urging and suavity.

---

1. This and the following chapter are well founded on source material. The chief documents are gathered in the *Documentos,* the analysis of which is printed in the bibliographical note. Supplementary matter lies in the letters of Carrera and Armano, already quoted, and in the martyrological accounts cited in the appendix. This phase of Tapia's career was most attractive to contemporary writers and their immediate successors, who considered the martyrdom the crowning achievement of his life, forming the spiritual basis on which the subsequent successes would rest. See especially the excellent *Relacion* of Ruiz, ff. 34-36.
2. That this is no exaggerated account may be seen by consulting Albizuri, B, 84 sq.
3. See Albizuri, l. c., and letters of Santiago and Perez in the *Documentos.*

Some of the chiefs came to him and advised him to appoint the captain and chief justiciar of those frontiers, Miguel Ortiz Maldonato, to choose a reliable Indian who would insist on right conduct among his fellows.[4] The captain was to punish infractions of Christian Indians by corporal punishment.

Even this did not deter the older natives from continuing their practices. Tapia then ordered that no dances should be held without his express permission and in his presence, and that no Christian should go to them under pain of whipping. That put a stop to the affairs, but mortal hatred for Tapia arose among some of the old men of the tribe.

It fell out that he arranged a grand fiesta for all the Christians, a religious and social ceremony in which a large concourse of Indians came together.[5] As the affair was proceeding, some of them came to Tapia, the superior of the mission, and begged him to give permission for an old-time dance. He refused, knowing what it might mean. They urged him. Finally he yielded, but on condition that he be present the whole time, and that they act and dress with becoming decency.

During the dance several of the pagan old men held a secret meeting to determine what to do with this Christian priest.[6] He was, they said, the first to come among them and tell them what they must do. He was interfering with their tribal customs, dictating to them in their own land about their own personal conduct. He made laws for their tastes, for their most cherished ways of acting. It was intolerable. Satisfaction must be sought. This decided, they entered the dance, and began their lewd movements. Tapia noticed this, and called them to himself. He spoke kindly to them, and asked them to go their way to other parts and sate themselves in their villainies.

"I am," he said, "the interpreter of morals here. I am bound to live as I teach, and to tell my people plainly what they must avoid. The law of Christ lays obligations on me, but I can carry

---

4. The narrative of Father Albizuri is most detailed on these events. Perez de Ribas, the scholar, is a constant control of the former's citations of fact and saying.

5. This event occurred about a month before the end. See Albizuri, B, 87.

6. Thus Albizuri, Ruiz, Santiago, Armano.

them with His help. We must not say one thing at our baptism and act the opposite afterward. God does not shut His eyes at our faults. Remember He is our judge as well as our father."[7]

After this affair he sat down and wrote to his friend and confidant, Francisco Ramírez, Rector of Pátzcuaro,[8] He told him all that had gone on, and concluded with an earnest request that he pray for him in the battle that was coming in his martyrdom. For he felt certain that with this fiesta he had written the close of his mortal life. Ramírez received this letter at the very time that Tapia passed out of this world.

One of these old men who had come to the dance was Nacabeba.[9] He was the chief Indian and cacique of the neighboring pueblo of Tovoropa, three miles north of San Felipe. By profession he was a pagan in morals, a public disturber of the peace, and a ruination of Christianity. He seems to have acted as the leader in the pagan rites, as something of a priest or medicine man.

These medicine men were the moving spirits of the obstructionist party, singled out in the documents as those over thirty years of age. This party, called Semencanaan by the missionaries, was the crowd that bothered the Fathers. They knew little but license and vice, drunkenness, women, war and death. They never adopted the Christian ways. Habituated in their vices since childhood, they refused to listen to the new teachers.

"They have always," writes Santiago,[10] "started the insurrections. They were the ones who spoke to the Suaqui, a nation of the fourth river, to get help for burning the mission at the Nativity in 1593. They threatened death to Pedro, cacique of Ocoroni,

7. Albizuri, B, 87 sq., quotes these speeches. Ramirez is his main source. Ramirez learned the essence of the facts from eye-witnesss, some of whom were still on the mission when Albizuri arrived.

8. Ramirez was then Rector of Valladolid. Soon he was made Rector of the Casa Profesa in Mexico, a tribute to his integrity and sound judgment. This letter is preserved only in Albizuri's citations.

9. Nacabeba was the arch-villain, a cacique, and a native priest. His power over his people has a striking similarity to the case of Sitting Bull and the Sioux. That potentate was the actual cause of Custer's Massacre, though at the time he was seventeen miles from the battle of the Little Big Horn near Hardin, Montana.

10. See Santiago in *Documentos*, and in Alegre, Cuevas, Ribas. Mange in his *Diario*, 336, gives an impassioned account of these events.

when measles and smallpox attacked their people, for they said that he brought it on them by harboring a priest. They tried to bring María, the servant of Father Tapia, into the conspiracy in the Lent of 1593. They said it was hard to have to give up their old customs of having many women and their religious carousals."

No one in all Sinoloa had been a greater obstacle to the work of the mission than Nacabeba, ever since the first Fathers came. He ridiculed Tapia everywhere, with insults and jibes against the *doctrina* and the teacher. He taunted the new Christians, and afflicted them in many ways in his capacity as cacique. He called them cowards, weaklings, to accept the strange law in their land. He blamed the priests for the intolerable burdens on his own conduct.

Tapia was grieved over the harm this chief caused, and he tried many times to bring him to change his ways. But the barbarian would not listen, and he called on his people to do justice to those who introduced strange ways and laws into their land. He found others of kindred feeling among the gentiles, and also a few discontented Christians. Chief of these was the apostate Alonso Sobota of Lopoche, who appeared before in this story, a man infamous in life and blasphemous in tongue. Another was Sebastián of Baboria, a wicked man and a traitor to Tapia, who had kept him as a member of his own household.[11] Not understanding the true liberty that would come from the new law, they complained against the restrictions.

Nacabeba worked with bribe and argument, and Sobota with him. They held secret meetings at Lopoche, Tovoropa, Acaucua, Matapan, Cubiri, and other places, but they could get little assistance from their brother Indians who were loyal to Tapia. Each meeting was a violent attack on the new law and the priests. They compared their own ways with the new morals, and bemoaned the dissolution of their customs in the modesty of the innovating religion. They thought it unbearable to stop their abuses of women, their drunken revels, their eating of human flesh, at the insufferable demand of Christianity. Finally, they would not tolerate hearing any more of this new law of clean living in their land.

---

11. See Albizuri, B, 87 sq.

The priests must go, and their leader first of all.[12] After the deed they would leave that abominable race that had yielded its mind to the intruders, and go to their ancient fellows, the Yaquis, in the northern wilds,[13] there to live according to the ways of their ancestors.

When Nacabeba continued his evil conduct in public, Tapia decided that he was powerless to change him with kindness. He asked the alcalde mayor, Maldonato, to threaten him with whipping for his harm to the converts. This was done, but the old man was much wrought up over the warning and created a public scene, ending the fracas by kidnapping several Christians and hiding out in the foothills to the east. Brought back by Ruiz and a searching party, he was confronted by the alcalde, who ordered him to be whipped and to have his hair cut off,—a shameful thing to those Indians who were so proud of their long hair. Angered at this treatment, and persuaded that Tapia was the cause of it all—for a message from Tapia came to Maldonato at the very moment— he went off to the mountains. They always went off that way for shame at their shorn head, till the hair grew again. There he planned the acts that were to follow. He called to the mountain rendezvous all his relatives and friends. He recounted his wrongs, and asked their help in getting his redress.

The conspirators met at Cavihuri, and with much wine and many speeches, and tobacco burning in their hands—their custom during solemn deliberations—they voted the death of the Father. The charge of executing the sentence fell on Nacabeba, the chief mover in the plot, and Tahaa, a brave and bellicose native. They agreed to act without delay. They would gather at Tovoropa on the following Sunday.

These meetings were not so secret that some of the Christians did not hear of the conspiracy.[14] They told Father Velasco, who advised Tapia of his danger.[15] Tapia, used to such perils of life, showed no special emotion at the news. He felt that he had long

---

12. Note that this decision was reached before Nacabeba was roused by personal injury at the hands of Maldonato. Tapia did not die because of a private grudge.

13. "Mountains" that is, the wild country near the mouth of the Yaqui.

been preserved by some unseen power. If now his time was come, if the protection was not to endure, he accepted the change in the plans of Providence. For himself, he had not been afraid up to now, and he had no intention of changing his attitude or his principles.

The Spaniards at San Felipe also asked him to avoid the snare of death, or at least to take a personal guard when he went among the savages. He replied that he had injured no man. He had given no just occasion for hatred. He loved them as children. He need have no fear when there was no blameworthy deed.

The following Saturday, July 9, 1594,[16] Tapia went on his customary ride from the headquarters at Ocoroni to the pueblo of Tovoropa.[17] He was accompanied by Don Pedro, the cacique, and the servant of the chief, a mulatto named Francisco. María and her little son went as servants of the Father.

Sunday morning Mass was said. Afterward the natives sent word to Tapia through Pedro that they saw Nacabeba and the others lurking about. Pedro asked Tapia to return with him at once to Ocoroni, where he could protect him. Tapia refused to do this. He had work to do here, and he did not believe that the Indians would carry out their threat. Nor did he want to show any fear and weaken his position with them. Sadly Pedro departed with Francisco. Old María took care of the cleaning and cooking, while her little boy aided Tapia in the catechetical work that occupied him all day.

Toward evening Tapia was very tired, and he decided to retire early. He was on his knees at the door of his hut, facing the

---

14. See Albizuri, B, 94.

15. See *Relacion* of Velasco in *Documentos,* fol. 122 sq., and Albizuri, l. c.

16. This date presents a peculiar difficulty. The first documents all place the death on Sunday, July 11, 1594. According to all methods of calculation, it is impossible that July 11, 1594, fell on a Sunday. It was a Monday. Astrain and other first-rate historians retain the original dating, probably for sentimental reasons. The author prefers to follow what became a general custom with regard to this date after 1600, and so to call Sunday, July 10, 1594, in accordance with rational chronology. Hence Tapia died on Sunday, July 10, 1594.

17. Tovoropa was a league north of San Felipe, say Cuevas, II, 382. Today it is generally included in the city of Sinaloa. No mark of the spot of martyrdom remains.

church and telling his beads.[18] Of a sudden figures stole out of the dusk and walked slowly to the door. At their head was Nacabeba. He approached quietly to Father Tapia and bent down as if to whisper some favor. Tapia suspected danger from the circumstances of the strange group before his eyes. He distrusted the visit at this hour of the day, the smooth words, the evil look in their eyes, for he knew the crowd well. But contrary to their expectation he kept a serene face. Unperturbed, rosary in hand, he spoke kindly to them.[19]

At the sign from Nacabeba, Tahaa threw back his cloak quickly. He drew out his *macana* and struck Father Tapia heavily on the head, making him slump to the earth as though dead. They stood back, terrified a moment at thought of what they had done.

Tapia saw that his death was near. He moved to the patio, and called on God with trustful and forgiving groans. Then he said: "What is this, my children, this evil thing that you have done?" Then, reaching out with his arms to the cross that stood in the cemetery between his door and the church, he folded his arms to die with the sign of salvation on him.

The villains had thought him dead. They wondered at the movements of the body, the words it spoke. Then they came on, and struck him with knives and *macanas*. Tapia, lurching forward with his last sigh, and seeing that he could not reach to the cross, made a cross with the fingers of his right hand,[20] as a sign of his mission to the Indians, and then lay quiet. The Father of the Missions was dead.

Struck by his last words, the conspirators went off like whipped dogs. They wanted to be away from the scene, for their hearts were afraid. But Nacabeba, reviling what Tapia had said, shouted: "do we listen to him, our enemy, the destroyer of our law?"[21]

---

18. All the sources agree on the details of this picture. Mange, 338, has the best brief sketch.

19. This calmness on his part dispels any idea that he died as a personal enemy. He died willingly, as a profession of faith.

20. This crossing of thumb and finger is a part of the Spanish way of making the sign of the cross.

21. These words were reported by Maria, by her child, and by the Indians who gave the alarm. There were many witnesses, and some of them later repented of their deed. Their corroboration made the facts morally certain for the writer.

The others, roused by this, returned and with savage glee mangled the body. With an axe they cut off his head and his left arm, but they could not sever the right. It lifted suddenly, with the fingers crossed, and it was found in this position the next day.

Then they vented their hate on all his belongings. His servants had run away. The murderers scattered the papers in his box in the church and tore them up and stamped on them. They killed his mule, and his devoted dog, such was their frenzy. They roused up all the little children who had come to catechism that day, but these fled into the darkness when they saw the murder, and escaped. The scoundrels then robbed the church of its sacred articles. The tabernacle was torn apart, the chalice taken away for later violation, the vestments put on their shoulders. They then set fire to the compound and burned the buildings to the ground.

As the fire was starting, Nacabeba turned to the truncated body and cried: "if you were a son of *Virigeva,* would He not free you from my hands? It is no help to you that you came down from heaven, for you cannot escape from me now. Now it is plain that your doctrine is false, though you pretend it is not." And he slashed the body up and down with his knife.

Then they set up a great shout in the pueblo. They had killed the Father. Let each one hide himself before the Spaniards come to avenge him. Afterward they spread fire round the pueblo, and over to the nearby Baboria and Lopoche and other places where there were churches. The natives, cowed by fear, let them have their way. All gathered their goods and left the pueblos depopulated, ruining in a few hours what had been won by such painful labor. A savage procession was now formed, as many as possible being clothed in the vestments from the church. At the front as a standard was the head of Tapia on a pole. On another was his left arm, fixed and held aloft. The fire spread beyond the pueblos, but by good fortune three days of rain followed, or the same fate might have come to the two Fathers who were in the vicinity, Pérez and Velasco.

As the wildly reveling cavalcade rode onward, they came to the pueblos of Sosoborimpo, Huricabi, and Zuaqui.[22] Hearing

---

22. They were heading for the Suaqui tribe along the Rio del Fuerte. See Ruiz, f. 36.

that Tapia was dead, a large crowd joined the conspirators in celebrating the infamous victory. Again the lascivious dances, the abominable sacrifices commenced, and they gave thanks for their deliverance from this priest of the Christian God. Nacabeba made a horrifying speech: "if you are a priest of God, come back to life!", and he held high the head of Tapia filled with wine. Then he tore the flesh from the head and arm to roast it, but as the fire did not burn it they ate it raw.[23]

Two Indians of Tovoropa who had run off in fear, reached San Felipe early in the morning and told what had happened. The Spaniards and Brother Castro roused themselves and went over to see the sad sight. All but Castro were armed, the *caudillo*, Antonio Ruiz, and the notary, Sebastián de Acosta, leading the way. At the door of the house they found the body, the breast supporting the two *macanas* that had struck him dead. A maniple lay nearby, drenched in blood. The right arm, elevated, was marked with the cross of the thumb and index finger.

They brought the body over to San Felipe and put it in the house of the Company to await the solemn funeral. The Spaniards and Father Velasco, who arrived in time, knelt round the corpse. The priest sang the office of the dead. Afterward the body was put into the ground near the high altar of the church. The Indians in tears passed to and fro all day long. Many touched articles to the grave of the holy missionary. The little son of María, constant companion of Tapia, was stricken with grief as he looked at the body and fell dead at the grave. A few days later the two new Fathers, Hernando de Santarén and Pedro Méndez, reached San Felipe. Their first act was to kneel before the sepulchre and pray to Tapia to give them his spirit of zeal and love. Santarén was to have a like death twenty-two years later.[24]

---

23. The documents all refer to this fact, that the fire did not burn the flesh; and the Indians present considered it a marvel.

24. On Santaren see *Documentos,* Nieremberg, Tanner, Alegre, Astrain, Ribas, Decorme.

CHAPTER XVII

The Black Night and After

I

The death of Tapia was a catastrophe for the mission.[1] He had been the mainstay of his fellows,[2] as he was the inspiration of the neophytes. His fearlessness, his marvelous talent for languages, his endurance in work, his constant jovial cheeriness, his solid judgment and prudence: all these were now taken away from them. Their leader was gone, and the pueblos he built broken up. Pagan priests had overthrown the missionary and destroyed his works. Black despair came over them all, even the Fathers who had been his colleagues. He had borne a charmed life, and they could not conceive themselves getting along without him.

Fear, the fear of a like fate, began to spread like wildfire. The missioners feared; they were not like Tapia in courage and in the wild abandon of heroes. The Indians, too, fell into utter collapse. Not yet long enough in their new religion, the triumph of the medicine men shook their faith, and the thought of a fresh war with those rampant savages haunted them. Who was now to protect them against the pagans? Who would guard them against grasping Spaniards? Many of their churches were in ruins, and their pueblos dispersed. In a word, all the organization of three intense years was shattered.

The plague of fear struck even the enemy. The gentiles and those converts who had a part in the murder felt insecure and fled to the forest regions. They hurried to get away from the avengers and from themselves, for their breasts were ready to open and reveal their horrible crime.[3]

---

1. Thus all the historians of the mission, in their accounts of the five years immediately following. See Alegre, I, lib. iv; also Ribas, Albizuri, *Documentos,* Venegas, Clavigero, Ortega, Davila, Kino, Mange, Nieremberg.

2. His name was an inspiration for two centuries of mission work. See the above-mentioned historians, and the documents in the *Documentos, Memorias,* etc.

3. Albizuri has a graphic account of this situation, in B, 133 sq.

Many Christians, too, in the natural inconstancy of an immature civilization, gave in to the infidels and forgot their faith. Again they returned to their superstitions, their irregular appetites, savage desires, unbridled passions. They took back their old idols and became one with the pagans in hatred for the name of Christian.

In the general dismay Captain Maldonado came to the front, to gather the scattered forces into some sort of security.[4] He called the Fathers of the Company to come back from their stations to the villa of San Felipe. They obeyed and gathered in the settlement. They were disheartened without their leader. Through it all, their only comfort was the sepulchre where the dead hero lay. They waited as though for their doom, like sheep for the slaughter, expecting death any hour.

The Spaniards fortified the villa. There was a rumor about that the savages had held a council and decided to kill them all and destroy their homes so that no living person should escape. They were few, and with no ammunition supply they could not hopefully face the multitude of enemies. Their only trust was in Spanish fortitude, for their stockade was nothing but thin poles.

Maldonado meantime sent for help to San Miguel de Culiacán, the nearest Spanish settlement to the south. There Don Diego de Robles, who presided over all Sinaloa, called a meeting of the *cabildo*. That body responded to the call by naming Alonso de Galarraga, the mayor and peace officer of the villa, to act as chief of the rescue force. It was Sunday, July 17, 1594.

Armed and on horseback they set out for San Felipe.[5] The soldiers are named in the document. They were Alonso de Galarraga, Juan Carlos his son, José Pérez Roacho, Juan Carlos his son, Diego Rodríguez, Pedro de Robles, Juan de Acosta, Martín de Armenta, Baltásar Quintero, Pedro Ochoa, Francisco Llanes, Pedro de Elgueeta, Gerónimo de Berriarza, Baltásar de Tapia. With this military aid Sinaloa could breathe easier.

At the same time the Suaqui country was visited[6] by a series of

---

4. Ibid., 135.
5. Ibid., 136
6. Again Albizuri is the main chronicler. Perez de Ribas has many pages on these events. See Alegre, I, 305-307.

disasters: storms, earthquakes, hurricanes, famine from a hot and dry summer. A mountain broke open and covered the old pueblo of Mochica, leaving it a heap of stones. All this put terror into the savages, and made them realize that they had done a great wrong. The Suaquis had been the bravest of the Sinaloa peoples. Now they were stunned. They moved from place to place, fugitives from nature and the elements. And the memory of those days became a tribal tradition.

Moved to action, they sent an embassy to the Fathers. They knelt at their feet and begged pardon for abetting Nacabeba, and they asked to become a Christian tribe. Father Albizuri says that the events here narrated put the fear of God so deeply into their hearts that they were still exemplary and pious in his day.[7]

In Sinaloa the frightened natives sent a petition to the viceroy for new Fathers. He ordered a troop of war to avenge the death of Tapia, and sent a captain to the *presidio* with twelve soldiers. This order was carried out by Fernández de Velasco, the Governor of Nueva Vizcaya, and Alonzo Díaz was named captain. He came down from Guadiana (Durango) on January 15, 1595, with the rector, Peláez, and Brother Vicente Beltran. Peláez collected information on the death of Tapia. He also moved the seminary and residence of Ocoroni to San Felipe, which from that day became the permanent center of the Sinaloa mission.

But the war was not over in Sinaloa. Turmoil continued until in August of 1596 a general insurrection broke out.[8] Then the incoming viceroy, the Conde de Monterey, increased the *presidio* with a complement of twenty more soldiers, and he appointed the famous chief, Captain Diego Martínez de Hurdaide. This strong character reached San Felipe in February of 1598, and a vigorous campaign followed.

After a long chase through the mountains above the Fuerte the conspirators were at last cornered and captured. They were then brought back to San Felipe for summary punishment. Nacabeba,

---

7. See Albizuri, writing at Vamopa in 1633; also Cuevas, II, 510. Mange, 339, has a fine note on the work of Ribas among these savages. See also Alegre, I, lib. iv.

8. See Mange, 338,—a man who knew Indians well; also Bancroft, *North Mexican States,* I, passim, on Hurdaide.

faced with certain death, asked to become a Christian, and Father Martín Pérez baptized him. The murderers were hanged and quartered. Other guilty persons were sentenced to slavery, if they had not already died in the battles with Hurdaide. The towns of Tovoropa, Lopoche, Matapan and Cavihuri, once so populous, passed out of memory, and of the tribe of Nacabeba only four persons remained.[9]

II

From the day of his death the dead hero began to receive marks of highest veneration. His beloved Tarsacan Indians, who were in Topia in the mountains, quickly sent a touching letter to their brethren in Michoacán. Its simplicity is charming:

"All governors, alcaldes, rulers, and more important men: see this letter, and send it to all the pueblos of the province of Michoacán. Tell them that we, the Tarascan Indians, send word that we in Topia give notice to all that in Cinaloa some Indians martyred the saintly Father Gonzalo de Tapia, the father of us all."[10]

This letter, written in Tarascan, came to Pátzcuaro on the feast of Saint Jerome, September 30. It was the first news of the event to reach New Spain. Father Ramírez opened it and announced the sad story. The Tarascans and Spaniards were struck with grief, and the Indians at once commenced to pray to Tapia as a saint.

The Tarascans of Culiacan wrote a similar letter:[11]

To our esteemed lords, resident in Pátzcuaro, Suiran, Maguaten, Gueran, Arantela, and all the other pueblos of the province of Michoacán, where our tongue is spoken: to all of you we give notice that you may tell it to the other smaller pueblos: our very reverend Father Gonzalo de Tapia is dead. He had come to Sinaloa to teach the faith of Christ to these nations, and they killed him and made a great martyrdom.

---

9. That is, in 1633.
10. This letter is copied in Albizuri, A, 298, from Ramirez. The Anua of 1597 speaks of Tarascans and Mexicans aiding the padres in Sinaloa.
11. Copied from "Documentos," fol. 45. A note says Tapia had brought them from Michoacan. They loved him. He used them in learning new languages and in instructing the neophytes. Cuevas prints the letter in the appendix to II.

They cut off his head and his left arm, and with his right hand alone he made the cross to signify how he died. He was found lying on the ground in this fashion after his death, with his right hand all bloody, and signing the whole body with the cross, to the left shoulder where they had cut off the arm while he was yet alive. And it was lying thus outside the house at the door where they attacked him. The pueblo called for aid when they murdered our very reverend Father Gonzalo de Tapia at Tovoropa. He died alone. The other Fathers are at Ocoroni. Thus we tell you of his death, that you may all recite a Pater Noster, and we are preparing to have a Mass said. And do not doubt about what we say, which is the very truth. He died, and we ask you to inform everybody. We who write this letter are the citizens and principal men in Culiacán. God be with you, and our holy Virgin Mary. Let this letter be delivered at Pátzcuaro and all the other pueblos. These things are written about what happened on the eleventh of July, Sunday, the night that the father died.

Father Santiago, a fellow missionary, writing of the death of Tapia, said:[12] "in saying the two prescribed Masses for him, I could not persuade myself to offer them for him, but I rather asked that he would beg God in heaven to pardon my sins by his merits. He was a truly apostolic man, a copy of our blessed Father Francis Xavier."

There is a large literature on Father Tapia.[13] After his death he was held in high esteem in America and Europe. His career led many others to come to the mission that he had begun, as it kept his name in honor in the Society for a hundred years. Unusual attention was given to him in the years immediately following 1594.

In Guadalajara a statue of him was set up and his relics were venerated there.[14] The people of his old pueblo of San Luis de la Paz had his picture painted, and it is said to be hanging in the church there even today. Likewise in San Felipe de Sinaloa, a Tarascan painted his picture and hung it in the church. His chief relics were recovered in 1599 and sent in the care of Brother

---

12. On Santiago see Alegre, I, 291-292.
13. See writings cited in Alegre, I, 292, and Nieremberg, III, 331.
14 See Albizuri, A, 297-302; B, 126-132. Albizuri says he has in his hands the memorials of Ramirez and many others.

Juan de la Carrera to Mexico, where they were honored in the college of San Pedro y San Pablo.[15]

The *regidores* of his birthplace, León in Castile, asked for a memento of him. Father Villafane, a Leonese, sent the bones of a finger of his right hand and a rib to the college of Sanmillán. The Fathers there made a summary *relacion* of his death, and it was sent all over Europe. The authorities wanted to have a public celebration, but the fathers would not permit it as Tapia had not yet been given public honor by the official Church.[16]

Father Martín Pérez, his first companion on the mission, wrote to his Provincial in 1616 that in that year the Hermitage of Father Tapia was built on the spot of his martyrdom.[17] Part of the head was placed in the altar stone as a relic. The house was intended as a place where the Fathers might rest from time to time or make their retreats. The Indians built this hermitage. Some of the workmen were connected with the conspiracy of 1594, but now they were loyal Christians. The stone on which they had cut off the head of Tapia they now preserved honorably at Tovoropa. This letter of Pérez contains a fine appreciation of his first mission superior.

His fellow Jesuits gave him a more striking testimonial in 1619.[18] In that year the Fathers who convened for the Provincial Congregation under Father Nicolás Arnaya, the Provincial, devoted their sessions to his heroic virtues, the veneration paid to him, and the place and manner of his death. They had a monument dedicated to him at Tovoropa, bearing the following inscription:

LUGAR DEL MARTRIO DEL BIENAVENTURADO PADRE GONZALO DE TAPIA, EL PRIMERO DE LA COMPANIA DE JESUS, QUE ENTRO EN ESTAS PROVINCIAS, A PREDICAR EL SANCTO EVANGELIO, Y

---

15. Tanner, 469, tells a beautiful story in this connection. Brother Carrera was bringing the relics from Father Perez to Mexico. On the way he stopped at the home of a certain Tovar. The child of the family, Juan, seeing the box and the relics, said to his mother: "Mother, that box is too small for the relics of such a great martyr. Some day I too am going to be a martyr like him." This is recorded by Tanner in his life of Tovar, where appropriate references may be found. Tovar, born in 1581 and become a Jesuit in 1598, died a martyr in 1616. Cf. Decorme, l. c.

16. See Albizuri, l. c.

17. Relacion of M. Perez in *Documentos*.

18. See Albizuri, B, 131.

FEE CATOLICA. FUE MARTYRIZADO A MANOS DE IMPIOS IN-
FIELES, EN ODIO DE LA MISMA FEE SANCTA, Y DOCTRINA CATO-
LICA EN ESTE PROPRIO LUGAR, ANO DE MDXCIIII, A X DIAS DE
JULIO.

Translated this would read:

The site of the martyrdom of the blessed Father Gonzalo
de Tapia, the first of the Company of Jesus to enter into those
provinces to preach the holy Gospel and the Catholic Faith.
He was martyred at the hands of heartless infidels, out of
hatred for the same holy Faith and Catholic doctrine, in
this very spot, July 10, 1594.

Over the monument a church was built. The principal altar
was on the spot of the martyrdom, and the stone on which Tapia
died was the consecrated altar stone. There too was the picture
of Tapia which was painted at San Felipe by the Tarascan artist.

It is certain that a movement was begun to canonize Tapia,
along with similar heroic figures of his age. In 1637 the Fathers
of the Provincial Congregation sent a petition to the Father General Mutius Vitelleschi.[19] They entreated him to forward with
all possible success the matter of the beatification of Father Gonzalo de Tapia, of the ten Tepehuan and Chinipas martyrs, and
the martyrs of Ajacán, Juan Bautista de Segura and his companions, with Father Martínez who was killed in Florida. The
history of this petition is still unknown to the present author. The
case was halted temporarily, and the Church has never reopened it.

One would expect some mention of miracles in connection with
so notable a life. The first one noted is difficult of proof.[20] It
is a story told by a Tarascan woman, that sometime in the fall of
1594 Tapia appeared to her one day in church, while she was
preparing for Confession. He upraided her for her past life, her
unconfessed sins; and he helped her make a good Confession and
live a good life afterward. Two or three stories of the same nature

---

19. See Postulata Cong. Prov. Mex. 1637, in Arch. Gen. S. J.
20. This and other marvelous accounts are given by Perez de Ribas,
137-138, and Albizuri, A, 312. The author makes no effort at proof of
these wonders. His purpose is to gather the original documents and let
them speak for themselves.

are found in early narratives, but no historical control is possible
in any of them.

A much more provable event was the finding of his relics in
the City of Mexico in 1900.[21] The writer does not here intend
to examine the case from all points of view, but simply to give
a brief recital of the facts. The story first appeared in an article
in the *Messajero del Sagrado Corazón,* in January of 1901.[22]
It was entitled "La Relacion del Hallazgo de las Reliquias del
P. Tapia," and it was written by Bishop Laureano Veres y Acevedo.

The facts as narrated by Acevedo are these. The relics of
Tapia were kept in the college of San Pedro y San Pablo until
1769. On the suppression of the Society they were given over to
the care of a Community of nuns, the "Religiosas de la Compania
de Maria." In the course of time, these Sisters had the box
of relics embedded in one of the stone walls of their house for safe
keeping and to avoid the desecration of unbelievers. The oral
tradition of their location died out. There was no written record
or diagram, so that no one knew where they were and no veneration was given to them.

Then the unusual occurrence took place. It was in 1900. One
corner of the room whose walls housed the relics, though unknown
to all, was much frequented by the Sisters. They began to hear
strange sounds from the direction of the street. They thought
these to be simply the ordinary noises caused by the cars and
wagons, but they persisted even in the quiet hours of the night.
The sounds were "like voices from the other world," and their
repetition and instancy made the nuns uneasy. The superioress
was called, and at last she decided to have a stone mason come
and open the wall at the spot in question. This was done in the
presence of all the Community. A hollow chamber was found,
and in it a box, covered and decorated. The box was drawn out
and the sounds never recurred.

They did not know what the box contained and they hesitated

---

21. This story, though not well known, is here set down as narrated by
competent witnesses.
22. Printed monthly in Mexico City.

to pry into the mysterious matter. But one day when Bishop Acevedo was visiting them, they brought the box for his inspection.
He opened it before them all and found that it held four packages,
wrapped in silk and fine cloths. Each package was marked with a
ticket and a clearly written name. One was "Cabeza del P. Gonzalo de Tapia, Primer Martyr y Fundador de las Misiones de
Sinaloa. Trajola el P. Martin Peláez, Visitador de Aquellas
Misiones. 1610." Another was "P. Gonzalo de Tapia, Fundador y
Primer Martyr de las Misiones de Sinaloa."

When opened the first package contained part of the skull, and
the second a tibia bone. Father Cuevas, the distinguished author
of the *Historia de la Iglesia en Mexico,* photographed both relics
and used the pictures in his history.[23] He likewise testifies to the
fact that he visited these same nuns in 1921 and found that they
still told exactly the same story. To ensure complete identi-
fication, he compared the part of the skull—it had been cloven
by Nacabeba—with the other half that had been kept in the possession of the Fathers Provincial since the early days. He says
that the two parts matched perfectly.

These and many other facts evidence the high honor in which
Tapia was held by his companions and successors. His career was
the subject of letters, *relaciones,* articles, sketches; and for over
a hundred years he was one of the great personages of the Company. In time other names came to displace his, and he fell back
into the obscurity of the ages.

One of his early biographers gives a very exact picture of his
personal appearance and disposition:[24]

> He was slightly less than middle height. His face was
> oval, his complexion swarthy and browned, lips red, cheeks
> colored, forehead wide and calm, eyebrows arched, beard
> full and black. His eyes were small and gracious, but with
> such short sight that he could scarcely see an object unless
> it were immediately in front of him. His voice was clear,
> suave, and sonorous. He had an amiable and joyous bear-
> ing, and a smile played continually about his lips. With his
> gravity he was not moody; collected, yet not absorbed in him-

23. Cuevas, II, 306.
24. Albizuri, B, 116 sq., relying on Ramirez, Villafane, and others.

self; discreet, but with moderation. His speech was so gentle, soft, and even, that he won hearts at first meeting. But his words had a ring and a drive that ensured response in his hearers.

He never spoke ill of others, aside from his letter to the General, and there he had a right to state the exact case. He was an optimist, always looking for good. His zeal was strong. Experience in handling men taught him to understand them better. He had to learn, as does every man. He was very young when he came into his superior position, and the affection of his subjects proves that he mastered himself and treated them with true courtesy and friendship.[25]

The great memorial to Tapia is not so much what is written, nor the relics and marvels and monuments, but the mission system that arose on him as its foundation. He worked a very short time, but in those three years he set the pace and the method, the line of attack that was followed and developed for the next hundred and seventy-five years. His untimely death did not take away the effect of his life. For though the first results were depressing, in time his martyrdom came to be esteemed as the most important single fact in the rise of the missions. As the Fathers moved up the coast from year to year, winning over to culture and religion hundreds of thousands of barbarians, they often thought and wrote and spoke of the man who had driven the first wedge into solid savagery, and burst open the way to conquer those fierce hearts. Ribas and Kino and Salvatierra, and all the rest of that army, marched through the breach opened by Tapia. They frankly imitated him, a most sincere sign of the reverence they felt for his famous name.

---

25. This affection and devotion may be seen in the *relaciones* on his death written by Perez, Velasco, Santiago, and by other friends such as Armano, Carrera, and Antonio Ruiz.

APPENDIX

Note on the Patronato Real

Throughout the preceding chapters a fact has been taken for granted that may well call for explanation. It is the constant and entire dependence of the Spanish Jesuits on the Spanish crown.

The question first appeared in finding the reason[1] why the Order came so late to New Spain. It would be injudicious, even incorrect, to solve this difficulty by alleging hostility on the part of the government and the crown. Quite the opposite was the case. The King and the General of the Jesuits entertained the highest regard for each other, and the Order itself was given a hearty welcome[2] into the Iberian peninsula from the first days.

The same problem, approached from various directions, is seen throughout this biography. The King asks the Religious if they are willing to go to his Indies, and he has their General appoint a chosen personnel.[3] The consent once obtained, he gives orders[4] that they go, with his permission, and taking his direction as to destination, method and means of transportation, outfit and supplies. On their arrival they are to begin the works that he has approved, under superiors whom he has ratified. Reports[5] on their activities are sent back to him, both by the civil officials and by the Visitor or the Provincial of the Jesuits.

Tapia is wanted[6] by the viceroy to evangelize the Chichimecos; the governor must approve and summon him. The Sinaloa mission is desired;[7] the viceroy must send letters patent authorizing the expedition: he designates the type of work to be opened, the limitations in material equipment, the particular front to be in-

---

1. Cf. p. 17.
2. Cf. p. 43.
3. Cedula of Philip to Borgia, 1566, as on p. 17; also pp. 18, 19.
4. Cedula of Philip to Casa de Contratacion, 1571, as on pp. 24, 25.
5. E. g., Don Martin Henriquez to Philip, 1572, as on p. 27; Avellaneda to Philip, 1592, on p. 89; Astrain, IV, 410-417.
6. Governor of Michoacan to Ramirez, as on p. 66; Velasco to Philip, 1590, as in Cuevas, II, 391.
7. Cf. on Rio y Loza, and Velasco, pp. 78-81.

spected and attacked. Then the governor must despatch the two on their way, making provision for them as far as frontier life permits. Later on at San Felipe, Tapia must write[8] the viceroy, to get more missionaries. He travels to Mexico[9] for the same purpose, and for a pecuniary grant from this official. A *presidio* must be provided by the government to protect the mission field from depredation. Each new contingent of missionaries must report, even at San Felipe, to the representatives of the crown. The Visitor, Avellaneda, returning to Europe, must see the King[10] to give a personal account of what he has found on his visitation.

Here is seen in the smallest detail the hand of a sovereign whose system reaches over the vast domains of the Emperor of all the Indies. Much further regulation of the same character may be discovered in the *Recopilacion de las Leyes*.[11] This code of laws devotes many sections to the royal wishes in religious affairs.

The Jesuits, like every other ecclesiastical person or corporation, came under the kingly control. They might not move from college to college,[12] or province to province, without permission of the King, the viceroy or governor, as the case happened to be. If any Jesuit wished to go to the Indies, he might not to do it without the placet of the King, of the Bishop in question, and of the Provincial. He might not stop and remain at the Canaries. In all things he was to be subject to regal orders, relying always on the help, and obedient to the direction, of His Majesty.

From this brief sketch it is clear that an understanding of the *Patronato Real* is absolutely necessary to one who would comprehend mission history. The missions, to the King, were part of his vast plan of action. From a political standpoint, he had a paramount interest in this most efficient force for colonization and national expansion, for peace and prosperity. Moreover, into his hands was committed the responsibility for the religious welfare of all those lands.

His position is summarized in the expression: *"the Patronato*

---

8. See page 124.
9. See Chapter Fifteen.
10. Astrain, IV, 410.
11. E. g., I, xiv, edition 1681.
12. Ibid., xiv, 22. (Vol. I, 109).

Real de las Indias,"[13] the royal right of patronage over the colonies. It was often referred to as the *Regio Vicariato de las Indias.* The crown acted as the agent, the vicar, of Rome; and it was an omnipresent and almost omnipotent vicar. Broadly speaking the royal patronage was twofold, acquisitive and distributive. The king collected all revenues coming regularly to the Church, and he saw to their proper disbursement. And as the power of the purse was then, as now, the power of regulation, the ruler was the master of ecclesiastical life, embracing under his prerogative every grade from top to bottom in the material equipment and official machinery of the Church. All ecclesiastical appointments were in his hands, all questions of building new edifices or new administrative districts, outlays and permits for every religious contingency; protection for the rights of the Church, clergy and laity; directions for the minutest matters from the tithes of the poor to the services of a cathedral. The public law abounded in ecclesiastical privileges and controls, in provisions for subsidy as well as for check and correction. Cases settled on this basis are scattered plentifully through the records of the *Cabildo* of Mexico[14] and the *Audiencia Real.* They show how completely the regime dominated all phases of colonial religion.

The system required a mighty genius at the head of the state, and as a matter of fact the rulers of Spain in the first colonial century were men of remarkable ability. Due to their large natural endowments and their zeal, a wonderful chapter was written into the history of world improvement.

It will be interesting to give a summary account of the rise of the *Patronato.* Royal influence in the appointment and conduct of churchmen was no new thing in 1500. The famous Investiture Controversy[15] furnishes a familiar example of early medieval

13. Best summary sketch is by Crevelli, in *Cath. Ency.,* X, art. "Mexico." (5. "The Royal Patronage and the Clergy"). Cf. Smith in *Historical Bulletin,* V, 4, 1927, "Control of the Church in Spanish America by the State"; also Wernz, *Jus Decretalium,* l. c.; Astrain, VI, 373-404; Desdevises du Dezert, in *Revue Hispanique,* Feb. 1917, "L'Eglise Espagnole des Indes a fin du 16me siecle"; Cuevas, II, c. ii; Solorzano, *Politica Indiana;* recent articles noted in *A. H. S. I.* 1932, pp. 183 sq., by Leite, Leturia, Montalban.
14. Actas de cabildo del ayuntamiento o constitucional de Mexico.
15. Carlyle, *Medieval Political Theory,* and MacIlwain, *Growth of Political Thought in the West from the Greeks to the End of the Middle Ages,* passim. Best biographical studies are by Fliche and Villemain.

intervention of lay potentates in religious administration. Hildebrand marked the breakup of unjustifiable interference in the nomination and election of officials in the spiritual polity. Still, his death did not seal the end of the difficulty. Throughout the centuries and on into modern times, kings and princes[16] received or appropriated many rights whose tendency operated to limit the episcopacy, church courts, tithes, and functions of all Orders.

But the opening of the sixteenth century saw a wide departure in policy from earlier practice. Spain and Portugal were given tremendous power over the Church in their possessions. For eight hundred years preceding the discovery of the new world, the peninsular peoples kept up an unabating war[17] against their Moorish overlords for civil and religious liberty. The struggle grew into a death grip between the united and battling Christian nations and the equally determined hosts whose key point was Granada. At last, in the climax of the Reconquest, Queen Isabella and her consort Ferdinand saw that a drastic move was needed to win their cause.

The obstacle to complete success was internal division in matters of belief. From olden times the Jews had invited the Africans to come to the peninsula, and down to the very end of the servitude Morisco influence undid whatever Spanish bravery and sacrifice had begun. Summary steps were necessary. Isabella petitioned Sixtus IV for a court of Inquisition;[18] her request was given her. Now whatever may be the tales of cruelty and hate in the life of this institution, it certainly destroyed the one element in Spain that prevented a united attack on the rule of the Alhambra.

The rulers then got hold of a greater religious power.[19] At the outset Isabella and Ferdinand set for themselves a definite

---

16. E. g., kings of England. See Gasquet, *Henry III and the Church;* Smith, *Church and State in the Middle Ages;* Brookes, *English Church and the Papacy;* Thurston, *No Popery.*

17. See Chapman, *History of Spain;* Walsh, *Isabella of Spain;* Madden, "Church in Contemporary Spain" in *Cath. H. R.,* Apr., 1932.

18. Leturia, in *Historisches Jahrbuch,* 46 Band, I Heft, "Der Heilige Stuhl und das Spanische Patronat in Amerika."

19. Ibid. See also, for brief analysis, Pastor, *Geschichte der Päpste seit dem Ausgang des Mittelalters,* XIII, 720-721.

goal. They would prevent by any means within their reach the appointment of men to episcopal sees or other benefices, who were not in their eyes loyal and dependable. For both Castile and Aragon, they could get no such blanket permission from the Pope. But when Granada fell, they had a virgin field where everything must be begun anew.

As early as 1486 they had in their hands the papal document that would guide their policy in the new territory. It was the "Bull of Granada," granted by Clement VIII. This paper conceded to the sovereigns the right of nomination to all ecclesiastical positions in conquered territory, from the archbishopric to the village curacy. Along with this they received all the tithes which the Moors, in the event of their future conversion, would pay to the Church.

How this local grant grew into the wide system of the *Patronato* is part of the international story. Alexander VI in 1493 settled a dispute between Spain and Portugal, over the boundary line in the newly discovered lands. The pontiff was anxious to spread the Gospel. The sovereigns were urgent, not only to justify the legality of their possessions (the Pope still had theoretical jurisdiction over all islands, according to medieval law), but they wished to lay a firm foundation for the future Church overseas. To induce them to fulfill their duties in this regard more perfectly, Alexander gave them the exclusive right to evangelize, withdrawing it from every other nation. And in the bulls *Inter Caeteras* and *Eximiae Devotionis* (1493 and 1501)[20] he granted to Spain all the ecclesiastical privileges which he had hitherto awarded to the Portugese throne, in view of its "apostolic conquests." A year before he died he sent to the Spanish rulers a formal grant in perpetuity, of all tithes and nominations in their colonial dominions. This grant he made dependent on royal foundation of all future churches, and the outlay became a matter of conscience with them.

By a legal device the tithes which had been donated to the crown were redonated to the Church, and from them the funds

---

20. These two bulls form the basic constitution of the Patronato. Cf. Bullarium Rom. Pont.

were drawn for the maintainance of churches and salaries of bishops and lower clergy. Finally, Julius II in his *Universalis Ecclesiae Regiminis* gave to the king of Spain and to his successors for all time the fullest rights of patronage and presentation to all Church benefices. Such is the origin of the celebrated *Patronato Real de las Indias.*

This control of affairs in the hands of one sovereign was quite in line with the contemporary ideas of absolutism. The history of all governments is a series of oscillations between autocracy and popular control. Medieval Europe,[21] though seriously threatened, had definitely rejected a theocracy, and the trials of the Innocents were ended forever. But the sixteenth century is full of examples of rulers overriding parliaments and councils, in the effort at sole domination within their domains. The man who could master the dual fields of Church and State obviously had within his grasp every line of power in his realm. Not that Philip II was a singular type. Each of his contemporary rulers aimed at the same thing, and each, alike with him, claimed to originate all authorization in colonial operations. He incited every advance, received and certified reports on each check or gain, ordered all retreats or forward movements.

This unifying of power was bound to lead to trouble. It was inevitable, in the compromise that is found in all human affairs, where the limitations of men, their minds, their passions, their weaknesses and ambitions come into play, that there be conflict between the issues of ecclesiastical and political purposes. Centralizing both functions in the hands of one man may appear to have lessened conflict, by avoiding the opposition of two wills. But within the one man there are many forces,—an idea that has been recognized ever since Saint Paul wrote his famous passage on the law in his mind and the law in his members. It

---

21. Dawson, *Progress and Religion.* Also Gasquet, *Henry III and the Church,* that Gregory IX and Innocent IV implicitly claimed temporal lordship and exercised it as to England, Scotland, Italy, and Sicily. Carlyle, vid. supr., rejects this opinion in its baldest statement, e. g., IV, 391, but inclines to the idea that the Popes were dangerously near the claim which some of their contemporary defenders made without equivocation, such as John of Salisbury, Manegold, etc., q. v. in Gettell, *History of Political Theories.*

is true that there were not wanting men in the sixteenth century who thought that the direction of these multiple affairs was too much for the abilities of any one man. They felt that he was bound to crack under the strain, and give undue prominence to one or other of his functions according to the time and circumstances of his personal life, the pull of his advisers, friends, special interests, or the condition of different parts of his realm. Francis Borgia[22] was such a man, however great a friend of Philip he might have been. And the project of a Congregatio de Propaganda Fide which he originated was simply a recognition of the royal limitations, and an effort to provide a workable substitute for reliance on the finite powers of even so great a ruler as Philip.

The series of concessions constituting the rights of the *Patronato* went far beyond what makes up legitimate supervison of ecclesiastical concerns. Though the kings took their obligations seriously and fulfilled them with energy and zeal, the time would come when less pious monarchs would usurp the liberty of religion. The Church cannot be nationalized[23] and continue Catholic. Similar cases have arisen before and since. William the Conqueror had a position not unlike that of Ferdinand, and his successors showed how it might be abused. So too the Hapsburgs long enjoyed unique privileges, among them the veto of a papal election,[24] and the exercise of these powers caused constant confusion.

The *Patronato* was abolished in 1824, and with its ending passed an outworn and anomalous institution. In its best usage it gave fine assistance to religious work. Turned to opposite purposes, it meant domination by the State and enslavement of the Church. Rather than a union, it became a separation and a subjugation, for it was a weapon with a double edge. In 1767 the Jesuits felt the sharp edge of royal disfavor,[25] and in the

---

22. Cf. p. 18, and Note 13 supra, on Leturia, etc. On Philip II see Loth "Philip II."

23. See Kurth *Catholic Church at the Turning Points of History*, passim; also Gosselin, *Pouvoir de Pape au Moyen Age*.

24. It was abolished by Pius X.

25. See Weld, *Suppression of the Society of Jesus in the Portuguese Dominions*. Astrain's volume VIII on the suppression has not yet appeared. Cf. also Cretineau-Joly, op. cit.

system it was an easy task to remove their Order from the scene. Nor were they alone in suffering, for within a generation others met a similar misfortune. The problem of union of Church and State will always be a vexing situation. But careful consideration will show that the union envisaged by Pius XI is much closer[26] to the admired American idea of separation of the two, than it is to the ancient theocracy or to the *Patronato Real de las Indias.*

---

26. Cf. documents connected with settlement of Roman Question in 1929; also articles by the present author in *America,* Dec. 3-10-17, 1927. It is interesting to note the opinion of such a thinker as Suarez on the papal power as connected with the *Patronato Real de las Indias.* "Potest Pontifex inter Principes seu Reges temporales distribuere provincias et regna infidelium, non ut illas suo arbitrio occupare possint, -hoc enim tyrannicum esset, ut infra dicam, - sed ut praedicatores Evangelii ad illos mittendos procurent et sua potestate eos tueantur, etiam justum bellum indicendo, si ratio et justa causa postulet." Taken from *De Fide, Vives* edition, 439.

BIBLIOGRAPHICAL NOTE

The Jesuit Order in keeping with its close organization has a large system for recording the salient facts of its operations. Thanks to this profuse stock of written documents, the historian is able to ascertain with fulness and exactness an immense amount of data for the construction of his story.

Paramount among these sources of history are the regular catalogues compiled by each house or college and sent to the central house in Rome at stated times. Next in order are the routine confidential reports made to headquarters by those in charge of local movements, or by the Visitors who are sent out to inspect the affairs of individual Provinces in the Order.

A third class of documents is the annual letters. These letters are sent to Rome to report the positive advances recorded in each Province. They are gathered by the Provincial from local correspondents, boiled down to a unified composition, and transmitted to the General. They are the common matter of history, the story of the achievements and outstanding characters in the different parts of the Order throughout the world. Not infrequently they are given to the public in one way or another, as they are likewise sent round to the various Provinces for the inspiration and education that is contained in their broad narrative of Jesuit activity.

For the sake of charity and the reputation of good men, the first two types of documents are not accessible to strangers. They are used in the ways of government within the Order, in assigning men to different stations, in choosing superiors, in recommending changes of policy or regulation. Only after a long lapse of time are they opened to inspection, in a way similar to the common practice of departments of State which retain private information for a minimum of fifty years after the events have transpired.

Of course the accidents of history, which so commonly despoil people of their property, have wrought similar misfortune to the Jesuit archives. But the careful watching of historians has succeeded in bringing most of this lost material into depositories that are now accessible to scholars. A notable example of this is the marvelous collection of Spanish American Jesuit documents dating from the times before the suppression of the Order, and now preserved in the Biblioteca Nacional of Santiago de Chile.

Besides the documents that are by nature internal to the Order, there exist in many places groups of governmental or ecclesiastical files and records dealing intimately with the activities of the Order. The Archivo General de Mexico contains several large volumes of unprinted matter of this character.

The above-named sources are obviously the best material for the history of the Jesuits. Still much valuable matter lies scattered through the tremendous volume of printed works written about the Order and its members at every period of modern times. Some of these books are the work of the Fathers themselves. Others are done by competent scholars outside the organization. Many more are the product either of admiring imaginations or of equally imagining dissidents. A detailed sketch of such writing may be seen in the masterly introduction to Hughes' history that is cited in the accompanying list.

In spite of this plethora of books and documents, it must be said in all truth that the materials for the present work are none too abundant, for the reason that this is the first effort at an account of the subject in the last three hundred years. The author admits the sketchiness of the account, though at the same time he feels that he has consulted all the available material.

The story would probably never have been written, were it not for a man who enjoys a rather stigmatized reputation, King Carlos the Third of Spain. In 1784 this sovereign, who had used his secret breast to conceal the motives for suppressing the Jesuits, ordered his viceroy at Mexico, Revillagigedo, to gather for him a report on the California missions. The viceroy complied in a famous document which is preserved in the viceregal correspondence in the Mexican national archives. It is entitled: *Copia del informe general instruido en cumplimiento de la Real Orden de 31 de Genero 1784 sobre las Misiones del Reino de Nueva Espana, comparando su actual estado con el que tenian las que entregaron los ex-Jesuitas al tiempo de la expatriacion.**

Revillagigedo thought it worth while for future history that

---

*See Cuevas, IV, 300 sq.

someone collect all the existing documents bearing on the Sinaloa, Sonora, and California missions. In accordance with that design, a diligent scholar, very likely a Franciscan historian whom ungrateful memory has left unnamed, gathered together the materials which are partially represented in the volumes soon to be mentioned as *Documentos* and *Memorias para la historia de Sinaloa.* For an introduction the compiler attached as his first seventeen folios a large section of the history of Alegre, I, 230-241. Bancroft supposes that the copying was done in the reverse order, but a careful comparison of both passages, together with the inserts in the redactor's introduction, reveal him as the one who made convenient use of a sketch already drawn. Alegre is himself a copyist at intervals, but he always acknowledges his debts, particularly to Perez de Ribas.

The mention of Bancroft introduces the character who by all odds deserves first rank for gathering the materials of this history and for making them available to others in his donation, of the Bancroft Library. His story** is by this time well known to American historians. In a word, he collected and left to the public the largest group of primary sources dealing with the history of the Pacific Slope of North America. His own thirty-nine volumes are a perfect gold mine in the riches they furnish the searcher into this field. Henry Morse Stephens, and particularly Herbert Eugene Bolton, have added to the same library over 86,000 pieces, so that today a student of Jesuit affairs in the Colonial West finds ample store from which to gather his story.

The manuscript history of Albizuri, and the works of Perez de Ribas and Alegre, furnish the groundwork for the history of the early Jesuit missions on the Pacific Slope. The second of these is especially deserving of respect, and he stands far off from those whom Astrain (I, 159) characterizes as the meretricious chroniclers of the sixteen hundreds. Alegre is a fine literary work, resting on copious first rate sources. Albizuri is almost a contemporary of the events discussed. For the rest, the present book is a problem of reconstruction. The chief materials used are to be found in the following list.

**See Langlois and Seignobos, 19-23; also Chapman, *Hist. Calif. Spanish Period,* 507-508, and Bancroft, *Native Races,* I, Introd.

UNPRINTED DOCUMENTS

A. Archivum Generale Societatis Jesu.

1. Documents taken from *Codex Vocationes Illustres*, II, nn. 66, 67, 70. On this collection see *Polanci Complementa*, I, xxxiii (cod. 18).

> **66.** *Letter of Brother Angelo Armano to Father General Aquaviva, from Mexico, October 26, 1594.* Fol. 1-1/2, autograph. On the death of Father Tapia, as learned from a letter of Father Alonzo de Santiago. (Italian).

> **67.** *Letter of Father Francisco Gutierrez to the Spanish Assistant, Father Antonio de Mendoza, from Puebla, October 23, 1594.* Fol. 3, autograph. On his own journey to Mexico, and on the death of Father Tapia, as learned from the *relacion* of Father Martin Pelaez, and from the letters of Tapia's companions, Fathers Juan Bautista Velasco and Martin Perez, written in Sinaloa and Guadiana July 11, 1594. (Spanish).

> **70.** *Letter of Brother Juan de la Carrera to the Spanish Assistant in Rome, from Puebla de los Angeles, March 1, 1600.* Fol. 7, autograph. On the life and death of Father Tapia, and containing a copy of a part of a letter from Tapia to Carrera. (Spanish).

2. Documents from *Historia Mexicana* and *Vitae.*

Mex. 1, 95 Apr. 17, 1590. Father General Aquaviva to Father Gonzalo de Tapia, praising his zeal for missions. (Reg. orig.)

Mex. 1, 125 Mar. 9, 1594. Father General Aquaviva to same, in praise of the fruits of the Sinaloa mission. (Reg. orig.)

Mex. 4, 32 1585. Catalogus primus (one page) noting Tapia.

Mex. 4, 33 1585. Catalogus secundus, marking personality value of Father Tapia.

Mex. 4 45v 1592. Catalogus brevis (one page) including Sinaloa.

Mex. 50 1592. Catalogus triennalis (one page) including Sinaloa.

Mex. 4, 61 1594-1595. Catalogus defunctorum Mex. Prov. (one page).

Mex. 16, 107 Aug. 1, 1592. Autograph letter of Father Gonzalo de Tapia to Father General Aquaviva. Fol. 2, plus signature.

Vitae 12 1619. Catalogus d'alcuni Martiri . . . whose reading was begun in the Casa Profesa of Rome after July 31, 1619. For July 11 the entry deals with the martyrdom of Father Tapia.

Vitae 116, 408 . . . Menologium . . . customarily read in Italian in the Casa Profesa of Rome after 1741.

Vitae 13 1650 circa. Breve notizie de Religiosi chi nella Compagnia di Giesu. A collection of eulogies, gathered by Father Gugliaris.

Mex. 19. Index of all documents contained in Codez Mex. 19, dealing with mission materials before 1600.

B. Albizuri, Juan de, S. J.

  1. *Historia de las Missiones Appostolicas de la Compania de Jesus en
      las Indias Occidentales de la Nueva Vizcaya.   Y Vida y Martyrio
      del P. Gonzalo de Tapia Fundador de las dichas Missiones y Apostol
      de los Cynaloas. Por el Padre Juan de Albiçuri Religioso Missionero
      de la misma Compania de Jesus.* Pp. 373. Vamopa, San Ignacio,
      1633.

      An engraved picture of Tapia forms the frontispiece. This copy,
      which reposes in the Bancroft Library, is cited in the text as Albi-
      zuri A. The substitution of "z" for "c" with the cedilla is in keeping
      with modern orthography.

  2. Another copy with the same title, but somewhat condensed in style
      and partially rearranged, is cited herein as Albizuri B. It has 144
      folios. The copy was loaned to the author by Carlos R. Linga of
      Mexico City. The frontispiece is a pen sketch of Tapia made from
      memory.

      The "A" copy is signed in person by Father Albizuri. Both copies
      are countersigned by the censors, Fathers Varela, Villafane, and Men-
      dez, designated by the Provincial to examine the book with a view
      to its worth for publication. It may well have been written to aid
      the process of the canonization of Tapia, a movement that was
      initiated in 1637 by the Mexican Province of the Order.

C. 1. *Documentos para la historia de Sinaloa.* Archivo General de
        Mexico, Historia, tomo xv, vols. 2, fol. 421. The contents of this
        pair of volumes are the following:

        folios 1-17 Description of Sinaloa borrowed from Alegre. On
                     folio 14 the writer omits Alegre's "de cujos com-
                     entarios bastemente exactos hemos tomado estas noti-
                     cias."

             17b   *Relacion of 1593,* on early works of Tapia and Perez.

             35b   *Relacion of 1594* noting results to middle of 1594.

             41b   *Relacion de la muerte de P. Gonzalo de Tapia.* Ribas
                     copies this document. Cuevas and Astrain both print
                     part of it. It is mentioned in Bancroft, *North Mex.
                     St.,* I, 120, as the best work on the death. It was
                     drawn up from shorter relaciones contributed by the
                     "Padres y Espanoles en Sinaloa." The date is fixed
                     as July 11, 1594. Later writers, such as Albizuri,
                     Tanner, Patrigani, changed the date to July 10, in
                     line with calendar requirements.

             45a   *Letter of the Tarascan Indians in Sinaloa to those
                     in Michoacan*—whence the former had come to found
                     colonies—on the death of Tapia. This is an im-
                     portant document both on the Indians and on Tapia.

46   *Relacion de la muerte de P. Tapia, por P. Alonzo de Santiago*, a companion of Tapia in Sinaloa. Fine details of Sinaloa life accompany the story of Tapia.

53b   *Relacion, etc., por P. Martin Perez, 1595*, the first companion of Tapia, in Sinaloa till 1626.

55b   *Carta, etc., por P. Pedro Mendez*, censor of Albizuri.

68b   *Anua of 1596*, with Sinaloa story of that year.

78a   *Anua of 1597*, mentioning holy memory of Tapia (86).

94b   *Anua of 1598*, telling fruits of Tapia's martyrdom.

99b   *Anua of 1599*, on capture of Nacabeba (114).

122a   *Relacion de P. Juan Bautista Velasco*, to Provincial.

150a   *Anua of 1602.*

172a   *Anua of 1604.*

177b   *Anua of 1606.*

184a   *Carta del P. Velasco*, on further mission movements.

197a   *Anua of 1611.*

211   *Anua of 1612.*

220   *Anua of 1613.* Mention of Perez de Ribas (222). Velasco is sketched in Memorias, pp. 474-480.

233   *Anua of 1614.*

247a   *Rio de Mayo, de esta mision.*

266b   *Anua of 1615.*

278a   *Carta del P. Martin Perez al Provincial*, describing fruits of the mission and building of hermitage of Tapia, with praise of Tapia.

308a   *Carta del P. Andres Perez de Ribas al P. Provincial, 1617.* M. Perez was with him on this journey.

321   *Anua of 1618.* Notes on school and seminary at San Felipe (321b).

330b   *Anua of 1619.* More on same and wonders therein.

365a   *Anua of 1621.* Spread of missions, with Franciscans in the towns. *El Padre y el capitan* now frequently mentioned together.

383b   *Anua of 1622*, on same matter.

391a   *Anua of 1623.*

393a   *Anua of 1624.*

394b   *Anua of 1625.*

397a   *Anua of 1626*, on extension of boundaries and works.

402a   *Carta del P. Juan Varela al P. Provincial, Feb. 16, 1628.* He is the new superior of Mision de San Ignacio. Ignatius Loyola was canonized in 1622.

405b   *Misiones de San Ignacio*, on boundaries, military expedition. First mention of Jesuits from other countries besides Spain and New Spain, such as Vandersipe, Castini.

407b   *Misiones de San Ignacio en Mayo, Yaqui, Nevornes, Chinipas, Sisibotaris, May 25, 1629.*

408b   *Carta del P. Diego de Guzman al P. Provincial, Sept. 16, 1629.*

412a   *Mision San Ignatio y sus Partidos.*

414a   *Anua of 1639,* on Mision de San Ignacio en Sinaloa.

415b   *Anua of 1639,* on Mision de San Xavier de Sonora which was opened in that year.

417   *Anua of 1655.*

419   *Anua of 1657.*

   N. B. This *Documentos* is a copy, written for Bancroft in 1880, of Tom. xv of the Archivo General de Mexico.

2. *Memorias para la historia de la Provincia de Sinaloa, 1530-1629.* Pp. 991. This and the above volumes of Documentos are in the Bancroft Library. Their genesis is treated by Bancroft *N. Mex. St.,* I, 120. The *Memorias* contains all the materials found in the former set, though differently arranged after fol. 67 in the *Documentos.* In addition the *Memorias* has documents, pp. 817-991, for other parts of Nueva Vizcaya taken from another tome of the Archivo General and not found in the *Documentos.*

3. *Documentos para la historia de Sonora,* a similar compilation copied from the Archivo General, and now reposing in the archives of Georgetown University, Washington, D. C.

D. Besides the numerous annual letters and *relaciones* contained in these three collections, several important isolated pieces must be noted:

   1. Letters of Father Martin Perez:

      a) *Letter of 1591,* printed in Hay *De Rebus Japonicis* (1605 Antwerp—Nutij) pp. 940-950; also in Atienza *Ragguaglio d'alcune missioni* (1592 Roma—Zannetti). cf. Sommervogel sub "Perez." Part of the same letter appears in *Purchas His Pilgrimes,* IV, 1552-1555.

      b) *Letter of 1592,* printed partly in Purchas, IV, 1854.

      c) *Letter of 1613,* in Alegre, II, 60-62.

      d) *Sucesos de la mision de Sinaloa, desde el de 1590 hasta el de 1620,* in Alegre, II, 169 sq.

   2. *Relacion de Antonio Ruiz,* on events in Sinaloa from 1564 to 1595. Fol. 39. Taken from Arch. Gen. Mex. tom. 316.

PRINTED MATERIALS

Actas de Cabildo del ayuntamiento o constitucional de Mexico, 1889, Mexico.

Adams, James T., *Epic of America,* 1931, New York, Little.

Alegambe, Philippus, S.J., *Mortes Illustres* 1657, Rome, Varesii.

Alegre, Francisco X., S.J. (Bustamante), *Historia de la Compania de Jesus en Nueva Espana* (1764) 1841, Mexico, Lara.

Allison-Fay-etc., *Guide to Historical Literature,* 1931, New York, Macmillan.

Andrews, Charles M., *Colonial Background of the American Revolution,* 1924, New Haven, Yale.

Archivum Historicum Societatis Jesu (polyglot review of Jesuit history, cited as *A. H. S. I.*) 1932 sq. Rome.

Astrain, Antonio, S.J., *Historia de la Compania de Jesus en la Asistencia de Espana* 1902-1928, Madrid, Razon y Fe.

Baegert, Jakob, S.J., *Nachrichten von der amerikanischen halbinsel Californien* 1772, Mannheim.

Bancroft, Hubert Howe, *Works* 1882-1891, San Francisco, Bancroft; *History of California* 1884-1890; *History of Mexico* 1883-1888; *Native Races* 1883 (groundwork of Bancroft project); *History of North Mexican States and Texas* 1884-1889.

Bandelier, Fanny R., *Journey of Alvar Nunez Cabeza de Vaca* 1905, New York.

Bartoli, Daniel, S.J., *Della Vita di S. Francesco Borgia* 1681, Roma, Tinassi.

Bassett, John J., *Middle Group of American Historians* 1919, New York.

Beach, W. W., *Indian Miscellany* 1877, New York, Munsell.

Beals, Ralph L., *Comparative Ethnology of North Mexico Before 1750* 1932, Berkeley, California.

Belloc, Hilaire, *How the Reformation Happened* 1928, New York, McBride.

Beristain y Sousa, Jose Mariano, *Biblioteca Hispano-Americana* 1883, Amecameca.

Bertrand, Jean T., *Histoire de l'Amerique Espagnole* 1929, Paris, Spes.

Bolton, Herbert E., *Anza Expeditions* 1930, Berkeley, California; *Colonization of North America* (with Marshall) 1920, New York, Macmillan; *Guide to Materials for the History of the United States in the Principal Archives of Mexico* 1913, Washington, Carnegie.; *Kino's Historical Memoir of Pimeria Alta* 1919, Cleveland, Clark; "Mission as a Frontier Institution," in *Am. Hist. Rev.,* Oct. 1917; *Padre on Horseback* 1932, San Francisco, Sonora; *Rim of Christendom* In Press; *Spanish Borderlands* 1921, New Haven, Yale; *Spanish Exploration in the Southwest, 1524-1706,* 1916, New York, Scribners; *Texas in the Middle Eighteenth Century* 1915, Berkeley, California; "The Epic of Greater America," in *Am. Hist. Rev.,* Apr. 1933.

Bourne, Edward G., *Spain in America* 1904, New York.

Branch, Edward D., *Westward* 1930, New York, Appleton.

Brinton, Daniel G., *American Race* 1891, New York.

Brooke, Z. N., *English Church and the Papacy* 1931, Cambridge.

Buelna, Eustaquio, *Compendio historico geographico y estadistico del Estado de Sinaloa* 1878, Mexico.

Bullarium Romanum 1733-1762, Romae, Mainardi.

Burke, Edmund, *European Settlements in America* 1808, London, Dodsley.

Campbell, Thomas, S.J., *Jesuits, 1534-1921* 1921, New York, Encyclopedia Press; *Pioneer Priests in North America* 1908 sq., New York, Fordham Univ. Press.

Carlyle, R. and J., *History of Medieval Political Theory* 1928, Edinburgh, Blackwood.

Carrez, Ludovicus, S.J., *Atlas Geographicus Societatis Jesu* 1900, Paris, Colombier.

Chandlery, P. J., S.J., *Fasti Breviores* 1910, Roehampton, Manresa.

Channing-Hart-Turner, *Guide to the Study and Reading of American History* 1912, Boston.

Chapman, Charles E., *Catalogue of Materials in the Archivo General de Indias for the History of the Pacific Coast and the American Southwest* 1919, Berkeley, California; *Founding of Spanish California, 1687-1783,* 1916, New York; *History of California, Spanish Period* 1925, New York, Macmillan; *History of Spain* 1918, New York.

Charlevoix, Francois X., S.J., *Histoire du Paraguay* 1756, Paris, Didot, Giffart et Nyon.

Chateaubriand, Francois A. R. Vicomte de, *Le Genie du Christianisme* 1847, Paris, Gonet.

Clarke, William, S.J., "First Christians in North America," in *Catholic Review,* Sept. 23, 1876.

Clavigero, Francesco X., S.J., *Storia de California* 1789, Venezia.

Clinch, Bryan J., *California and its Missions* 1904, San Francisco, Whitaker.

Corrigan, W. R., S.J., *Die Kongregation de Propaganda Fide und ihre Taetigkeit in Nord-Amerika* 1929, Muenchen, Joergen.

Cortes, Hernando (McNutt), *Letters of Cortes* 1908, New York.

Cotel, Pierre, S.J., *Catechism of Vows* 1875, Baltimore, Kelly, Piet.

Coulter, Edith, *Guide to Historical Bibliographies* 1927, Berkeley, California.

Cretineau-Joly, J., *Histoire religieuse, politique, et litteraire, de la Compagnie de Jesus,* 1846, Paris, Mellier.

Crevelli, Camillo, S.J., "Mexico" (in *Cath. Ency.*)

Cuevas, Mariano, S.J., *Historia de la Iglesia en Mexico* 1928, El Paso, Revista Catolica.

Davila, Gil Gonzales, S.J., *Teatro Eclesiastico de la Primitiva Iglesia de las Indias Occidentales* 1649-1655, Madrid.

Dawson, Christopher, *Progress and Religion* 1929, London, Longmans.

Decorme, Gerard, S.J., *La Obra de los Jesuitas en Mexico durante la Epoca Colonial* 1932, (to be printed).

De la Puente, Luis, S.J., *Vida del V. P. Baltasar Alvarez* 1615, Madrid, Sanchez.

Denziger-Bannwart, *Enchiridion Symbolorum* 1922, Freiburg, Herder.

Desdevises du Dezert, Georges N., "L'Eglise Espagnol des Indes a la fin du 16me siecle," in *Revue Hispanique*, Feb. 1917.

Diaz del Castillo, Bernal, *Historia de la Verdadia de Conquista de la Nueva Espana (1632)*, 1904, Mexico.

Drews, Joannes, S.J., *Fasti Societatis Jesu* 1723, Brunsberg.

Duell, Prent, *Mission Architecture as Exemplified in San Xavier del Bac* 1919, Tucson, Ariz., Archeol, and Hist. Soc.

Duhr, Bernard, S.J., *Deutsche Auslandsehnsucht im 17 Jahrhundert.* Aus der uberseeischen Missionsarbeit deutscher Jesuiten, 1928, Stuttgart, Ausland und Heimat; *Die Studienordnung der Gesellschaft Jesu* 1896, Freiburg, Herder; *Jesuitenfabeln* 1899, Freiburg, Herder.

Engelhardt, Zepherin, O. F. M., *Missions and Missionaries of California* 1908-1915, San Francisco.

Epistolae Praepositorum Generalium ad Patres et Fratres Societatis Jesu 1909, Rollarii, De Meester.

Epitome Instituti Societatis Jesu 1924, Romae.

Espasa, *Enciclopedia Universal Ilustrada Europea Americana,* Barcelona, Hijos de Jose Espasa.

Feder, Alfred, S.J., *Lehrbuch der geschichtlichen Methode* 1924, Regensburg.

Fine, Eduard, S.J., *Juris Regularis tum Communis tum Particularis Quo Regitur Societas Jesu* 1909, Prati, Giachetti.

Fish, Carl R., *Guide to Materials for American History in Roman and Other Italian Archives* 1911, Washington, Carnegie.

Fiske, John, *Discovery of America* 1892, New York, Houghton.

Florencia, Francisco, de, S.J., *Historia de la Provincia de la Compania de Jesus en Nueva Espana 1694,* Mexico, Carrascoso.

Forrest, Earle R., *Missions and Pueblos of the Old Southwest* 1933, Glendale, Clark.

Fouqueray, Henri, S.J., *Histoire de la Compagnie de Jesus en France des Origines a la Suppression, 1528-1762* 1910-1924, Paris.

Frank, Waldo, *America Hispana* 1931, New York, Scribners.

Gasquet, F. Aidan Card., *Henry III and the English Church* 1905, London, Bell.

Gettell, Raymond A., *History of Political Theories* 1924, New York, Century.

Goldie, Francis, S.J., *First Christian Mission to the Great Mogul* 1897, Dublin, Gill.

Goodier, Alban, S.J., *Jesuits* 1930, London, Macmillan.

Gosselin, Pere, *Pouvoir du Pape au Moyen Age* 1845, Paris, Perisse.

Graham, R. G. B. Cunningham, *Vanished Arcadia* 1924, London.

Guilday, Peter, "John Gilmary Shea," in HISTORICAL RECORDS AND STUDIES, XVII 1926, July, New York, U. S. Cath. Hist. Soc.

Guilhermy, Elesban de, S.J., *Menologie de la Compagnie de Jesus* 1892, Paris, Torrien.

Hackett, Charles W., "Retreat of the Spaniards from New Mexico in 1680," in *S. W. Hist. Ass'n. Quart.*, xvi, 137-168; 259-276; "Revolt of the Pueblo Indians of New Mexico," in *Tex. St. Hist. Ass'n. Quart.*, xv, 93-147.

Hakluyt, Richard, *Divers Voyages* (1582), 1850, London, Hakluyt Society.

Hallenbeck, Cleve, *Spanish Missions of the Old Southwest* 1926, New York, Doubleday.

Hammond, George P., *Juan de Onate and the Founding of New Mexico* 1927, Santa Fe; (with Rey) Obregon's *Sixteenth Century Explorations in Western America* 1928, Los Angeles, Wetzel.

Heredia, Jose G., *Bibliografia de Sinaloa Historica y geografica* 1926, Mexico.

Herman, J-B., S.J., *La Pedagogie des Jesuites aux xvie siecle* 1914, Paris, Picard.

Hernaez, Francisco X., S.J., *Coleccion de Bulas, Breves, y otros Documentos Relativos a la Iglesia de America y Filipinas* 1879, Brussels, Vromont.

Herrara, Antonio, *Historia general de Indias* 1601, Madrid.

Hollis, Christopher, *Saint Ignatius* 1931, New York, Harpers.

Hosea, Minnie, *Jesuits in New Spain in the Sixteenth Century* 1930, Thesis, University of California.

Hughes, Thomas, S.J., *History of the Society of Jesus in North America Colonial and Federal* 1908-1917, London, Longmans.

Huonder, Anthony, S.J., "Reductions of Paraguay," in *Catholic Encyclopedia.*

Icazbalceta, Joaquin Garcia, *Bibliografia Mexicana del Siglo XVI* 1886, Mexico; *Obra*, 1896, Mexico.

Imago Primi Saeculi Societatis Jesu 1640, Antwerp, Moreti.

Institutum Societatis Jesu 1892-1893, Florentiae.

Ixtlilxochitl, Don Fernando d'Alua, *Histoire des Chichimeques* 1840, Paris, Bertrand; *Historia de Chichimecos* 1891, Mexico, Chavero.

Jameson, John F., *History of Historical Writing in America* 1891, Boston.

Jones, Cecil K., *Hispanic American Bibliographies* 1922, Baltimore.

Joyce, Thomas A., *Mexican Archeology* 1914, New York.

Kenton, Edna, *Jesuit Relations and Allied Documents* 1925, New York.

Kino, Eusebio Francisco, S.J. (Bolton), *Favores Celestiales (Historical Memoir of Pimeria Alta)* 1919, Cleveland, Clark.

Krmpotic, Msgr. M. D., *Life and Works of the Reverend Ferdinand Konscak, S.J., 1703-1759* 1923, Boston, Stratford.

Kurth, Godefroid (Day), *Catholic Church at the Turning Points of History* 1918, Helena, Naegele.

Langlois, C. V. and Seignobos, C., *Study of History* 1898, New York, Holt.

Las Casas, Bartolome, *Historia de Indias* 1875, Madrid.

Leite, Serafin, S.J., "Le Statut legal des Missions dans les Colonies portu-gaises," in *Revue d'Histoire des Missions* 8 (1931) 197-205; "O Pad-roado e a Expansao portugesa no Oriente," in *Broteria* xiii (1931) 69-81.

Leonard, Irving A., *Don Carlos de Siguenza y Gongora* 1929, Berkeley, California; *The Mercurio Volante of Don Carlos de Siguenza y Gon-gora* 1932, Los Angeles, Quivira Society.

Leturia, Pedro, S.J., "Die Heilige Stuhl und das Spanische Patronat in Amerika," in *Historisches Jahrbuch,* 46 Band, 1 Heft; "Misiones his-pano-americanas segun la Junta de 1568," in *Illuminare* (Victoria), 8 (Nov.-Dic. 1930), Suppl. Cient., pp. 1-20.

Littleton, Mary Brabson, *By the King's Command* 1928, New York, Kennedy.

Longridge, W. H., *Spiritual Exercises of Saint Ignatius* 1909, London, Scott.

Loth, David, *Philip II* 1932, New York, Brentano.

Lowery, Woodbury, *Spanish Settlements Within the Present Limits of the United States* 1911, New York, Putnam.

Luchaire, Achille, *Manuel des Institutions Francaises* 1892, Paris, Hachette.

Lummis, Charles F., *Spanish Pioneers* 1893, Chicago, McClurg.

Lyser, Alice, and Ashby, Eleanor, *Spain and Spanish America in the Libra-ries of the University of California* 1928-1930, Berkeley, California.

McGucken, William J., S.J., *Jesuits and Education* 1932, Milwaukee, Bruce.

Maclagen, Edward, *Jesuits and the Great Mogul* 1932, London, Burns, Oates and Washburne.

Madden, Marie, "Church in Contemporary Spain," in *Cath. Hist. Rev.,* April 1932.

Maitland, F. W., *Roman Canon Law in the Church of England* 1897, Lon-don, Methuen; (and Pollock) *History of English Law before the Time of Edward I* 1898, Cambridge.

Mange, Juan Matheo (Fernandez del Castillo), *Diario de las Explora-ciones en Sonora, y Lus de Tierra Incognita en la America Septen-trional* 1926, Mexico, Tallares Graficos de la Nacion.

Marquis, T. G., "Jesuit Missions in Canada," in Wrong *Chronicles of Canada* 1914-1916, Toronto.

Maynard, Theodore, *De Soto and the Conquistadores* 1930, New York, Longmans.

Mechan, John L., *Francisco de Ibarra and Nueva Vizcaya* 1927, Durham, Duke.

Mendieta, Geronimo de, *Historia Eclesiastica Indiana* 1870, Mexico.

Miller, John, *Memoirs of General (George) Miller* 1828, London, Longmans.

Missiology—see bibliography in *A. H. S. I.,* 1932, pp. 143 sq.

Montalban, Francisco X., S.J., *Das Spanische Patronat und die Eroberung der Philippinen nach den Akten des Archivs von Indien in Sevilla* 1930, Freiburg, Herder.

Montalembert, Charles F. R. Comte de, *Monks of the West* 1896, London.

Monumenta Historica Societatis Jesu (see catalogue in 1932 *A. H. S. I.*), 1894-1925, Madrid, (Rome).

Moses, Bernard, *Establishment of Spanish Rule in America* 1908, New York; *Spain's Declining Power in South America* 1918, Berkeley, California.

Mullen, Elder, S.J., *Spiritual Exercises of Saint Ignatius Loyola* (text) 1914, New York, Kenedy.

Nadas, Joannes, S.J., *Annus Dierum Memorabilium Societatis Jesu* 1665, Antwerp, Muersius.

Nieremberg, Juan E., S.J. (and Andrade, Cassini), *Varones Ilustres de la Compania de Jesus* 1666 (1889) Madrid, Buendia.

North, Arthur W., *Mother of California* 1908, San Francisco.

Nos martyres; Catalogue des Peres et Freres de la Compagnie de Jesus qui ont sacrificie leur vives pour leur fois ou leur vocation 1905, Paris, Leroy.

O'Connor, John, S.J., *Autobiography of Ignatius Loyola* 1900 New York, Benziger.

"Ordenanzas de Su Majestad hechas para los nuevos descumbrimientos conquistas y pacificaciones, July 13, 1573 (en el bosque Sevilla)," in *Coleccion de Documentos Ineditos,* xvi, 142-187. 1871, Madrid.

Orozco y Berra, Manuel, *Geografia de las lenguas y carta etnografica de Mexico* 1864, Mexico, Andrade y Escalante.

Ortega, Francisco de, S.J. *Apostolicos Afanes de la Compania de Jesus* 1887, Barcelona.

Oswald, Augustinus, S.J., *Commentarius in Constitutiones Societatis Jesu* 1845, Paris, Desclee.

Pachtler, G. M., S.J., *Ratio Studiorum et Institutiones Scholasticae Societatis Jesu per Germaniam olim vigentes* 1887-1894, Berlin, Hofmann.

Parkman, Francis, *Jesuits in North America in the Seventeenth Century* 1867, Boston.

Pastells, Pablo, S.J., *Historia de la Compania de Jesus en la provincia del Paraguay* 1912, Madrid.

Pastor Ludwig von, *Geschichte der Päpste seit dem Ausang des Mittel-alters* 1891 sq. Freiburg, Herder.

Patrignani, Giuseppe Antonio, S.J., *Menologio di pie memorie d'alcuni Religiosi della Compagnia de Giesu* 1730, Venezia, Pezzana.

Paxson, Frederic L., *History of the American Frontier, 1763-1893* 1925, Boston.

Peixotto, Ernest, *Our Hispanic Southwest* 1916, New York, Scribner.

Pfefferkorn, Ignatius, S.J., *Beschreibung der Landschaft Sonora* 1794, Koln.

Phillips, W. Allison, "Spain" (in part), in *Ency. Brit.,* 14th ed.

Plinius Secundus, Gaius, *Naturalis Historia* (translated in Bohn's Classical Library.

Pockstaller, Theodore, S.J., *Juan Maria de Salvatierra and the Establishment of the First Permanent Settlements in California, 1698-1707* 1919, (doctorate thesis), Berkeley

Polanco, Joannes Alphonsus de, S.J., *Vita Ignatii Loyolae et Rerum Societatis Jesu Historia* 1894, Madrid.

Prescott, William A., *History of the Conquest of Mexico* (1843) 1922, New York.

Priestley, Herbert I., *Coming of the White Man 1929* New York, Macmillan; *Jose de Galvez, Visitor-General of New Spain, 1765-1771* 1916, Berkeley, California; *Mexican Nation* 1923, New York, Macmillan

Purchas, Samuel, *Hakluytus Posthumus,* or *Purchas His Pilgrimes* 1625, (1907), London.

Recopilacion de Leyes de los reinos de las Indias, 1681, (1841), Madrid.

Ribadeneyra, Pedro de, S.J., *Vida del P. Francisco Borgia* 1594, Madrid, Madrigal.

Ribas, Juan Perez de, S.J., *Historia de los Triunfos de nuestra Santa Fe* 1645, Madrid.

Riegel, Robert E., *America Moves West* 1930, New York, Holt.

Robertson, James A., List of Documents in Spanish Archives relating to the history of the United States, printed or preserved in transcript in United States Libraries. 1910, Washington, Carnegie.

Roosevelt, Theodore, *Winning of the West* 1900, New York.

Rousseau, Francois, *L'Idee missionnaire aux xvi et xvii siecles* 1930, Paris, Spes.

Salvat, *Diccionario Salvat:* Enciclopedico Popular Illustrado (no date) Barcelona, Salvat.

Santacilia, Jorge Juan, et Antonio de Ulloa, *Voyage Historique de l'Amerique meridionale fait par ordre du Roi d'Espagne par Don George Juan Santacilia et Don Antonio de Ulloa* 1752, Paris, Jombert.

Sauer, Carl O., and Brand, Donald D., *Aztatlan: prehistoric Mexican frontier on the Pacific Coast* 1932 Berkeley, California.

Schmidlin, Joseph (Braun), *Catholic Mission Theory 1932* Techny, Mission Press.

Schmitt, Ludovicus, S.J., *Synopsis Historiae Societatis Jesu* 1914, Ratisbon, Pustet.

Schurhammer, Georg, S.J. (Eble), *Saint Francis Xavier* 1928, Saint Louis, Herder.

Schwickerath, Robert, S.J., *Jesuit Education* 1904, St. Louis, Herder.

Sedgwick, Henry D., *Cortes, the Conqueror* 1927, London.

Shea, John Gilmary, *History of the Catholic Church Within the Limits of the United States* 1892, New York; *History of the Catholic Missions Among the Indian Tribes of the United States, 1529-1854,* 1855, New York; "Log Chapel on the Rappahannock," in *Cath. World,* Mar. 1875; "Spanish Mission Colony on the Rappahannock: first European settlement in Virginia, in W. W. Beach *Indian Miscellany, 333-344.*

Shepherd, William R., *Guide to Materials for the History of the United States in Spanish Archives,* Simancas, the Archivo Historico Nacional, and Seville 1907, Washington, Carnegie.

Simpson, Lesley B., *Encomienda in New Spain in the Sixteenth Century* 1929, Berkeley, California.

Slosson, Edwin E. *American Spirit in Education* 1921 New Haven, Yale.

Smith, A. L., *Church and State in the Middle Ages* 1905, Oxford, Oxford.

Smith, Francis J., S.J., "Control of the Church in Spanish America by the State," in *Hist. Bull.,* V, 4 (1927).

Solorzano, Pereira, Juan, *Disputatio de Indiarum Jure,* 1629, Matriti; *Politica Indiana* 1776, Madrid.

Sommervogel, Carlos, S.J., *Bibliotheque de la Compagnie de Jesus* 1909, Paris, Picard.

Stoecklein, Joseph, S.J., *Der Neue-Welt Bott mit allerhand Nachrichten der Missionariorum Societatis Jesu, 1642-1726* 1728-1761 Augsburg und Gratz Philipp, Martin und Veith.

Streit, Robert, O. M. I., *Bibliotheca Missionum* 1916-1929, Munster.

Suarez, Francisco, S.J., *De Fide* (See Vives Edition: 1856-1861 Paris).

Tanner, Mathias, S.J., *Societas Jesu usque ad sanguinis et vitae profusionem militans* 1675, Prague.

Taraval, Sigismond, S. J. (Wilbur) *Indian Uprising in Lower California,* 1734-1737 1931 Los Angeles, Quivira.

Thebaud, Augustin, S.J., *Three Quarters of a Century,* Hist. Records and Studies, Monograph Series 1904 New York, U. S. Catholic Historical Society.

Thomas, Alfred F. *Forgotten Frontiers* 1932 Norman, Oklahoma.

Thompson, Francis, *Saint Ignatius Loyola* 1910, London.

Thurston, Herbert, S.J., *No Popery* 1930 London, Longmans.

Torre, Juan Jose de la, S.J., *Constitutiones Societatis Jesu Latine et Hispanice cum earum Declarationibus* 1892, Madrid.

Turner, Frederick, *Frontier in American History* (1893) 1920 New York.

Thwaites, Reuben Gold, *History of Wisconsin,* in Scudder *American Commonwealths* 1885-1908, Boston; *Jesuit Relations and Allied Documents* 1893, Cleveland.

Uriarte, Jose Eugenio, S.J., and Lecina, Mariano, S.J., *Biblioteca de Escritores de la Compania de Jesus pertenecientes a la antigua Asistencia de Espana desde sus origines hasta el ano de 1773* 1929 Madrid, Razon y Fe.

Van Dyke, Paul, *Saint Ignatius Loyola* 1926, New York.

Venegas, Miguel, S.J., (Wilbur) *Juan Maria de Salvatierra of the Company of Jesus* 1929, Clark, Cleveland.

Venegas, Miguel, S.J., (Burriel), *Noticias de la California* 1757, Madrid.

Wagner, Henry R., *Spanish Southwest, 1542-1794* 1924, Berkeley, California.

Wallace, Lew, *Fair God* 1873, New York, Houghton.

Walsh, William T., *Isabella of Spain* 1931, London, Sheed.

Webb, W. P., *Great Plains* 1931, Boston, Ginn.

Weld, Alfred, S.J., *Suppression of the Society of Jesus in the Portuguese Dominions* 1877, London, Burns, Oates.

Wernz, Francis X., S.J., *Jus Decretalium* 1914, Romae.

Williams, Mary W., *People and Politics of Latin America* 1930, Boston, Ginn.

Winship George P., *Coronado Expedition, 1540-1542,* 1896, Washington, Gov. Print. Off.

Wissler, Clark, *American Indian* 1922, New York.

INDEX

Persons and Places

Topics